2nd Edition

THE BETTER-WRITING CENTER

SSAT

PRACTICE TESTS
UPPER LEVEL

By Won Suh, J.D.

I dedicate this book to my parents because they may be two of only a relative few in the world insane—and gracious—enough to continue to encourage my passion of writing and publishing workbooks and study guides, as I continue to forgo and shun opportunities presented to me as a licensed attorney.

Dear Student,

In 2013, I published my first practice test workbook for admissions to some of the best high schools in the nation. The reception to the book was truly awesome. It inspired me to continue publishing and providing students with access to high quality practice tests that will help them build their skills and be better prepared for whatever standardized tests they encounter.

Many of you are extremely bright and driven, and that is why I created this book for high-achieving students seeking to take the SSAT to gain admission to some of the best schools in the nation. If you find that the problems are challenging, don't let that worry you. I suggest taking a diagnostic test using an official SSAT practice test before you begin using this book. The primary function of this book is to teach the skillsets you will need to be successful. As you work through the questions and learn how to approach them, you will see your skills improve.

Thank you again for purchasing this book, and I wish you the best of luck in your studies and in your pursuit of your future aspirations. God bless. If you should have any questions, please feel to direct them my way. I have provided you with my personal work email for this purpose. I am happy to answer your questions, especially if there's any ambiguity or critical typographical error I've overlooked

Regarding the 2nd edition specifically, you have spoken, so I have listened.

I heard from many of you that *SSAT Practice Tests: Upper Level* was too difficult for the standards set by the SSAT. My goal has always been to provide rigorous questions to help students be extremely well prepared, but I became too eager. I crafted some of the most mindboggling questions I could conceive of for middle school, and that's not necessarily a good thing. To help this book be more accessible to more students, I have combed through the practice tests to find the questions—the math and analogies questions—that were especially problematic and rigorous for students. I either edited answer choices or wrote entirely new questions to replace them. This time around, I tempered the difficulty of the questions to be more useful to more students.

At the same time, however, I did not want to cripple this book by removing practice questions that would benefit some students. As a result, I have done something no one else has done before in a second edition of a book (at least to my knowledge): I have included all of the questions I removed from the practice tests—you'll find them after the practice tests in a separate section. I did this because I believe that products should continue to make forward progress, not compromise unnecessarily. I made absolutely no compromises to make this book a better value for you. I leave it up to you to decide whether you want to do attempt these additional questions.

Yours truly,

Won Suh
President & Director
The Better Writing Center
Email: won.suh@betterwritingcenter.com

Contents

FREE CONSULTATION

Thank you for your purchase. Your purchase entitles you to a complimentary hour of in-person private tutoring or academic consultation.* Just bring this book!

SCHEDULE YOUR CONSULTATION TODAY
won.suh@betterwritingcenter.com

*This offer is subject to scheduling and availability limitations and will be honored on a first come, first serve basis.

TUTORING OFFERED

LEARN FROM THE BEST. LEARN FROM THE AUTHOR.

TESTING	MATHEMATICS	SCIENCE	WRITING
CogAT	Algebra 1 & 2	Biology	School Assignments
SSAT	Geometry	Chemistry	AP History DBQs
SHSAT	Trigonometry	Physics	Personal Statements
ACT	Pre-calculus	Computer Science	Application Essays
SAT	AP Calculus AB & BC		

FIND THE BETTER WRITING CENTER

THE BETTER WRITING CENTER

7369 McWhorter Place
Suite 402
Annandale, Virginia 22003

THE TESTS

SSAT
UPPER LEVEL
TEST 1

ANSWER SHEET

Make sure to completely fill in the bubbles corresponding to your answer choices.

Section 1

1 Ⓐ Ⓑ Ⓒ Ⓓ Ⓔ	6 Ⓐ Ⓑ Ⓒ Ⓓ Ⓔ	11 Ⓐ Ⓑ Ⓒ Ⓓ Ⓔ	16 Ⓐ Ⓑ Ⓒ Ⓓ Ⓔ	21 Ⓐ Ⓑ Ⓒ Ⓓ Ⓔ
2 Ⓐ Ⓑ Ⓒ Ⓓ Ⓔ	7 Ⓐ Ⓑ Ⓒ Ⓓ Ⓔ	12 Ⓐ Ⓑ Ⓒ Ⓓ Ⓔ	17 Ⓐ Ⓑ Ⓒ Ⓓ Ⓔ	22 Ⓐ Ⓑ Ⓒ Ⓓ Ⓔ
3 Ⓐ Ⓑ Ⓒ Ⓓ Ⓔ	8 Ⓐ Ⓑ Ⓒ Ⓓ Ⓔ	13 Ⓐ Ⓑ Ⓒ Ⓓ Ⓔ	18 Ⓐ Ⓑ Ⓒ Ⓓ Ⓔ	23 Ⓐ Ⓑ Ⓒ Ⓓ Ⓔ
4 Ⓐ Ⓑ Ⓒ Ⓓ Ⓔ	9 Ⓐ Ⓑ Ⓒ Ⓓ Ⓔ	14 Ⓐ Ⓑ Ⓒ Ⓓ Ⓔ	19 Ⓐ Ⓑ Ⓒ Ⓓ Ⓔ	24 Ⓐ Ⓑ Ⓒ Ⓓ Ⓔ
5 Ⓐ Ⓑ Ⓒ Ⓓ Ⓔ	10 Ⓐ Ⓑ Ⓒ Ⓓ Ⓔ	15 Ⓐ Ⓑ Ⓒ Ⓓ Ⓔ	20 Ⓐ Ⓑ Ⓒ Ⓓ Ⓔ	25 Ⓐ Ⓑ Ⓒ Ⓓ Ⓔ

Section 2

1 Ⓐ Ⓑ Ⓒ Ⓓ Ⓔ	9 Ⓐ Ⓑ Ⓒ Ⓓ Ⓔ	17 Ⓐ Ⓑ Ⓒ Ⓓ Ⓔ	25 Ⓐ Ⓑ Ⓒ Ⓓ Ⓔ	33 Ⓐ Ⓑ Ⓒ Ⓓ Ⓔ
2 Ⓐ Ⓑ Ⓒ Ⓓ Ⓔ	10 Ⓐ Ⓑ Ⓒ Ⓓ Ⓔ	18 Ⓐ Ⓑ Ⓒ Ⓓ Ⓔ	26 Ⓐ Ⓑ Ⓒ Ⓓ Ⓔ	34 Ⓐ Ⓑ Ⓒ Ⓓ Ⓔ
3 Ⓐ Ⓑ Ⓒ Ⓓ Ⓔ	11 Ⓐ Ⓑ Ⓒ Ⓓ Ⓔ	19 Ⓐ Ⓑ Ⓒ Ⓓ Ⓔ	27 Ⓐ Ⓑ Ⓒ Ⓓ Ⓔ	35 Ⓐ Ⓑ Ⓒ Ⓓ Ⓔ
4 Ⓐ Ⓑ Ⓒ Ⓓ Ⓔ	12 Ⓐ Ⓑ Ⓒ Ⓓ Ⓔ	20 Ⓐ Ⓑ Ⓒ Ⓓ Ⓔ	28 Ⓐ Ⓑ Ⓒ Ⓓ Ⓔ	36 Ⓐ Ⓑ Ⓒ Ⓓ Ⓔ
5 Ⓐ Ⓑ Ⓒ Ⓓ Ⓔ	13 Ⓐ Ⓑ Ⓒ Ⓓ Ⓔ	21 Ⓐ Ⓑ Ⓒ Ⓓ Ⓔ	29 Ⓐ Ⓑ Ⓒ Ⓓ Ⓔ	37 Ⓐ Ⓑ Ⓒ Ⓓ Ⓔ
6 Ⓐ Ⓑ Ⓒ Ⓓ Ⓔ	14 Ⓐ Ⓑ Ⓒ Ⓓ Ⓔ	22 Ⓐ Ⓑ Ⓒ Ⓓ Ⓔ	30 Ⓐ Ⓑ Ⓒ Ⓓ Ⓔ	38 Ⓐ Ⓑ Ⓒ Ⓓ Ⓔ
7 Ⓐ Ⓑ Ⓒ Ⓓ Ⓔ	15 Ⓐ Ⓑ Ⓒ Ⓓ Ⓔ	23 Ⓐ Ⓑ Ⓒ Ⓓ Ⓔ	31 Ⓐ Ⓑ Ⓒ Ⓓ Ⓔ	39 Ⓐ Ⓑ Ⓒ Ⓓ Ⓔ
8 Ⓐ Ⓑ Ⓒ Ⓓ Ⓔ	16 Ⓐ Ⓑ Ⓒ Ⓓ Ⓔ	24 Ⓐ Ⓑ Ⓒ Ⓓ Ⓔ	32 Ⓐ Ⓑ Ⓒ Ⓓ Ⓔ	40 Ⓐ Ⓑ Ⓒ Ⓓ Ⓔ

Section 3

1 Ⓐ Ⓑ Ⓒ Ⓓ Ⓔ	13 Ⓐ Ⓑ Ⓒ Ⓓ Ⓔ	25 Ⓐ Ⓑ Ⓒ Ⓓ Ⓔ	37 Ⓐ Ⓑ Ⓒ Ⓓ Ⓔ	49 Ⓐ Ⓑ Ⓒ Ⓓ Ⓔ
2 Ⓐ Ⓑ Ⓒ Ⓓ Ⓔ	14 Ⓐ Ⓑ Ⓒ Ⓓ Ⓔ	26 Ⓐ Ⓑ Ⓒ Ⓓ Ⓔ	38 Ⓐ Ⓑ Ⓒ Ⓓ Ⓔ	50 Ⓐ Ⓑ Ⓒ Ⓓ Ⓔ
3 Ⓐ Ⓑ Ⓒ Ⓓ Ⓔ	15 Ⓐ Ⓑ Ⓒ Ⓓ Ⓔ	27 Ⓐ Ⓑ Ⓒ Ⓓ Ⓔ	39 Ⓐ Ⓑ Ⓒ Ⓓ Ⓔ	51 Ⓐ Ⓑ Ⓒ Ⓓ Ⓔ
4 Ⓐ Ⓑ Ⓒ Ⓓ Ⓔ	16 Ⓐ Ⓑ Ⓒ Ⓓ Ⓔ	28 Ⓐ Ⓑ Ⓒ Ⓓ Ⓔ	40 Ⓐ Ⓑ Ⓒ Ⓓ Ⓔ	52 Ⓐ Ⓑ Ⓒ Ⓓ Ⓔ
5 Ⓐ Ⓑ Ⓒ Ⓓ Ⓔ	17 Ⓐ Ⓑ Ⓒ Ⓓ Ⓔ	29 Ⓐ Ⓑ Ⓒ Ⓓ Ⓔ	41 Ⓐ Ⓑ Ⓒ Ⓓ Ⓔ	53 Ⓐ Ⓑ Ⓒ Ⓓ Ⓔ
6 Ⓐ Ⓑ Ⓒ Ⓓ Ⓔ	18 Ⓐ Ⓑ Ⓒ Ⓓ Ⓔ	30 Ⓐ Ⓑ Ⓒ Ⓓ Ⓔ	42 Ⓐ Ⓑ Ⓒ Ⓓ Ⓔ	54 Ⓐ Ⓑ Ⓒ Ⓓ Ⓔ
7 Ⓐ Ⓑ Ⓒ Ⓓ Ⓔ	19 Ⓐ Ⓑ Ⓒ Ⓓ Ⓔ	31 Ⓐ Ⓑ Ⓒ Ⓓ Ⓔ	43 Ⓐ Ⓑ Ⓒ Ⓓ Ⓔ	55 Ⓐ Ⓑ Ⓒ Ⓓ Ⓔ
8 Ⓐ Ⓑ Ⓒ Ⓓ Ⓔ	20 Ⓐ Ⓑ Ⓒ Ⓓ Ⓔ	32 Ⓐ Ⓑ Ⓒ Ⓓ Ⓔ	44 Ⓐ Ⓑ Ⓒ Ⓓ Ⓔ	56 Ⓐ Ⓑ Ⓒ Ⓓ Ⓔ
9 Ⓐ Ⓑ Ⓒ Ⓓ Ⓔ	21 Ⓐ Ⓑ Ⓒ Ⓓ Ⓔ	33 Ⓐ Ⓑ Ⓒ Ⓓ Ⓔ	45 Ⓐ Ⓑ Ⓒ Ⓓ Ⓔ	57 Ⓐ Ⓑ Ⓒ Ⓓ Ⓔ
10 Ⓐ Ⓑ Ⓒ Ⓓ Ⓔ	22 Ⓐ Ⓑ Ⓒ Ⓓ Ⓔ	34 Ⓐ Ⓑ Ⓒ Ⓓ Ⓔ	46 Ⓐ Ⓑ Ⓒ Ⓓ Ⓔ	58 Ⓐ Ⓑ Ⓒ Ⓓ Ⓔ
11 Ⓐ Ⓑ Ⓒ Ⓓ Ⓔ	23 Ⓐ Ⓑ Ⓒ Ⓓ Ⓔ	35 Ⓐ Ⓑ Ⓒ Ⓓ Ⓔ	47 Ⓐ Ⓑ Ⓒ Ⓓ Ⓔ	59 Ⓐ Ⓑ Ⓒ Ⓓ Ⓔ
12 Ⓐ Ⓑ Ⓒ Ⓓ Ⓔ	24 Ⓐ Ⓑ Ⓒ Ⓓ Ⓔ	36 Ⓐ Ⓑ Ⓒ Ⓓ Ⓔ	48 Ⓐ Ⓑ Ⓒ Ⓓ Ⓔ	60 Ⓐ Ⓑ Ⓒ Ⓓ Ⓔ

Section 4

1 Ⓐ Ⓑ Ⓒ Ⓓ Ⓔ	6 Ⓐ Ⓑ Ⓒ Ⓓ Ⓔ	11 Ⓐ Ⓑ Ⓒ Ⓓ Ⓔ	16 Ⓐ Ⓑ Ⓒ Ⓓ Ⓔ	21 Ⓐ Ⓑ Ⓒ Ⓓ Ⓔ
2 Ⓐ Ⓑ Ⓒ Ⓓ Ⓔ	7 Ⓐ Ⓑ Ⓒ Ⓓ Ⓔ	12 Ⓐ Ⓑ Ⓒ Ⓓ Ⓔ	17 Ⓐ Ⓑ Ⓒ Ⓓ Ⓔ	22 Ⓐ Ⓑ Ⓒ Ⓓ Ⓔ
3 Ⓐ Ⓑ Ⓒ Ⓓ Ⓔ	8 Ⓐ Ⓑ Ⓒ Ⓓ Ⓔ	13 Ⓐ Ⓑ Ⓒ Ⓓ Ⓔ	18 Ⓐ Ⓑ Ⓒ Ⓓ Ⓔ	23 Ⓐ Ⓑ Ⓒ Ⓓ Ⓔ
4 Ⓐ Ⓑ Ⓒ Ⓓ Ⓔ	9 Ⓐ Ⓑ Ⓒ Ⓓ Ⓔ	14 Ⓐ Ⓑ Ⓒ Ⓓ Ⓔ	19 Ⓐ Ⓑ Ⓒ Ⓓ Ⓔ	24 Ⓐ Ⓑ Ⓒ Ⓓ Ⓔ
5 Ⓐ Ⓑ Ⓒ Ⓓ Ⓔ	10 Ⓐ Ⓑ Ⓒ Ⓓ Ⓔ	15 Ⓐ Ⓑ Ⓒ Ⓓ Ⓔ	20 Ⓐ Ⓑ Ⓒ Ⓓ Ⓔ	25 Ⓐ Ⓑ Ⓒ Ⓓ Ⓔ

Writing Sample

Select one of the two essay prompts below and write an essay or story to address or answer the prompt you selected. Your writing sample will help schools understand you better as an applicant.

A. What is one thing that everyone should be doing to make his or her community a better place?

B. He hit the ground running.

Use this page and the next to write your essay or story.

Continue on the next page.

SECTION I
25 Questions
30 minutes

Work through each problem in this section. You may use the blank pace to the right of the page, if you need, to do your figuring. Then select the best one of the five suggested answer choices.

Note: Some of the problems are accompanied by figures, which are rendered as accurately as possible, EXCEPT when the problem explicitly states that its accompanying figure is not drawn to scale.

Sample Problem:

6,329	(A)	2,151
− 3,478	(B)	2,275
	(C)	2,807
	(D)	2,851
	(E)	2,951 Ⓐ Ⓑ Ⓒ ● Ⓔ

SPACE FOR FIGURING

1. Arnie is planning a Christmas party for his company, which employs 29 people, including himself. He needs to buy enough sodas for everyone to have two, but in his town sodas only come in cases of 12. How many cases of soda must he buy?

    (A) 2
    (B) 3
    (C) 4
    (D) 5
    (E) 6

2. Janie has x times as many stickers as Ronnie does. If Ronnie has 3 stickers, how many more stickers does Janie have?

    (A) $3(x-1)$
    (B) $3+x$
    (C) $3x$
    (D) $2x+1$
    (E) $2x$

3. If 35% of a number is 147, what is 18% of that number?

    (A) 9.261
    (B) 75.6
    (C) 77.91
    (D) 210
    (E) 420

GO TO THE NEXT PAGE.

SPACE FOR FIGURING

4. The dimensions of a rectangular prism are 2 inches by 3 inches by 4 inches. How many of these rectangular prisms would be needed to perfectly fill up a cube whose sides are 2 feet long?

    (A) 24
    (B) 96
    (C) 144
    (D) 432
    (E) 576

5. Which figure can be drawn without lifting the pencil or backtracking?

    (A) ⋈
    (B) ⊕
    (C) ⊤
    (D) ⱳ
    (E) ⊓

$$\frac{93,249}{6,070} =$$

6. The result of the above calculation is closest to which of the following?

    (A) 1.5
    (B) 1.6
    (C) 15
    (D) 16
    (E) 20

7. In the figure, segment AB is 24 centimeters long. How long is AC?

    (A) 48 cm
    (B) 72 cm
    (C) 96 cm
    (D) 108 cm
    (E) 120 cm

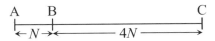

GO TO THE NEXT PAGE.

SPACE FOR FIGURING

8. If the average of six consecutive odd integers is 4, what is the largest integer?

(A) 5
(B) 7
(C) 8
(D) 9
(E) 10

9. When $3X + 4Y = 55$ and $2X + 2Y = 35$, what is the value of $X + Y$?

(A) 15
(B) 17.5
(C) 20
(D) 22.5
(E) 24.5

10. Solve for the value of m in the following equation: $\left(\sqrt[3]{m}\right)^2 = 64$

(A) 2
(B) 8
(C) 16
(D) 256
(E) 512

11. If 130 percent of w is 6.5, what is 70% of $4w$?

(A) 5
(B) 7.5
(C) 14
(D) 15
(E) 17.65

GO TO THE NEXT PAGE.

12. Which of the following could be the value of X if
$2 - X > 3X + 4$?

(A) $-\dfrac{5}{6}$

(B) $-\dfrac{1}{2}$

(C) $-\dfrac{4}{15}$

(D) $\dfrac{1}{4}$

(E) $\dfrac{1}{2}$

Questions 13-14 are based on the table in the figure.

13. If there were 15,000 criminal law attorneys in the United States in year X, about how many more of them were in the public sector than in the international sector?

(A) 5,000
(B) 5,750
(C) 6,000
(D) 6,750
(E) 7,500

14. What fractional part of the number of contract law attorneys in the United States work in the private sector?

(A) $\dfrac{13}{20}$

(B) $\dfrac{3}{4}$

(C) $\dfrac{4}{5}$

(D) $\dfrac{17}{20}$

(E) $\dfrac{19}{20}$

HOW ATTORNEYS IN THE
UNITED STATES WERE
EMPLOYED IN YEAR X

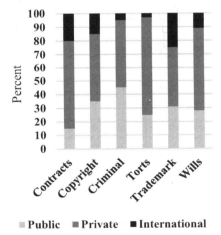

GO TO THE NEXT PAGE.

15. Lucius is collecting stamps that are each worth one-tenth of a cent. Every day, Lucius collects three times the number of stamps that he did on the previous day. If on the first day Lucius collected one stamp, how much would his entire stamp collection be worth by the end of the 6th day, to the nearest cent?

(A) $0.24
(B) $0.36
(C) $0.60
(D) $2.43
(E) $3.64

16. Let x be a positive prime integer less than 44. What is the probability that x is less than 22?

(A) $\dfrac{2}{5}$

(B) $\dfrac{19}{43}$

(C) $\dfrac{1}{2}$

(D) $\dfrac{3}{5}$

(E) $\dfrac{4}{7}$

17. Ramon is paid $1,800.00 for working 40 hours. At this rate, how much would he be paid for working 50 hours?

(A) $1,900.00
(B) $2,000.00
(C) $2,150.00
(D) $2,250.00
(E) $2,300.00

GO TO THE NEXT PAGE.

SPACE FOR FIGURING

18. 3 apples and 2 pears weigh 100 oz. 4 apples and 5 pears weigh 187 oz. May buys 1 apple and 1 pear. If the bag she puts her fruits in weighs 2 oz, how much do the bag and fruits weigh?

   (A) 41 oz
   (B) 43 oz
   (C) 45 oz
   (D) 52 oz
   (E) 54 oz

19. Kevin sold 30 games and then bought 18 more. If he originally had 62 games, what is the ratio of the number of games he has now to the number of games he originally had?

   (A) 9 to 15
   (B) 25 to 31
   (C) 18 to 31
   (D) 48 to 62
   (E) 12 to 18

20. Which of the following grids could be completely covered by placing the block shown to the right without any overlaps?

   (A)

   (B)

   (C)

   (D)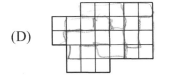

   (E)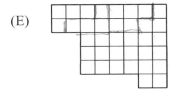

GO TO THE NEXT PAGE.

21. A square and isosceles right triangle have the same area. What is the ratio of the perimeter of the isosceles right triangle to the perimeter of the square?

(A) $1 : 2$

(B) $2 : 1$

(C) $1 + \sqrt{2} : 2$

(D) $\sqrt{2} : 1$

(E) $3 : 4$

22. The following table shows how many apples fell from Jack's apple tree during the first five days of picking season. If the total number of apples that fell during the first five days was y, how many apples fell on the fifth day, in terms of y?

(A) $x = y - 159$

(B) $x = y + 159$

(C) $x = 159 - y$

(D) $x = 3y - 53$

(E) $x = 5y - 49$

Daily Apple Totals

Day	Apple Count
1	33
2	42
3	35
4	49
5	x

23. If a line passes through the points $(3, -4)$, $(2, 9)$, and $(0, a)$, what is the value of a?

(A) 55

(B) 46

(C) 35

(D) -1

(E) -17

24. Jack and Jill operate Above the Hill, which is a relaxation spa for the weary who ran up the hill. Jack and Jill make a profit of $120.00 per customer, for an average weekly profit of $6,600.00. Not satisfied, however, Jack and Jill plan to reduce the price per customer by $40. How many more customers will Jack and Jill need at a minimum, at this newly reduced rate, to continue earning the same amount of money as before?

(A) 27

(B) 28

(C) 55

(D) 82

(E) 83

GO TO THE NEXT PAGE.

25. If the dots in the figure shown are connected by starting at 1 and then going to 2 before going to 3, for which of the following figures will it be necessary to retrace a line or lift the writing implement to draw?

(A)

(B)

(C)

(D)

(E)

STOP

IF YOU FINISH BEFORE TIME IS CALLED, YOU MAY CHECK YOUR WORK ON THIS SECTION ONLY.
DO NOT TURN TO ANY OTHER SECTION IN THE TEST.

SECTION 2
40 Questions
40 Minutes

After reading each passage, answer its accompanying questions. Select your answers on the basis of the information presented in the passage only.

Line 5

10

15

The notion of zombies has long been a source of fascination for us humans, with the success of shows such as *The Walking Dead* underscoring just how widespread our fascination with these undead persons of the horror and science fiction genre is. But what if the living dead were more than just a matter of fiction?

In fact, in the case of plants, certain parasitic bacteria called phytoplasma can infect healthy plants and cause a transformation in the plants' flowers, converting the flowers into leafy shoots that are unable to produce offspring. Moreover, these bacteria are able to attract insects to the plants that will spread the bacteria, rather than help disseminate pollen.

And, in the case of animals, there is always the Nematomorph hairworm, which develops inside grasshoppers and crickets until the worm is mature. But unlike other parasites, which feed off their hosts, the hairworm actually manipulates the behavior of its host. By altering the biochemistry of its host's brain, the hairworm is able to compel its host to dive into water and commit suicide by drowning—grasshoppers and crickets never, under normal circumstances, behave in such a manner—so that the hairworm can emerge and swim away to find a mate.

So the question that remains today is: How long will it be before a parasite, bacteria, or virus that can manipulate human brain behavior is discovered?

---

1. The Nematomorph hairworm controls its host by
   (A) compelling its host to try to find food underwater
   (B) feeding off its host's body
   (C) causing its host to panic and lose control
   (D) altering its host's brain's biochemistry
   (E) eating away at its host's brain slowly

2. The author alludes to *The Walking Dead* in order to
   (A) instill a fear of zombies into the reader
   (B) support his or her favorite show
   (C) delineate society's fascination with zombies
   (D) highlight the role of zombies in popular media
   (E) suggest that the day of zombies will soon be upon humankind

3. According to the passage, once the Nematomorph hairworm leaves its host, it
   (A) swims away to find a host for its eggs
   (B) consumes its host's dead body
   (C) makes its way to dry ground to find a mate
   (D) finds an aquatic shelter to provide for its mate
   (E) seeks out a mate

4. Phytoplasma interfere with their host plants' reproduction by
   (A) sabotaging insects' ability to spread pollen
   (B) rendering the plants infertile
   (C) damaging the plants leafy shoots
   (D) causing insects to choose to disseminate the bacteria instead of pollen
   (E) delaying the dissemination of the plants' pollen

GO TO THE NEXT PAGE.

Line 5

10

What do the letters QWERTY represent to you? Many people would correctly surmise that these 6 letters are not some bizarre acronym of randomly placed letters but rather the first 6 letters of a keyboard (starting from the upper left letter key). But beyond the recognition of the first six letters on a standard keyboard, how many more of the letters are instantly recognizable and identifiable?

Researchers at Vanderbilt University tried to answer this question in the scientific journal *Attention, Perception, and Psychophysics*. What they found in one experiment was that from a corps of typists who averaged 72 words per minute with an accuracy level of 94 percent, the typists could only correctly identify the placement of 15 of the 26 letters on a QWERTY keyboard, in 80 seconds. In a second experiment, in which a key on a blank keyboard lit up and the participants had to identify the key's letter, the participants only correctly identified 55 percent of the keys on the first try, further bringing to light new questions about our cognitive learning skills.

5. It can be inferred that the Vanderbilt researchers were
    (A) not at all surprised by the results
    (B) contemplating a retrial of the experiment to make sure they didn't make any mistakes
    (C) at least somewhat surprised by the results
    (D) unable to type as fast as the typists were able to
    (E) unable to correctly identify the placement of keyboard keys

6. It can be inferred that the letters QWERTY
    (A) make up a bizarre acronym of randomly placed letters
    (B) are among the more recognizable letters of a keyboard, in terms of placement
    (C) are absolutely recognizable by everyone
    (D) can be rearranged on a standard keyboard however the typist wants
    (E) have been placed in the most optimal position of the keyboard possible

7. It can be inferred that accurate typing
    (A) is impossible to achieve at slower speeds
    (B) is performed faster when the placement of the keys are not memorized
    (C) is preferred to handwriting
    (D) does not require a perfect active memory of the layout of the keyboard
    (E) is performed more slowly when being observed by third parties

8. The first and second experiments differed in that
    (A) the first involved identifying the placement of the letters on an entire keyboard, whereas the second involved identifying some of the letters of a keyboard, one at a time
    (B) the first involved seeing how quickly all of the letters of a keyboard could be identified, whereas the second involved identifying the letters in 80 seconds
    (C) the first involved identifying 15 out of 26 keys, whereas the second involved identifying one letter at a time
    (D) the first involved typing at 72 words per minute, whereas the second involved typing with an accuracy level of 94 percent
    (E) the first involved memorizing and reciting randomly placed letters on a scrambled keyboard, whereas the second involved watching letters flash briefly on a screen and then trying to correctly identify on a blank keyboard where they flashed

9. The author wrote the passage in order to
    (A) demonstrate the futility of memorization
    (B) figure out the most efficient way to type
    (C) promote a deeper understanding of the history of keyboards
    (D) support passive learning methods
    (E) indicate that there may be more to cognitive learning skills than previously understood

GO TO THE NEXT PAGE.

Neil Armstrong may have been the first man to set foot on the Moon, but he does not hold the distinction of being the first primate—humans are classified as primates, after all—to go into outer space. Depending on how "outer space" is defined, that distinction may belong to Albert I, a rhesus monkey that rode aboard a
Line 5 V-2 Blossom rocket that launched on June 11, 1948. But if what is known as the Kármán line is used to demarcate the boundary between Earth's atmosphere and outer space, then it would not be until June 14, 1949, that the first animal astronaut would reach outer space.

Because the Kármán line establishes that outer space begins 100 kilometers
10 above the Earth's surface, Albert I's flight would not qualify him to be the first primate to go into outer space, as his flight only reached an altitude of 63 kilometers. Instead, the first to reach outer space would be another rhesus monkey that scientists named Albert II, after he achieved an altitude of 134 kilometers. Rather tragically, it wasn't until September 20, 1951 that Yorick became the first
15 monkey to survive the entirety of a rocket flight—some mice had survived previous rocket flights, but Yorick was the first monkey to do so.

10. If the Kármán line is used to establish the boundary of outer space, then Albert I was not the first primate to into outer space because

   (A) his rocket only went up 63 kilometers above the surface of the Earth
   (B) he died on the descent back to Earth's surface
   (C) the Kármán line is an imaginary line that changes from time to time
   (D) The technology was not available at the time to propel rockets more than 100 kilometers above the surface of the Earth
   (E) Albert II's rocket went up higher than his did

11. It can be inferred that at least how many monkeys died during their trips to space?

   (A) 0
   (B) 1
   (C) 2
   (D) 3
   (E) 4

12. This passage would be most appropriate in

   (A) a science fiction novel
   (B) a reference book
   (C) a bibliography
   (D) a personal diary
   (E) a movie script

13. Yorick's flight was momentous because

   (A) he did something that previously only mice had achieved
   (B) it only took scientists a little over three years to figure out how to successfully send a primate into outer space and return safely
   (C) his survival during the rocket flight proved to scientists that space flight, as it was, had been perfected for human sustainability
   (D) he was superior genetically to any other rhesus monkey that had previously attempted a rocket flight into space
   (E) he was the first monkey to survive the entirety of a rocket flight into space

14. Which of the following would be the best title for the passage?

   (A) "Yorick's Success as an Astronaut"
   (B) "A Tale of Two Monkeys: Journeys into the Unknown"
   (C) "The Kármán Line: Defining the Boundaries of Outer Space"
   (D) "Behind the Scenes of the First Steps on the Moon"
   (E) "The Value of Sacrifices"

GO TO THE NEXT PAGE.

Line 5

10

No one else in the history of the world conquered as much land as Genghis Khan did. According to one estimate, he conquered almost 12 million square miles, from the easternmost coast of Eurasia to the Mediterranean and parts of the Middle East—by comparison, the United States has a surface area of 3.79 million square miles.

Though Genghis Khan left scores of millions of people dead in the wake of the ruthless expansion of his empire, he was intriguingly levelheaded and fair in the way he conducted his operations. For instance, he was amenable to peacefully assimilating into his empire other kingdoms and societies that he came across, so long as they did not offer resistance. And even when they did offer resistance, he was known to offering his talented adversaries trusted positions within the ranks of his military.

15. The author mentions the surface area of the United States in order to

(A) comment on the enormity of the land mass of the United States
(B) provide a reference point for comparison
(C) display nationalistic pride in the size of the United States
(D) argue for an expansion of United States borders
(E) offer an irrelevant piece of trivia

16. Genghis Khan's empire expansion could be described as merciless because

(A) he was barbaric and unreasonable in the way he dealt with people
(B) he caused the deaths of tens of millions of people
(C) he was extremely greedy and ambitious for power and conquest
(D) he slaughtered people for the sake of slaughtering them
(E) he did not consider the feelings of his soldiers when he began is military campaigns

17. All of the following words were or could be used to describe Genghis Khan except

(A) unrelenting
(B) reasonable
(C) fair
(D) ruthless
(E) glib

18. The author probably found it surprising that Genghis Khan

(A) wanted to take over the world
(B) offered worthy adversaries quick and painless deaths
(C) conquered territory as quickly and rapidly as he was able to
(D) was brutal but amenable to peaceful takeovers at the same time
(E) took advantage of the fears of the people he conquered

19. Genghis Khan is notable for

(A) being the most ruthless and deadly conqueror in history
(B) assimilating more foreign empires and societies than anyone else in history did
(C) offering the most fair terms and conditions of surrender than any other conqueror in history did
(D) conquering more territory than anyone else in history did
(E) finding a good middle ground between being ruthless and friendly to his opponents

GO TO THE NEXT PAGE.

Line 5

10

15

20

25

Ancient Athens is often credited as being the progenitor of the modern concept of democracy. There is some debate as to which Athenian introduced the idea of democracy to Athens, but there is no debate that an aristocrat named Cleisthenes was the one who ushered in the acceptance of democracy as a form of governance by a people who had just two years prior ousted the tyrant Hippias in 510 B.C. But perhaps there is more to the story than a desire to end the reign of a tyrant who had grown increasingly repressive after the assassination of his brother Hipparchus in 514.

Greece, which was comprised of hundreds of city-states, or poleis, was fixated on war—wars were the norm, not the exception—and it was this fixation that led to the rise of the hoplite phalanx in the 7th century B.C. as the centerpiece of Greek militaries, so formidable the phalanx was. The phalanx's formidability came from its formation of densely packed soldiers standing in long parallel lines, with six to eight lines per phalanx. The phalanx soldiers, called hoplites, wore heavy armor, carried spears and swords, and bore shields that covered each warrior's left side and the right side of the man standing to his left. In this way, when the hoplites raised their shields and spears and started to march in complete synchronization, the phalanx transformed into an armed and impenetrable barrier that advanced methodically and relentlessly on its foes.

Moving a mass of people simultaneously and keeping them in formation were no easy tasks. It was imperative that there was a complete homogeneity of effort; there was no place for laziness or individual heroics. If one soldier leapt or fell out of place, the phalanx could be fatally compromised. Thus, each soldier depended on the others around him, and it is this codependency on one another that fostered an egalitarian ethos in the hoplites—socioeconomic class mattered little in a phalanx; everyone fought as equals.

And with 20 to 40 percent of the free males of every polis serving as a hoplite, the evidence convincingly suggests that the hoplite phalanx played a nontrivial role in the history of Athenian democracy; the question is how much.

20. The main idea of the passage is that
(A) phalanxes were essential to Greek poleis
(B) democracy became accepted in Athens because Cleisthenes drove out the tyrant Hippias
(C) phalanxes were effective because the hoplite soldiers wore heavy armor and carried heavy weapons
(D) military needs may have paved the way for the adoption of democracy in Athens
(E) the city-states of Ancient Greece developed the phalanx concept because they were so fixated on war

21. Which of the following was not true of Greek phalanxes or hoplites?
(A) Hoplite shields were designed to protect the hoplite's right side and the left side of the man standing to his right.
(B) Phalanxes were comprised of rows of soldiers.
(C) Phalanxes were formidable because they essentially transformed into impenetrable and weaponized moving walls.
(D) Hoplites standing in a phalanx formation wore heavy armor and carried spears and swords.
(E) Synchronization was critical to the success of a phalanx.

GO TO THE NEXT PAGE.

22. Which of the following best describes the significance of the phalanx in 7th century B.C. Greece?

    (A) Greek militaries had no possible hope of victory without at least one phalanx.
    (B) Phalanxes were optional for the militaries of Greek poleis.
    (C) The phalanx was the focal point of Greek militaries.
    (D) Greek militaries that did not use phalanxes relied heavily on cavalry and chariots.
    (E) Without the rise in prominence of the phalanx formation, democracy would never have been adopted in Athens.

23. How did the phalanx promote the mindset necessary for the acceptance of democracy?

    (A) Athenian phalanxes were behind Hippias's ouster in 510 B.C.
    (B) Hoplites depended on their fellow soldiers for survival, which led to a breakdown of the segregation typical of socioeconomic classes.
    (C) Because a homogeneity of effort was required of the hoplites, the soldiers developed an understanding of each other's frustrations and hardships.
    (D) 20 to 40 percent of free males of every polis served as hoplites, making freedom a priority.
    (E) There was no connection between phalanxes and the adoption of democracy.

24. Which of the following questions is left unanswered by the passage?

    (A) Why was Hipparchus assassinated?
    (B) Who ushered democracy into Athens?
    (C) Why did Hippias become an increasingly repressive tyrant?
    (D) How many rows of soldiers made up a typical phalanx formation?
    (E) Did the phalanx contribute at all to the adoption of democracy?

25. Overall, Greece's organizational structure as a nation in 7th century B.C. was one of

    (A) a totalitarian government
    (B) a constitutional monarchy
    (C) absolute chaos and anarchy because of all of the wars were waged on a regular basis
    (D) a communistic state that permitted city-states to operate independently
    (E) a collection of hundreds of city-states

GO TO THE NEXT PAGE.

As humans, we are naturally prone to fear the dark and the things that thrive in the dark. Our fear derives primarily from our vulnerability at night; it does not help that "we are accustomed to mastering our world by day," as Diane Ackerman writes in *The Moon by Whale Light*, since this contrast makes us all the more painfully

Line 5 aware of how vulnerable we are at night. For ages, storytellers have played (or preyed, as the case may be) on our fear of the dark. Ghosts, ghouls, and demons come out at night, and monsters wait in hiding for us until we're about to sleep; the list goes on, but instead of driving us away, these tales of nighttime terrors hold us raptly captive and even have us coming back for more, a phenomenon many

10 behavioral researchers have dubbed "the horror paradox."

Studies have shown that watching scary scenes induces in us a similar response to as if we were directly experiencing those same scenes, which is why our heartbeats increase by as many as 15 beats per minute, palms sweat, skin temperature drops several degrees, muscles tense, and blood pressure spikes. We

15 experience these physiological shifts because "[t]he brain hasn't really adapted to the new technology [of movies]," explains Glenn Sparks, a professor of communications at Purdue University. "We can tell ourselves the images on the screen are not real, but emotionally our brain reacts as if they are ... our 'old brain' still governs our reactions."

20 So why is it that a significant number of people enjoy being scared so much? Many theories exist. Some claim that we watch horror movies as sort of a tribal rite of passage, while others claim that by watching violence, we forestall the need to act it out, a phenomenon some refer to as "symbiotic catharsis." Still others suggest morbid curiosity as the reason we enjoy scary movies and stories. Whatever the root

25 cause of our preoccupation with horror is, one thing is certain: movie box office numbers don't lie—from 1995 to 2012, 21 horror movies had grossed (after adjusting for inflation) over $100 million each.

26. The author's tone in the passage is
   (A) ignorant and illogical
   (B) analytical but biased
   (C) shocked and offended
   (D) amused yet agitated
   (E) objective and informative

27. Which of the following is not specified by the passage as a physiological shift that results from watching a scary scene?
   (A) sweaty palms
   (B) raised blood pressure
   (C) lowered body temperatures
   (D) anxiety-induced rashes
   (E) increased rate of heartbeats

28. The horror paradox can be defined as
   (A) the mechanism by which violent desires and tendencies are forestalled by consuming media of the horror genre
   (B) the brain's inability to adapt to the new technology of movies
   (C) the phenomenon of being drawn to the things that are the most terrifying
   (D) the irony of horror stories being set at night, even though people are likelier to encounter scary phenomena during the day, when they are awake
   (E) the movie industry's ability to generate revenues in excess of $100 million

GO TO THE NEXT PAGE.

29. It can be inferred from the passage that
    (A) everyone enjoys the horror genre
    (B) ghosts, ghouls, demons, and monsters are not capable of scaring people in the daytime
    (C) it is not possible to go through a tribal rite of passage without undergoing a terrifying ordeal
    (D) the author considers $100 million in box office sales to be at least fairly successful for a movie
    (E) Diane Ackerman is an expert on human psychology who has done considerable research on the causes of fear

30. The author wrote this passage primarily to
    (A) recommend watching horror movies as a tribal rite of passage
    (B) show how profitable the horror genre is
    (C) explain why people are afraid of the dark
    (D) explain what drives fear and speculate about why the horror genre is as popular as it is
    (E) illustrate how vulnerable people feel at night

31. According to the passage, it may be the case that we as humans are more acutely aware of our vulnerability at night because
    (A) we are used to mastering the world by day
    (B) the drop in temperature at night causes us to feel greater levels of fear
    (C) horror movies and storytellers have brainwashed us into believing that terrifying supernatural phenomena occur more frequently at night
    (D) we normally spend the nights indoors safe and protected
    (E) we understand that horror stories and tales are for the most part fictional

GO TO THE NEXT PAGE.

Line 5

10

15

The English idiom "to cry wolf" comes from Aesop's Fable "The Boy Who Cried Wolf" and means to complain about something when nothing is actually wrong. Many other similar moralistic idioms and fables and anecdotes are used to teach us early on that honesty is the best policy and that lying ultimately leads to ruin. Few would argue that these moral lessons are erroneous or fallacious, per se; it is, after all, far easier to imagine how dishonesty can result in disaster and far simpler and safer to teach young children that lying is absolutely bad.

One of the problems with teaching that dishonesty is an absolutely morally reprehensible device, though, is that it causes unnecessarily difficult struggles with guilt, even when a situation calls for, or even requires, dishonesty and deception. Moral struggle is, of course, generally good—it keeps us anchored and helps us to better understand ourselves—but too much struggle can be more counterproductive than good and it gives people the impression that morality is black and white. Because life is rarely black and white, a balanced approach to moral education is needed—at some point, children need to be weaned off uncompromisingly absolute ideals and taught how to maintain integrity as they react to situations flexibly.

32. The author would most likely agree with the idea that
(A) lying is always good and perfectly acceptable
(B) certain situations require some degree of dishonesty
(C) fables and moral lessons teach impractical lessons
(D) white lies are always permissible
(E) honesty is always the best policy

33. The passage implies that few would argue that the lessons of honesty taught by fables are fallacious because teaching such lessons is
(A) due to ignorance
(B) obligatory
(C) regretful
(D) done out of hesitation
(E) convenient

34. Moral struggle is generally good because it
(A) helps us to understand others
(B) prevents us from becoming counterproductive
(C) allows us to feel less regret and remorse in the future
(D) keeps us anchored
(E) helps us to find the most morally effective solutions

35. The author's tone in the passage is
(A) opinionated and practical
(B) aggressive yet objective
(C) scornful yet amused
(D) appreciative and passive
(E) respectful and impractical

GO TO THE NEXT PAGE.

Line 5

10

15

20

In antiquity, when the human body was not as well understood as it is today, medical practitioners believed that many illnesses could be cured or treated by a process known as bloodletting or, more scientifically, phlebotomy. As the term suggests, bloodletting involved letting blood out of the body, typically by making some sort of incision to draw blood or by using leeches to suck blood out. And while it may seem baffling as to why people would consent to such a procedure, which started probably some 3,000 years ago with the ancient Egyptians or Sumerians and continued with the Greeks and Romans and gained traction even into the Renaissance, reaching its peak in the 19th century, it is important to understand the paradigm of medicine of that time.

It was widely believed by preeminent physicians such as Hippocrates that the human body was comprised of four primary substances or "humors": blood, phlegm, yellow bile, and black bile. It was further posited that illnesses resulted when the humors were out of balance. Thus, depending on which humor was believed to be in excess, a different purging technique was used. One of these techniques was of course bloodletting, which was to be used when the body contained an excessive imbalance of blood. Though accidental deaths due to bloodletting were not uncommon, its various implementations continued to thrive for an extended time, as it took on even greater societal significance when people realized that blood was the most dominant humor.

36. Hippocrates believed all of the following to be humors of the body except:

(A) yellow bile
(B) blood
(C) cartilage
(D) phlegm
(E) black bile

37. It can be inferred from the passage that

(A) if there was an excess of yellow bile, then black bile would be purged because black bile is the opposite humor of yellow bile
(B) if there was an excess of phlegm, then both phlegm and yellow bile would be purged because yellow bile is similar to phlegm
(C) if there was a deficiency of a humor, then that humor would be obtained from someone else who had an excess of that particular humor
(D) modern medicine has discovered that humors do actually comprise the four primary substances of the human body
(E) doctors until sometime in the 19th century believed that death was an acceptable risk that had to be taken in order to try to cure a patient

38. Phlebotomy was a common practice in antiquity because

(A) leeches were particularly effective at drawing blood out
(B) it was believed then that letting blood out could cure or treat illnesses
(C) bloodletting was the most convenient method of treatment
(D) doctors were greedy and lazy, so they didn't want to provide legitimate treatments
(E) people enjoyed the relief they experienced when bad blood exited their bodies

39. According to Hippocrates and his contemporaries, illnesses resulted when

(A) the humors of the body were out of balance
(B) doctors accidentally made incisions that resulted in excessive blood loss
(C) proper sanitation measures were not employed
(D) an ill person spent too much time around others who weren't ill
(E) bacteria and viruses were spread to others

GO TO THE NEXT PAGE.

40. The practice of bloodletting probably originated
   - (A) with the ancient Greeks and Romans
   - (B) during the Renaissance
   - (C) several millennia ago with the Egyptians or Sumerians
   - (D) in the 19th century, once people realized blood was the most dominant humor
   - (E) when it was realized that people who found leeches feeding on them felt better after having some of their blood drawn out than they did before the leeches feeding on them

STOP

IF YOU FINISH BEFORE TIME IS CALLED, YOU MAY CHECK YOUR WORK ON THIS SECTION ONLY.
DO NOT TURN TO ANY OTHER SECTION IN THE TEST.

SECTION 3
60 Questions
30 Minutes

There are two types of questions in this section: synonyms and analogies.

Synonyms
Each question consists of one word in capital letters, followed by five answer choices. Select the answer choice consisting of the word or phrase closest in meaning to the word in capital letters.

Sample Question:

TORRID:

(A) mild
(B) painful
(C) pleasant
(D) hot
(E) sticky

 Ⓐ Ⓑ Ⓒ ● Ⓔ

---

1. VIVID:

    (A) stubborn
    (B) bland
    (C) comfortable
    (D) striking
    (E) humorous

2. MUTINY:

    (A) kowtow
    (B) rebel
    (C) jest
    (D) pray
    (E) augment

3. THRIFTY:

    (A) fake
    (B) economical
    (C) wise
    (D) flamboyant
    (E) wasteful

4. JARGON:

    (A) gibberish
    (B) container
    (C) error
    (D) healthy
    (E) communication

5. FUNDAMENTAL:

    (A) sophisticated
    (B) routine
    (C) essential
    (D) entertaining
    (E) unimaginative

6. PARCH:

    (A) incinerate
    (B) stand
    (C) desiccate
    (D) observe
    (E) predate

7. HUMILITY:

    (A) meekness
    (B) moderation
    (C) reluctance
    (D) exuberance
    (E) haughtiness

8. AGGRAVATE:

    (A) curse
    (B) soften
    (C) explain
    (D) worsen
    (E) brighten

GO TO THE NEXT PAGE.

9. COMMENCE:
   (A) begin
   (B) submerge
   (C) afflict
   (D) pause
   (E) purchase

10. MELLOW:
   (A) jumpy
   (B) relaxed
   (C) fearsome
   (D) edgy
   (E) fruity

11. POSTERITY:
   (A) descendants
   (B) stationery
   (C) caboose
   (D) adhesives
   (E) engine

12. CONTRITE:
   (A) relaxed
   (B) vengeful
   (C) ecstatic
   (D) sorrowful
   (E) relevant

13. EFFICACY:
   (A) residence
   (B) effectiveness
   (C) desirability
   (D) monetization
   (E) innateness

14. TENUOUS:
   (A) unsound
   (B) consistent
   (C) persistent
   (D) unruly
   (E) disastrous

15. NEOPHYTE:
   (A) commander
   (B) editor
   (C) veteran
   (D) amateur
   (E) performer

16. VORACIOUS:
   (A) perceptive
   (B) odoriferous
   (C) lackadaisical
   (D) ravenous
   (E) vibrant

17. DEPLETE:
   (A) discover
   (B) restock
   (C) covet
   (D) exhaust
   (E) convert

18. ATROPHY:
   (A) victory
   (B) bitterness
   (C) defeat
   (D) finality
   (E) degeneration

19. HACKNEYED:
   (A) overused
   (B) unclean
   (C) original
   (D) felicitous
   (E) ludicrous

20. EXTRANEOUS:
   (A) unnecessary
   (B) superb
   (C) unintelligible
   (D) inherent
   (E) antiquated

GO TO THE NEXT PAGE.

21. BLASPHEMY:

    (A) disrespect
    (B) sacrilege
    (C) honor
    (D) trick
    (E) loyalty

22. PERFUNCTORY:

    (A) thorough
    (B) hasty
    (C) flawed
    (D) perfect
    (E) fastidious

23. FORTUITOUS:

    (A) deliberate
    (B) grateful
    (C) generous
    (D) unpredictable
    (E) serendipitous

24. COERCE:

    (A) convince
    (B) force
    (C) resign
    (D) wheedle
    (E) beguile

25. VIRULENT:

    (A) noxious
    (B) unyielding
    (C) lenient
    (D) viral
    (E) sympathetic

26. INDEFATIGABLE:

    (A) unbeatable
    (B) tireless
    (C) vulnerable
    (D) overwhelming
    (E) cunning

27. REMINISCE:

    (A) remember
    (B) lament
    (C) respond
    (D) begrudge
    (E) enjoy

28. FLUMMOX:

    (A) flap
    (B) spin
    (C) inebriate
    (D) capitulate
    (E) confound

29. GAFFE:

    (A) accomplishment
    (B) cue
    (C) misstep
    (D) crime
    (E) cliché

30. ABLUTION:

    (A) annulment
    (B) cleansing
    (C) grief
    (D) pollution
    (E) touch

GO TO THE NEXT PAGE.

Analogies

These questions will ask you to find the relationships between words. For each question, select the answer choice that best completes the analogy relationship.

Sample Question:

Glove is to hand as shoe is to

(A) mouth
(B) head
(C) finger
(D) foot
(E) sock

Ⓐ Ⓑ Ⓒ ● Ⓔ

31. Chicken is to pig as

   (A) cow is to cheetah
   (B) turtle is to shark
   (C) donkey is to giraffe
   (D) bear is to snake
   (E) penguin is to moose

32. Baker is to bread as

   (A) waiter is to food
   (B) bank teller is to money
   (C) woman is to baby
   (D) dentist is to teeth
   (E) sculptor is to statue

33. Star is to galaxy as

   (A) needle is to haystack
   (B) photograph is to album
   (C) beach is to ocean
   (D) continent is to country
   (E) planet is to moon

34. Whine is to tantrum as

   (A) punch is to slap
   (B) desire is to want
   (C) squeak is to roar
   (D) moan is to groan
   (E) smile is to grin

35. Program is to performance as

   (A) shopping is to checklist
   (B) itinerary is to journey
   (C) poem is to stanza
   (D) prelude is to symphony
   (E) plan is to schedule

36. Glove is to pugilist as

   (A) shoe is to nomad
   (B) cane is to elderly
   (C) bow is to archer
   (D) crown is to king
   (E) lure is to bait

37. Odometer is to distance as

   (A) radar is to sonar
   (B) altimeter is to flight
   (C) scale is to obesity
   (D) barometer is to pressure
   (E) thermometer is to fever

38. Pacemaker is to cardiac as

   (A) crutch is to cerebral
   (B) prosthetic is to scalp
   (C) hearing aid is to auditory
   (D) bandage is to stitch
   (E) splint is to fracture

GO TO THE NEXT PAGE.

39. Walk is to ambulate as plod is to

(A) trudge
(B) jog
(C) dash
(D) scurry
(E) sprint

40. Oaf is to acumen as

(A) novice is to experience
(B) police is to courage
(C) servant is to master
(D) veteran is to skill
(E) millionaire is to poverty

41. Curator is to gallery as

(A) firefighter is to flames
(B) editor is to newspaper
(C) mayor is to state
(D) jury is to law
(E) anthology is to books

42. Defoliate is to tree as

(A) remove is to wart
(B) defrost is to window
(C) trim is to hair
(D) peel is to orange
(E) misplace is to belonging

43. Omnipotent is to power as omniscient is to

(A) knowledge
(B) senses
(C) presence
(D) artistry
(E) divinity

44. Doctor is to apothecary as

(A) pastor is to church
(B) driver is to racecar
(C) architect is to engineer
(D) electrician is to fireman
(E) employee is to occupation

45. Rural is to barn as

(A) urban is to building
(B) cosmopolitan is to fashion
(C) suburban is to city
(D) metropolitan is to skyscraper
(E) celestial is to sky

46. Quash is to incite as

(A) tout is to proclaim
(B) blemish is to defile
(C) amphibian is to aquatic
(D) loud is to deaf
(E) animus is to affection

47. Infantile is to puerile as

(A) homely is to royal
(B) miserly is to generous
(C) juvenile is to adolescent
(D) grueling is to effortless
(E) apathetic is to personable

48. Toady is to lionize as

(A) misanthrope is to loathe
(B) president is to impeach
(C) farmer is to fodder
(D) coward is to aggrandize
(E) conductor is to orchestra

49. Descent is to plummet as

(A) father is to children
(B) ascent is to skyrocket
(C) brother is to sister
(D) reputation is to damage
(E) interpretation is to literal

50. Census is to population as

(A) survey is to questions
(B) poll is to voters
(C) assessment is to examination
(D) inventory is to stock
(E) questionnaire is to optional

GO TO THE NEXT PAGE.

51. Enervate is to energize as

    (A) ponder is to teach
    (B) cultivate is to plant
    (C) immolate is to sacrifice
    (D) obstruct is to block
    (E) deny is to admit

52. Pulverization is to erode as

    (A) havoc is to wreak
    (B) convey is to inform
    (C) foreshadow is to forecast
    (D) compulsion is to cajole
    (E) excision is to destruction

53. Key is to lock as

    (A) password is to username
    (B) clue is to mystery
    (C) hint is to suggestion
    (D) index card is to notes
    (E) alphabet is to word

54. Agility is to acrobat as

    (A) fairness is to arbiter
    (B) brush is to painter
    (C) words is to orator
    (D) clarity is to vision
    (E) integrity is to thief

55. Appendage is to auxiliary as

    (A) addendum is to useless
    (B) muscle is to strength
    (C) limb is to expendable
    (D) engine is to movement
    (E) core is to essential

56. Telephone is to voice as

    (A) car is to passenger
    (B) shoe is to sprinter
    (C) novel is to chapter
    (D) airplane is to flight
    (E) box is to clothes

57. Frugal is to spendthrift as

    (A) erudite is to scholar
    (B) athletic is to gamer
    (C) pious is to atheist
    (D) scientific is to survey
    (E) strategic is to gambit

58. Acre is to field as

    (A) second is to year
    (B) watt is to kilowatt
    (C) millimeter is to size
    (D) hour is to flight
    (E) degree is to magnitude

59. Shot is to needle as

    (A) infection is to antibiotic
    (B) cheese is to cow
    (C) incision is to scalpel
    (D) suture is to stethoscope
    (E) laser is to light

60. Favorable is to propitious as

    (A) lethal is to salubrious
    (B) auspicious is to opportune
    (C) vulnerable is to invincible
    (D) awkward is to careless
    (E) militant is to chaotic

STOP

**IF YOU FINISH BEFORE TIME IS CALLED, YOU MAY CHECK YOUR WORK ON THIS SECTION ONLY.
DO NOT TURN TO ANY OTHER SECTION IN THE TEST.**

SECTION 4
25 Questions
30 Minutes

Work through each problem in this section. You may use the blank pace to the right of the page, if you need, to do your figuring. Then select the best one of the five suggested answer choices.

Note: Some of the problems are accompanied by figures, which are rendered as accurately as possible, EXCEPT when the problem explicitly states that its accompanying figure is not drawn to scale.

Sample Problem:

6,329	(A) 2,151
$-$ 3,478	(B) 2,275
	(C) 2,807
	(D) 2,851
	(E) 2,951 Ⓐ Ⓑ Ⓒ ● Ⓔ

SPACE FOR FIGURING

1. If q is a positive real number less than 1, which of the following statements is true?

      I. q^2 is less than q.
      II. q may be negative.
      III. q^3 is greater than q^2.

(A) I only
(B) I and II
(C) II only
(D) II and III
(E) I, II, and III

2. If $25 \times B^2 = 9$, and $B + C = 1$, which of the following can be C?

(A) $\dfrac{16}{25}$

(B) $\dfrac{1}{5}$

(C) $\dfrac{2}{5}$

(D) $\dfrac{3}{5}$

(E) $\dfrac{4}{5}$

GO TO THE NEXT PAGE.

3. $355\frac{8}{17} - 196\frac{12}{17} =$

    (A) $169\frac{4}{17}$
    (B) $168\frac{13}{17}$
    (C) $159\frac{1}{4}$
    (D) $158\frac{4}{17}$
    (E) $158\frac{13}{17}$

---

4. $1.675 \div 10^{-3} =$

    (A) 0.001675
    (B) 0.01675
    (C) 167.5
    (D) 1,675
    (E) 1,675,000

---

5. Find the least common multiple of 32, 36, and 40.

    (A) 360
    (B) 720
    (C) 1,440
    (D) 5,760
    (E) 46,080

---

6. If the average of three consecutive integers is 17, what is the sum of the largest of these three integers and the next consecutive integer that follows the largest of these three integers?

    (A) 19
    (B) 20
    (C) 34
    (D) 36
    (E) 37

GO TO THE NEXT PAGE.

7. A log is cut into three equal-sized pieces. If one cut takes 3 minutes and 45 seconds, how long would it take to cut the three log pieces into six equal-sized pieces?

    (A) 10 minutes, 15 seconds
    (B) 10 minutes, 45 seconds
    (C) 11 minutes, 15 seconds
    (D) 11 minutes, 25 seconds
    (E) 18 minutes, 30 seconds

8. Simplify the variable expression: $\dfrac{92a^3b^{-2}c^4d}{23a^2b^3d^{-1}}$

    (A) $4ab^5c^4d^2$

    (B) $\dfrac{4ac^4d^2}{b^5}$

    (C) $\dfrac{3a^{1.5}c^4}{b^{1.5}}$

    (D) $3ab^{-5}c^4d^{-2}$

    (E) $\dfrac{3a^6c^4d^2}{b^6}$

9. The mean weight of three watermelons is 8.8 pounds, while the mean weight of five pumpkins is 6.4 pounds. What is the mean weight of all eight produce items?

    (A) 7.3 pounds
    (B) 7.4 pounds
    (C) 7.6 pounds
    (D) 7.7 pounds
    (E) 8.2 pounds

10. All of the following products are equal EXCEPT

    (A) $3 \times \frac{7}{21}$

    (B) $\frac{8}{17} \times \frac{51}{24}$

    (C) $1\frac{3}{10} \times \frac{20}{26}$

    (D) $5 \times \frac{25}{150}$

    (E) $\frac{19}{2} \times \frac{4}{38}$

GO TO THE NEXT PAGE.

11. United States pennies weigh 2.50 grams per coin. If a roll of pennies contains 50 pennies, and the roll paper weighs 1.50 grams, how many grams does a roll of pennies, including the roll paper that wraps the pennies, weigh?

   (A) 120.0 grams
   (B) 121.5 grams
   (C) 125.0 grams
   (D) 126.5 grams
   (E) 151.5 grams

12. Combine and simplify:
    $(6x^4 - 5x^2 + 9x) - (x^4 - 4x^3 - 7x) + 1$

   (A) $5x^4 - 9x^3 + 16x + 1$
   (B) $5x^4 - x^3 + 2x - 1$
   (C) $5x^4 - 5x^3 + 4x^2 + 16x + 1$
   (D) $5x^4 - 4x^3 - 5x^2 + 16x + 1$
   (E) $5x^4 + 4x^3 - 5x^2 + 16x + 1$

13. If $2M + 5 < 22$, and M is a positive integer, what is the maximum value of $5M + 19$?

   (A) 64
   (B) 61
   (C) 59
   (D) 57
   (E) 53

14. A fence $15\frac{2}{3}$ feet long is barbed every 4 inches, starting with a barb at the very beginning of the fencing. How many barbs does the fence have?

   (A) 48
   (B) 47
   (C) 46
   (D) 45
   (E) 43

GO TO THE NEXT PAGE.
SPACE FOR FIGURING

15. If $4x^4 + 5y^4 = 0$, and x and y are real numbers, what is the value of $5x^2 + 4y^2$?

    (A) -1
    (B) 0
    (C) 1
    (D) 2
    (E) It cannot be determined from the information given.

16. What is the value of the second smallest of five consecutive even integers, if the smallest is one-third of the greatest?

    (A) 4
    (B) 6
    (C) 8
    (D) 10
    (E) 12

17. Cassandra purchased a plot of real estate for $560,000. If the lot was 10 hectares (1 hectare = 10,000 square meters), what was her cost per square meter?

    (A) $0.05
    (B) $0.06
    (C) $0.56
    (D) $5.60
    (E) $56.00

18. In a survey, 900 people indicated that they owned at least one dog, one cat, or both. 550 people said they had dogs, while 420 people said cats. How many of the people surveyed own both at least one cat and one dog?

    (A) 60
    (B) 70
    (C) 90
    (D) 130
    (E) 150

GO TO THE NEXT PAGE.
SPACE FOR FIGURING

19. $9 \times 4{,}265 =$

    (A) $9 \times 4{,}000 + 265$
    (B) $9 \times 4{,}000 + 9 \times 26 + 9 \times 5$
    (C) $9 \times 4{,}000 + 9 \times (200 + 60) + 5$
    (D) $9 \times 4{,}000 + 9 \times 260 + 9 \times 5$
    (E) $9 \times 4{,}200 + 9 \times 60 + 5$

20. A sphere's volume is given by the formula $V = (4 \times \pi r^3) \div 3$, where r represents the radius of the sphere. If two spheres are tangent to each other (they're touching at exactly one point), what is the distance between the centers of the spheres, if the smaller one has a volume of 36π in.^{3} and the larger one has a volume of 288π in.^{3}?

    (A) 9 in.
    (B) 18 in.
    (C) 72 in.
    (D) 252 in.
    (E) 324 in.

21. What is the value, in cents, of $23p$ pennies and $47d$ dimes, where p and d are integers?

    (A) $(23 + 47)(p + d)$
    (B) $23p + 47d$
    (C) $70p + d$
    (D) $493pd$
    (E) $23p + 470d$

22. In the figure, O is the center of the circle that has diameters $\overline{AB}$ and $\overline{CD}$, as shown. The two diameters intersect to form $\angle AOC$ that measures $x°$. If the measure of $\angle AOD$ is twice that of $\angle AOC$, and the radius of circle O is 15 centimeters, what is the area of sector COB?

    (A) 45π cm^2
    (B) 55π cm^2
    (C) 65π cm^2
    (D) 75π cm^2
    (E) 112.5π cm^2

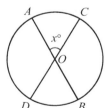

GO TO THE NEXT PAGE.
SPACE FOR FIGURING

23. If a box measuring 4 feet by 5 feet by 6 feet is filled to capacity by 200 equal-sized snow globes, what could be the dimensions of a box filled to capacity by 450 snow globes?

   (A) 4 feet by 5 feet by 13.5 feet
   (B) 6 feet by 6 feet by 6 feet
   (C) 8 feet by 12 feet by 12 feet
   (D) 8 feet by 5 feet by 9 feet
   (E) 8 feet by 10 feet by 12 feet

Questions 24-25 refer to the graph.

24. If Mallory's monthly budget is $8,000, how much money does she put into savings in one year?

   (A) $960
   (B) $5,000
   (C) $9,600
   (D) $11,520
   (E) $12,000

25. How much more does Mallory spend on rent in 3 months than she does on utilities in 3 months?

   (A) $1,200
   (B) $3,200
   (C) $3,600
   (D) $6,000
   (E) $9,600

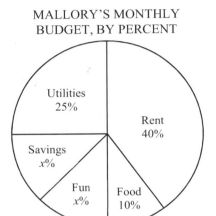

MALLORY'S MONTHLY BUDGET, BY PERCENT

Utilities 25%
Rent 40%
Savings $x\%$
Fun $x\%$
Food 10%

STOP

IF YOU FINISH BEFORE TIME IS CALLED, YOU MAY CHECK YOUR WORK ON THIS SECTION ONLY.
DO NOT TURN TO ANY OTHER SECTION IN THE TEST.

SSAT
UPPER LEVEL
TEST 2

ANSWER SHEET

Make sure to completely fill in the bubbles corresponding to your answer choices.

Section 1

1	(A)(B)(C)(D)(E)	6	(A)(B)(C)(D)(E)	11	(A)(B)(C)(D)(E)	16	(A)(B)(C)(D)(E)	21	(A)(B)(C)(D)(E)
2	(A)(B)(C)(D)(E)	7	(A)(B)(C)(D)(E)	12	(A)(B)(C)(D)(E)	17	(A)(B)(C)(D)(E)	22	(A)(B)(C)(D)(E)
3	(A)(B)(C)(D)(E)	8	(A)(B)(C)(D)(E)	13	(A)(B)(C)(D)(E)	18	(A)(B)(C)(D)(E)	23	(A)(B)(C)(D)(E)
4	(A)(B)(C)(D)(E)	9	(A)(B)(C)(D)(E)	14	(A)(B)(C)(D)(E)	19	(A)(B)(C)(D)(E)	24	(A)(B)(C)(D)(E)
5	(A)(B)(C)(D)(E)	10	(A)(B)(C)(D)(E)	15	(A)(B)(C)(D)(E)	20	(A)(B)(C)(D)(E)	25	(A)(B)(C)(D)(E)

Section 2

1	(A)(B)(C)(D)(E)	9	(A)(B)(C)(D)(E)	17	(A)(B)(C)(D)(E)	25	(A)(B)(C)(D)(E)	33	(A)(B)(C)(D)(E)
2	(A)(B)(C)(D)(E)	10	(A)(B)(C)(D)(E)	18	(A)(B)(C)(D)(E)	26	(A)(B)(C)(D)(E)	34	(A)(B)(C)(D)(E)
3	(A)(B)(C)(D)(E)	11	(A)(B)(C)(D)(E)	19	(A)(B)(C)(D)(E)	27	(A)(B)(C)(D)(E)	35	(A)(B)(C)(D)(E)
4	(A)(B)(C)(D)(E)	12	(A)(B)(C)(D)(E)	20	(A)(B)(C)(D)(E)	28	(A)(B)(C)(D)(E)	36	(A)(B)(C)(D)(E)
5	(A)(B)(C)(D)(E)	13	(A)(B)(C)(D)(E)	21	(A)(B)(C)(D)(E)	29	(A)(B)(C)(D)(E)	37	(A)(B)(C)(D)(E)
6	(A)(B)(C)(D)(E)	14	(A)(B)(C)(D)(E)	22	(A)(B)(C)(D)(E)	30	(A)(B)(C)(D)(E)	38	(A)(B)(C)(D)(E)
7	(A)(B)(C)(D)(E)	15	(A)(B)(C)(D)(E)	23	(A)(B)(C)(D)(E)	31	(A)(B)(C)(D)(E)	39	(A)(B)(C)(D)(E)
8	(A)(B)(C)(D)(E)	16	(A)(B)(C)(D)(E)	24	(A)(B)(C)(D)(E)	32	(A)(B)(C)(D)(E)	40	(A)(B)(C)(D)(E)

Section 3

1	(A)(B)(C)(D)(E)	13	(A)(B)(C)(D)(E)	25	(A)(B)(C)(D)(E)	37	(A)(B)(C)(D)(E)	49	(A)(B)(C)(D)(E)
2	(A)(B)(C)(D)(E)	14	(A)(B)(C)(D)(E)	26	(A)(B)(C)(D)(E)	38	(A)(B)(C)(D)(E)	50	(A)(B)(C)(D)(E)
3	(A)(B)(C)(D)(E)	15	(A)(B)(C)(D)(E)	27	(A)(B)(C)(D)(E)	39	(A)(B)(C)(D)(E)	51	(A)(B)(C)(D)(E)
4	(A)(B)(C)(D)(E)	16	(A)(B)(C)(D)(E)	28	(A)(B)(C)(D)(E)	40	(A)(B)(C)(D)(E)	52	(A)(B)(C)(D)(E)
5	(A)(B)(C)(D)(E)	17	(A)(B)(C)(D)(E)	29	(A)(B)(C)(D)(E)	41	(A)(B)(C)(D)(E)	53	(A)(B)(C)(D)(E)
6	(A)(B)(C)(D)(E)	18	(A)(B)(C)(D)(E)	30	(A)(B)(C)(D)(E)	42	(A)(B)(C)(D)(E)	54	(A)(B)(C)(D)(E)
7	(A)(B)(C)(D)(E)	19	(A)(B)(C)(D)(E)	31	(A)(B)(C)(D)(E)	43	(A)(B)(C)(D)(E)	55	(A)(B)(C)(D)(E)
8	(A)(B)(C)(D)(E)	20	(A)(B)(C)(D)(E)	32	(A)(B)(C)(D)(E)	44	(A)(B)(C)(D)(E)	56	(A)(B)(C)(D)(E)
9	(A)(B)(C)(D)(E)	21	(A)(B)(C)(D)(E)	33	(A)(B)(C)(D)(E)	45	(A)(B)(C)(D)(E)	57	(A)(B)(C)(D)(E)
10	(A)(B)(C)(D)(E)	22	(A)(B)(C)(D)(E)	34	(A)(B)(C)(D)(E)	46	(A)(B)(C)(D)(E)	58	(A)(B)(C)(D)(E)
11	(A)(B)(C)(D)(E)	23	(A)(B)(C)(D)(E)	35	(A)(B)(C)(D)(E)	47	(A)(B)(C)(D)(E)	59	(A)(B)(C)(D)(E)
12	(A)(B)(C)(D)(E)	24	(A)(B)(C)(D)(E)	36	(A)(B)(C)(D)(E)	48	(A)(B)(C)(D)(E)	60	(A)(B)(C)(D)(E)

Section 4

1	(A)(B)(C)(D)(E)	6	(A)(B)(C)(D)(E)	11	(A)(B)(C)(D)(E)	16	(A)(B)(C)(D)(E)	21	(A)(B)(C)(D)(E)
2	(A)(B)(C)(D)(E)	7	(A)(B)(C)(D)(E)	12	(A)(B)(C)(D)(E)	17	(A)(B)(C)(D)(E)	22	(A)(B)(C)(D)(E)
3	(A)(B)(C)(D)(E)	8	(A)(B)(C)(D)(E)	13	(A)(B)(C)(D)(E)	18	(A)(B)(C)(D)(E)	23	(A)(B)(C)(D)(E)
4	(A)(B)(C)(D)(E)	9	(A)(B)(C)(D)(E)	14	(A)(B)(C)(D)(E)	19	(A)(B)(C)(D)(E)	24	(A)(B)(C)(D)(E)
5	(A)(B)(C)(D)(E)	10	(A)(B)(C)(D)(E)	15	(A)(B)(C)(D)(E)	20	(A)(B)(C)(D)(E)	25	(A)(B)(C)(D)(E)

Writing Sample

Select one of the two essay prompts below and write an essay or story to address or answer the prompt you selected. Your writing sample will help schools understand you better as an applicant.

A. How much of a role does convenience play in your decision-making process?

B. There was no time to panic, only time to act.

Use this page and the next to write your essay or story.

Continue on the next page.

SECTION I
25 Questions
30 minutes

Work through each problem in this section. You may use the blank pace to the right of the page, if you need, to do your figuring. Then select the best one of the five suggested answer choices.

Note: Some of the problems are accompanied by figures, which are rendered as accurately as possible, EXCEPT when the problem explicitly states that its accompanying figure is not drawn to scale.

Sample Problem:

6,329	(A)	2,151
− 3,478	(B)	2,275
	(C)	2,807
	(D)	2,851
	(E)	2,951 Ⓐ Ⓑ Ⓒ ● Ⓔ

---

1. Which of the following could NOT be the side lengths of a right triangle?

   (A) 2, 2, $2\sqrt{2}$
   (B) $\sqrt{3}$, 3, $2\sqrt{3}$
   (C) 10, 24, 25
   (D) 7, 24, 25
   (E) 15, 20, 25

---

2. Ernest has 600 marbles. He gives his little sister 54 of them. What percent of the original number of marbles does he have left?

   (A) 91%
   (B) 90%
   (C) 45%
   (D) 10%
   (E) 9%

GO TO THE NEXT PAGE.

3. Triangles A and B are similar. If the length of one of the sides
    of triangle B is 45 cm, and the length of the corresponding side
    of triangle A is 9 cm, what is the ratio of the area of triangle A
    to that of triangle B?

    (A) $1 : 25$
    (B) $1 : 5$
    (C) $5 : 1$
    (D) $25 : 1$
    (E) It cannot be determined from the information given.

4. Dillon has 51 comics in his collection that he plans to give away
    to his friends at his birthday party. At his party, 15 of friends
    come over. If he gives out the same number of comics to each
    friend, how many comics will he have left over?

    (A) 0
    (B) 2
    (C) 3
    (D) 6
    (E) 9

$$\left(-\frac{6}{7}\right)^{3} \div \left(\frac{6}{7}\right)^{2} =$$

5. The result of the above calculation is closest to which of the following?

    (A) $\left(\dfrac{6}{7}\right)^{5}$

    (B) $\left(\dfrac{6}{7}\right)^{6}$

    (C) $\left(-\dfrac{7}{6}\right)$

    (D) $\left(-\dfrac{6}{7}\right)$

    (E) $\left(-\dfrac{6}{7}\right)^{5}$

GO TO THE NEXT PAGE.

SPACE FOR FIGURING

6. $\dfrac{99,346}{4,013}$ most closely equals which of the following?

 (A) 2.4
 (B) 2.5
 (C) 24
 (D) 25
 (E) 247.5

7. When $C + D = 7$ and $(E + D) \div 3 = 6$, what is the value of $E + C$?

 (A) 1
 (B) 6.5
 (C) 11
 (D) 13
 (E) It cannot be determined from the information given.

8. In the figure, the semicircle A and trapezoid B share a common boundary. The top base of trapezoid B is congruent to the diameter of semicircle A and the height of trapezoid B is 3 inches. If the bottom base of trapezoid B is 1.5 times the length of that of trapezoid B's top base, and the area of semicircle A is 18π square inches, what is the area of trapezoid B? (The formula for the area of a trapezoid is $A = \frac{1}{2} \times (b_1 + b_2) \times h$, where b_1 represents the length of one base, b_2 the other base, and h the height.)

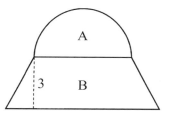

 (A) 36 sq. in.
 (B) 45 sq. in.
 (C) 60 sq. in.
 (D) 96 sq. in.
 (E) 108 sq. in.

9. If Karl scored 55, 63, 57, 72, and 81 on five tests, what was his average for those five tests?

 (A) 63
 (B) 64
 (C) 64.7
 (D) 65
 (E) 65.6

GO TO THE NEXT PAGE.

SPACE FOR FIGURING

10. If 65 percent of $4x$ is 5.2, what is 30 percent of 50 percent of x?

   (A) 0.3
   (B) 0.39
   (C) 1.2
   (D) 1.3
   (E) 1.5

11. In the figure, if s is a whole number, which of the following
    could be half of the length of segment AB?

   (A) 23
   (B) 23.5
   (C) 25
   (D) 25.5
   (E) 28

12. Which of the following could be the value of T if
    $0.5(T + 3) < 4$?

   (A) 3
   (B) 5
   (C) 7
   (D) 8
   (E) 9

13. In the figure, what is the measure of $\angle BCD$, if the measure of
    $\angle ABC$ is 40° more than the measure of $\angle BAC$?

   (A) 35°
   (B) 45°
   (C) 70°
   (D) 80°
   (E) 110°

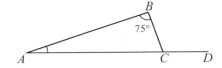

14. If a winter coat, originally priced at $185.00, is discounted 45%
    during a spring cleaning sale, what is the coat's spring sale
    price?

   (A) $83.25
   (B) $83.50
   (C) $92.50
   (D) $101.75
   (E) $103.25

GO TO THE NEXT PAGE.

15. The lengths of two roads have a ratio of 7:5. If the shorter road is lengthened by 20 miles, the shorter road will still be shorter than the longer road by 20 miles. What is the length of the longer road?

 (A) 100 miles
 (B) 120 miles
 (C) 140 miles
 (D) 160 miles
 (E) 180 miles

16. Roald lives 14 miles from school, and Porter lives 15 miles from school. If Roald's house, Porter's house, and the school are collinear, meaning that they are all on the same line, what is the distance from Roald's house to Porter's house?

 (A) 1 mile
 (B) 9 miles
 (C) 14.5 miles
 (D) 29 miles
 (E) It cannot be determined from the information given.

17. If the average of two numbers, A and B, is equal to the sum of two other numbers, C and D, what is the value of C, in terms of A, B, and D?

 (A) $A + B - D$
 (B) $2A + 2B - 2D$
 (C) $A + B - 2D$
 (D) $A + B \div 2 - D$
 (E) $(A + B) \div 2 - D$

18. Tracy needs to provide shoes for his school's track team, which has 165 members. The shoes are originally $50.00 per pair. If he orders more than 200 pairs of shoes, he will receive a 45% discount on the total order. How much more would it cost Tracy to order two pairs of shoes for every member of the track team than it would to order one pair of shoes per member?

 (A) $750.00
 (B) $825.00
 (C) $907.50
 (D) $1,250.00
 (E) $2,500.50

GO TO THE NEXT PAGE.

SPACE FOR FIGURING

19. Three watermelons weigh the same as 40 apples. To the weight of the nearest apple, what is the weight of seven watermelons?

    (A) 80
    (B) 85
    (C) 93
    (D) 94
    (E) 95

20. Nick, a volunteer at an orphanage, wants to bring the children some more holiday cheer, so he plans to celebrate Christmas with them for 12 days. On each day, he will give each child one more gift than he gave the child the previous day. (For example, if he gives a child x gifts on one day, he'll give the child $x + 1$ gifts the next day.) If he gives each child 1 gift on the first day, and there are 13 children at the orphanage, how many gifts will he have given in total by the end of the 6th day?

    (A) 78
    (B) 96
    (C) 126
    (D) 273
    (E) 343

21. In the addition of the four-digit numbers shown, the letters A, B, and C each represent a unique single digit. Which of the following accurately lists the correct value for each digit?

    (A) A = 4, B = 8, C = 1
    (B) A = 3, B = 7, C = 1
    (C) A = 3, B = 7, C = 6
    (D) A = 4, B = 7, C = 6
    (E) It cannot be determined from the information given.

$$\begin{array}{r} A\ B\ 2\ C \\ +\ A\ C\ B\ C \\ \hline B\ 4\ 0\ 2 \end{array}$$

22. Two congruent circles are externally tangent to one another. A line segment is then drawn from one circle's center to the other circle's center. If this line segment is the radius of a third circle, what is the ratio of the area of the third circle to that of one of the first two circles?

    (A) 4 : 1
    (B) 3 : 1
    (C) 2 : 1
    (D) 1 : 2
    (E) 1 : 4

GO TO THE NEXT PAGE.

SPACE FOR FIGURING

23. The table shows how many millions of barrels of crude oil were produced by a particular oil field over a period of six months. During which month was there the greatest percent increase in crude oil output compared to the previous month?

    (A) April
    (B) May
    (C) June
    (D) July
    (E) August

CRUDE OIL PRODUCTION	
March	12
April	18
May	25
June	35
July	40
August	57

24. A clothes store sells, on average each month, 100 pairs of shoes for $75.00 each and 200 pairs of pants for $55.00 each. In order to increase sales, the store plans to bundle a pair of pants and a pair of shoes. If the bundle costs $120.00, how many bundles must the store sell per month to make sure the monthly revenue does not decrease? Assume customers will no longer buy shoes and pants separately.

    (A) 124
    (B) 135
    (C) 137
    (D) 154
    (E) 155

25. A certain region with an area of 163 square kilometers is divided up into five regions. The smallest region has an area of 15 square kilometers, the largest has an area of 59 square kilometers, and no two regions have the same area. If the area of each region is an integer number of square kilometers, what is the greatest possible median area?

    (A) 36 square kilometers
    (B) 37 square kilometers
    (C) 38 square kilometers
    (D) 57 square kilometers
    (E) 58 square kilometers

STOP

**IF YOU FINISH BEFORE TIME IS CALLED, YOU MAY CHECK YOUR WORK ON THIS SECTION ONLY.
DO NOT TURN TO ANY OTHER SECTION IN THE TEST.**

SECTION 2
40 Questions
40 Minutes

After reading each passage, answer its accompanying questions. Select your answers on the basis of the information presented in the passage only.

In our current day and age, with our modern technology and innumerable nature documentaries, it is easy to believe that we have discovered every animal species alive. At the very least, we expect that we should have at least discovered every mammalian species in existence. Yet, in the June of 2007, in the town of
Line 5   Opala in the Democratic Republic of Congo, researchers spotted a new type of monkey, which they subsequently named *Cercopithecus lomamiensis*.

     And after years of study and evaluation, the researchers finally officially unveiled the *Cercopithecus lomamiensis*, or lesula, to the world in a *PLOS ONE* publication dated September 12, 2012. The discovery of the lesula is significant
10   because it is the second primate species to be discovered since the sun-tailed monkey was discovered 28 years ago in 1984, the first being the kipunji, which was discovered in 2003. The discovery is further significant because it promises the possibility of the discovery of more animal species in the future.

---

1. The discovery of the lesula was significant in that the lesula was
   (A) previously thought to be extinct
   (B) so genetically similar to the kipunji that scientists had long believed they were the same species
   (C) just the second primate to be discovered since 1984
   (D) found living in an extremely remote part of Opala, a city in the Democratic Republic of Congo
   (E) believed to be a creature of legend, according to the people of Opala

2. The author makes the assumption that
   (A) no other mammalian species will be discovered henceforth
   (B) as technology advances so too does the rate of discovery of animals increase
   (C) the discovery of new animal species is predominantly based on luck
   (D) technology is advanced enough to make the discovery of most animal species feasible
   (E) new species of mammals will only be discovered once every 28 years

3. It is possible to infer that
   (A) it takes time for a scientists to officially reveal a species of animal publicly
   (B) new mammalian species will only be found in more remote parts of the world
   (C) Africa is the most likely place new species of animals will be discovered
   (D) *PLOS ONE* is one of the most prestigious science journals for unveiling new animal species
   (E) the sun-tailed monkey was thought to be the last discoverable monkey species, for nearly two decades

4. The author's tone is one of
   (A) feigned interest and subjectivity
   (B) forced enthusiasm and veiled sarcasm
   (C) subtle derision and doubt
   (D) blatant scorn and amusement
   (E) scientific fascination and optimism

GO TO THE NEXT PAGE.

Line 5

10

15

20

25

30

The word *tort* is borrowed from Old French, in which it means "an injury or a wrong," although it can be traced back etymologically to the Middle Latin words *tortum, tortus,* and *torquere*. In the present day, it is reserved almost exclusively for legal contexts and can be defined as "a wrongful act that results in some manifestation of harm to a person's body, property, or reputation, for which a legal remedy may be sought."

The process of commencing a lawsuit in tort begins with the plaintiff establishing a prima facie case against the defendant—*prima facie* is Latin for "on the first surface" or "at first glance." If the case does not appear to be viable on its face, then it should not be able to proceed, and the defendant can move to dismiss the plaintiff's claim. If, somehow, the case does proceed, then the defendant may be able to obtain a summary judgment or directed verdict in his favor. With several different ways for the defendant to win almost automatically, it becomes apparent why the plaintiff has to establish his prima facie case.

Establishing a prima facie case is not a simple matter of asserting that a defendant's actions caused the plaintiff harm. Each type of tort has unique elements or factors that must be proven in order for the plaintiff to establish a prima facie case. Only when every element of a tort is satisfied will the burden shift to the defendant to raise an appropriate defense—assumption of risk, consent, self-defense, and defense of others are some of the more common defenses. If he cannot, then the plaintiff will win the case, possibly by summary judgment or directed verdict, and the defendant will be held liable for the plaintiff's injury. If the defendant is able to raise a viable defense, however, then the burden shifts back to the plaintiff to overcome that defense.

Ultimately, the party who is best able to refute and rebut the claims of the other will stand victorious, but in the vast majority of cases and situations, it is better to avoid going to court altogether. Litigation should be the last possible recourse for people to consider. The media may portray lawsuits as glamorous ordeals—wars waged valiantly and brilliantly in court; the truth is that they are expensive, time consuming, and emotionally harrowing; the vast majority of problems are better resolved outside of the courtroom.

5. The author wrote this passage primarily to
   (A) discuss the etymology of the word *tort*
   (B) provide a brief and simple overview of tort law
   (C) caution against engaging in lawsuits
   (D) detail the steps one needs to take in order to initiate an action in tort law
   (E) explain how to get out of a tort action

6. The author discourages litigation for all of the following reasons except that
   (A) it is expensive
   (B) it is not as glamorous as the media makes it out to be
   (C) it is time consuming
   (D) it is emotionally draining
   (E) it is the only option available sometimes

7. All of the following are cited as possible tort claim defenses except
   (A) consent
   (B) negligence
   (C) defense of others
   (D) self-defense
   (E) assumption of risk

GO TO THE NEXT PAGE.

8. It can be inferred about summary judgments and directed verdicts that
    (A) they are rulings made in favor of a party when either the opposing party fails to properly make his case or the facts make it clear that the party should win
    (B) only the defendant can obtain a summary judgment or directed verdict
    (C) they are exceedingly rare in the vast majority of instances, since most parties to lawsuits will have lawyers who help them prepare for trial
    (D) if a party wins in a case with a summary judgment or directed verdict, it will be impossible for the losing party to bring the case back to trial on the same facts and issues
    (E) they are the quickest ways cases can be decided

9. Which of the following examples would not allow a defendant to raise a proper defense against a prima facie tort case?
    (A) The plaintiff knows that the defendant doesn't know how to operate a tractor but gives the defendant the keys to his anyway; the defendant subsequently drives the tractor into the plaintiff's house.
    (B) The plaintiff instructs the defendant to hit him, stating that he wants to know how strong the defendant is.
    (C) The defendant severely injured the plaintiff after the plaintiff attacked him first.
    (D) The plaintiff assaults the defendant's friend, so the defendant steps in and punches the plaintiff.
    (E) The plaintiff accuses the defendant of being a snitch, so the defendant steals and totals the plaintiff's car.

10. In order to establish a prima facie case, the plaintiff must
    (A) present an airtight case that the defendant cannot refute
    (B) prove his case beyond a reasonable doubt
    (C) satisfy all of the elements of the tort he is asserting
    (D) satisfy the majority of the elements of the tort he is asserting
    (E) satisfy at least one of the elements of the tort he is asserting

GO TO THE NEXT PAGE.

Line 5

10

15

In the history of music, innumerable artists have come and gone, but most have either never risen to prominence or faded into obscurity after but a brief stint in the limelight. Fewer than a relative handful of these artists are timelessly successful enough to be able to permanently embed themselves into the public conscious. Few, if any at all, would argue that singers such as Whitney Houston, Elvis Presley, Bob Dylan, and Michael Jackson do not belong in this pantheon of the elite, but listeners and fans often wonder and debate whom history considers the all-time best. With so many different genres of music, consumer preferences, and musical traditions, to say that there is a definitive best would be logically fallacious. Still, despite the subjectivity that is inherent in determining the best musician, performer, or act of all time, much empirical data point to one group as reigning supreme above all others, at least in the twentieth century, and that group is the Beatles. The group has won numerous awards, including seven Grammys, ranked first on *Billboard* magazine's "Hot 100 Top All-Time Artists" list, produced more #1 singles and albums than any other performer in history, and has sold over a billion tapes and discs worldwide, making them the best-selling group of all time.

11. It can be inferred from the passage about musical success that

(A) the more successful one is, the more likely it is that even audiences who don't enjoy the genre will willingly listen to the artist's music

(B) the longevity and profundity of success can be at least somewhat determined by sales of musical media

(C) the more musically talented one is, the more money one will earn

(D) the more albums one releases, the more money he or she will earn

(E) musical brilliance can be measured by how many new genres one can invent

12. The word "relative" is used in the passage to

(A) stress that the word *handful* is being used literally

(B) point out that many of the artists are related to each other

(C) emphasize that no one should ever attempt music as a career because of the extremely low odds of success as a musician

(D) underscore the lack of musical talent most people possess

(E) indicate figurative comparison

13. Of whom among the following can it not be inferred that the author believes to be ranked among the elite musicians of all time?

(A) Michael Jackson
(B) Whitney Houston
(C) Mariah Carey
(D) Elvis Presley
(E) Bob Dylan

14. The Beatles have achieved all of the following except

(A) composing thousands of songs in order to sell over a billion tapes and discs worldwide

(B) being ranked first on *Billboard* magazine's "Hot 100 Top All-Time Artists" list

(C) winning multiple Grammys—seven, to be exact

(D) being the best-selling group of all time

(E) produced more #1 albums and singles than any other performer

GO TO THE NEXT PAGE.

Line 5

10

15

20

25

Rent seeking is not, as one might expect, necessarily the process of landlords seeking higher rent payments from their tenants. Rather, the term "rent" in economics refers to the value given for something in excess of the value necessary to retain that thing. In other words, rent is the amount an entity profits from another without reciprocating in kind to the same extent.

For instance, if an employee is paid $200,000, but he would have just as effectively and willingly performed his job for $150,000, then he is said to make $50,000 per year in rent. Rent seeking, then, is the concept of an entity seeking to increase the amount of rent it makes. There is nothing inherently wrong with the concept of rent seeking—it is natural for individuals to want greater profits—but, as Professor Emeritus Gordon Tullock, the iconic inventor of the concept of rent seeking, keenly observed, rent seeking is problematic because it leads to economic waste.

Tullock saw that many industries lobby the government for financial benefits and expend considerable resources in doing so, meaning that the net rent an entity makes is rarely equal to the benefits it receives. To determine net rent, it is necessary to offset the benefit received by the amount spent seeking rent. What this means is that if a company receives $2 million in tax benefits, but spent $500,000 while lobbying, it has only truly made a rent of $1.5 million.

Society bears the cost, in the form of tax dollars, of the rent that the industries make, but the real problem is that industries receive less than what society pays for; that is, there is waste. To go back to the prior example, there was an economic waste of $500,000 because there was an imperfect transfer of resources—the amount society gives is more than what the company receives. Unfortunately, it is unlikely that the practice of rent seeking will ever end because people are less concerned about the economic efficiency of society than they are about their bottom dollars.

15. Economic waste is bad because

(A) the taxpayers have to shoulder the burden of rent seeking
(B) it leads to economic inefficiency
(C) lower income families, who pay the greatest percentage of the nation's taxes, have to pay so that the rich get richer
(D) it encourages people to be more selfish
(E) when entities can't perfectly transfer their resources, much tension, anxiety and frustration ensue

16. It can be inferred about economic waste that

(A) as long as the resources are transferred between parties without any loss, there is no economic waste
(B) lobbying efforts don't produce economic waste
(C) economic waste is the same thing as being wasteful
(D) economic waste is bad because it results in a loss of jobs
(E) industries will stop their lobbying efforts soon because they are aware of the amount of economic waste that lobbying produces

GO TO THE NEXT PAGE.

17. Which of the following would most likely be considered an example of rent seeking?

    (A) An employee asks his company for a contribution of $50,000 to a charity that he is very passionate about.
    (B) An employee demands a raise of $50,000, even though he's actually content with his current salary and has no interest in working elsewhere, even for higher pay.
    (C) An employee asks his company for a raise of $50,000 because a competitor offered him $50,000 above his current salary.
    (D) An employee does not ask for a raise and does no additional work.
    (E) An employee asks for a pay decrease but an equivalent increase in his stock options.

18. The main purpose of this passage is to

    (A) demand industries to cease their wasteful rent seeking efforts
    (B) credit Gordon Tullock for coming up with the idea of rent seeking
    (C) discuss an economic concept and explain its ramifications
    (D) suggest that rent seeking will one day become possible
    (E) inform readers about rent seeking and urge them to never ask for pay raises

19. The author would most likely agree with the idea that

    (A) Gordon Tullock's fame in economics is limited to his ideas of rent seeking
    (B) Tenants should not go for great deals on housing rentals because the landlords are sure to hike prices up eventually
    (C) The practice of rent seeking by individuals and corporations alike should be a jailable offense
    (D) The government can end rent seeking by always agreeing to give industries the financial benefits they are looking for
    (E) On a large scale, rent seeking wastes many resources that could otherwise be used productively in and for society

GO TO THE NEXT PAGE.

Box locked secrets maintain a steel fortress,
And never will these whispers of the heart
Escape their dungeon cells, for they impose
Upon their Master grave circumstances.

Line 5   Weary in his heart, and forlorn in his mind
Does the rigid heart sailor, traversing through
Waves chaotic, find solace in Man's best friend,
Neither Beast nor Material, neither Woman nor
Child; rather, the sweet tympanic swashings of
10   Liquid gold barley flow through his veins melodiously
In Delightful Pentameter Iambic.

Box locked prison, oh how thou prisoners yearn
So fervently to flee the confines of thine sturdy
Walls, thou prisoners seek asylum and refuge
15   On the isles of Lady Liberty; but what thou
Doesn't perceive is the treachery awaiting around
Ev'ry turn and corner.

20. In the poem, the phrase "steel fortress" (line 1) represents

(A) defense against criminals
(B) sturdy determination
(C) a massive structure
(D) resolution not to commit crimes
(E) a daunting obstacle

21. What is the overall tone of the passage?

(A) desperate and enthusiastic
(B) unconscionable and hesitant
(C) anguished and melancholy
(D) compassionate and capricious
(E) onerous and redemptive

22. "Lady Liberty" represents

(A) the freedom from a literal prison camp
(B) the freedom of speech and press
(C) the freedom from a self-imposed burden
(D) the freedom to travel and explore the world freely
(E) absolute freedom and autocracy

23. The "liquid gold barley" helps the "rigid heart sailor" find solace most likely by

(A) erasing his memories
(B) increasing his heart rate, and therefore heartbeat, like a percussion instrument
(C) changing the way he views the past
(D) helping him feel relaxed
(E) giving him the opportunity to overcome his fears

24. "Prisoners" in the last stanza refers to

(A) "secrets" (line 1)
(B) "dungeon cells" (line 3)
(C) "grave circumstances" (line 4)
(D) "best friend" (line 7)
(E) "treachery" (line 16)

GO TO THE NEXT PAGE.

Genetic engineering, the process of directly manipulating the genome of an organism, bacterium, or virus may have become possible only relatively recently, but the notion of gene manipulation itself has existed for thousands of years.

Line 5 Using the process of artificial selection, early breeders, including farmers and herders, would only permit crops and animals with desirable traits to reproduce in an effort to increase the chance that these traits would manifest in the offspring. It probably baffled them when anomalies appeared seemingly randomly in the offspring of the parents they had carefully bred.

10 It wasn't until after Gregor Mendel, an Augustinian monk, came along that did the mechanisms behind heredity become more apparent. Mendel published his findings in a research paper in 1866, but decades elapsed before anyone took heed of his findings. It wasn't until 1900, more than a decade after his death, when Hugo de Vries of Holland and Karl Korrens of Germany independently arrived at the same conclusions that Mendel had arrived at; de Vries rediscovered Mendel's

15 research and republished it in 1901.

From 1854 to 1856, Mendel ran hybridization experiments with the common edible pea plant (*Pisum sativum*), testing to see how the phenotypes, or physical characteristics, of the descendants differed from the parent plants. After selecting seven readily differentiable and easily qualifiable phenotypes, and breeding multiple

20 generations of the plants, he discovered that the phenotypes of the progeny emerged in a specific, patterned ratio and that each of the seven traits he had selected were passed down independent of the other traits.

These findings helped him come to the greater and revolutionary understanding that each parent only contributes half of its genetic material to its

25 offspring and that some traits are expressed in the offspring more dominantly than others are, thus effectively refuting the "blending theory," which was the leading theory of inheritance at the time and proposed that inherited traits blended together from generation to generation. It is no wonder that Mendel's conceptually simple pea experiment would earn him, albeit posthumously, the title of "the father of

30 genetics."

25. Which of the following examples would best represent the strongest case for the blending theory?

(A) The offspring of two curly-haired parents has straight hair.

(B) A man who sustains a serious injury during a work-related accident passes a scar half the size down to his child

(C) The offspring of two animals has triple its parents' combined strength when it becomes fully mature

(D) A white flower and a red flower are bred together and a fourth of the offspring have white flowers, half have pink flowers, and the remaining fourth have red flowers.

(E) The size of the offspring of two parents is always the average of sizes of the parents

26. The main idea of the passage is that

(A) genetic engineering is the process of manipulating genomes

(B) Mendel wasn't the only one to discover the mechanisms behind heredity

(C) *Pisum sativum* was the easiest species of plants that could have been chosen for hybridization experiments

(D) Mendel performed revolutionary experiments in the field genetics that would, for a long time, go unappreciated

(E) Mendel's work inspired Hugo de Vries and Karl Korrens to perform more genetics experiments

GO TO THE NEXT PAGE.

27. The definition of *phenotype*, as it is used in the passage, is
    (A) anything that can be passed on to others
    (B) an inherited physical trait
    (C) any genetic trait
    (D) a physical trait not genetically acquired
    (E) the collective of all physical traits, genetic and otherwise

28. According to the passage, what was one of the limitations of artificial selection that early breeders faced?
    (A) Artificial selection limited breeders in the number of traits that could be bred.
    (B) Artificial selection was a much more time consuming process than genetic engineering was.
    (C) Carefully selected parents would at least occasionally produce genetic anomalous offspring.
    (D) Carefully selected parents would once in a while produce offspring that were of a completely different species.
    (E) Carefully selected parents would be unable to produce offspring, due to fertility issues.

29. The author would most likely agree with the idea that
    (A) Mendel needed to breed more generations of offspring before coming to his specific conclusions
    (B) artificial selection and genetic engineering are synonymous
    (C) had it not been for de Vries, Mendel's contribution to science would have remained lost
    (D) if Mendel's work had been taken seriously from the outset, then the field of genetics could have been propelled along more quickly in its infancy
    (E) without Mendel, there would be no field of genetics today

30. Through his findings, Mendel was able to disprove that
    (A) traits are passed down in specific, patterned ratios
    (B) traits are passed down independently of other traits
    (C) inherited traits blend together from generation to generation
    (D) some traits are expressed more dominantly than others are
    (E) each parent passes down half of his, her, or its genetic material

GO TO THE NEXT PAGE.

Line 5

10

The greatest misnomer among office and consumer products has to be "pencil lead," which contains no lead whatsoever. Rather, the majority of the writing core in a pencil is a composite of graphite and clay, with a higher percentage of graphite in the mix producing a darker pencil lead color and a lower percentage of graphite producing a lighter color. As the story goes—there seems to be some debate as to the factual accuracy of the history—when graphite was first discovered, supposedly sometime between 1564 and 1565, it was initially mistaken for coal. Unlike coal, however, this lead-colored substance did not burn, though it did easily stain the fingers and make dark marks upon objects, perfect for writing. The only problem was that it was too soft and brittle to be properly used as a writing material—people realized that some sort of holder was necessary if they wanted to use graphite effectively for writing. It was this need for a graphite holder that eventually led to the placement of graphite in wooden cases; with that, the first incarnation of the modern pencil was born.

31. "Pencil lead" is a misnomer because

    (A) only the color is the same as that of lead
    (B) pencil shells are made from wood
    (C) it contains no pencil lead
    (D) lead is toxic and pencils are not
    (E) pencil lead is made from graphite and clay, in addition to lead

32. It is believed that graphite was discovered sometime

    (A) in the early 1560s
    (B) in the mid-1560s
    (C) in the late 1560s
    (D) in the middle of the 15th century
    (E) in the early 16th century

33. A holder was necessary to use graphite for writing because graphite was

    (A) too soft and brittle
    (B) too free-flowing like liquid
    (C) too messy to hold in one's hand
    (D) too evaporative
    (E) not stable enough atomically

34. Which of the following can be inferred about the color of pencil lead?

    (A) If clay comprises a smaller percentage of pencil lead, the color of the lead will be darker.
    (B) If clay comprises a larger percentage of pencil lead, the color of the lead will be darker.
    (C) If graphite is not used in pencil lead, then the pencil lead will be an extremely light shade of gray.
    (D) Colored pencils only contain a small percentage of graphite and clay so that dyes can be mixed in.
    (E) Clay is used in pencil lead because it provides the lead with increased structural integrity.

35. The best title for the passage is

    (A) "Misnamed Office Supplies"
    (B) "The Consistency of Pencil Lead"
    (C) "The History of Writing Implements"
    (D) "How the Pencil Came to Be"
    (E) "Graphite: Coal's Lookalike"

GO TO THE NEXT PAGE.

Cars are an indispensable part of our daily lives, facilitating travel immensely. We often neglect to think about how important the roads on which they travel are, but roads have, for a very long time, been essential to civilization.

Line 5

Take the Roman Empire, for instance. It depended heavily on its roads, building more than 55,000 miles of highways throughout Europe over about seven centuries, in order achieve the success it did. These roads helped Rome move supplies and soldiers quickly, allowing the Romans to outpace their enemies and to ensure tighter control over their cities and colonies. Moreover, because the Roman Empire built an extensive network of roads, it was able to better map its empire.

10

That, in turn, further allowed for the Romans to keep its empire more tightly under control.

But if the roads had not been brilliantly engineered for efficiency, perhaps the Roman Empire would not have flourished as much as it had. Before the road construction process began, surveyors would use sighting poles to plot the most

15

direct route from one location to another. And once the construction process began, the roads were not just haphazardly thrown together with cobble and stone. These roads consisted of several layers to ensure durability and flatness, with each layer conforming to a specific "recipe" to maximize traveling effectiveness and efficiency. To top it all off, the sides of Roman roads were punctuated with stone

20

pillars that bore relevant information to the traveller, such as the distance to the nearest town.

36. The author believes that

(A) without its vast network of highways, the Roman Empire would not have been as successful
(B) the Roman Empire had the most extensive network of highways in the ancient world
(C) enemy invaders would have razed the Roman Empire to the ground much earlier on, if it hadn't been for the empire's network of roads
(D) more people in the Roman Empire would have been permanently and severely deprived of supplies without the network of roads
(E) without the Roman Empire's vast network of highways, people would not have been able to leisurely travel to faraway locations

37. The stone pillars that punctuated the sides of Roman roads are most analogous to modern

(A) shoulder or exit lanes
(B) rest stops
(C) highway dividers
(D) compasses
(E) highway signs

38. The primary purpose of the passage is to

(A) detail the ramifications that the invention of cars had on our society
(B) expound on how valuable roads are in the process of transporting supplies and people
(C) explain how modern roads share the same engineering principles with roads of ancient Rome
(D) discuss the significance of roads in the Roman Empire and how they were constructed
(E) offer a hypothesis on the most efficient way of constructing roads

GO TO THE NEXT PAGE.

39. Before construction began on roads in ancient Rome,

   (A) the most direct route between the intended destinations was determined

   (B) the cost of construction of a road was weighed against the need for that road

   (C) surveyors used sighting poles to measure the distance from one point to another

   (D) tunnels were dug through terrain that proved too treacherous to construct roads over

   (E) slaves laid down the cobble and stone necessary for construction on the roads to begin

40. Roads in ancient Rome consisted of multiple layers in order to

   (A) make the roads softer and thus easier for horses and carriages to travel on

   (B) ensure durability and ease of travel

   (C) make the roads harder and thus easier for horses and carriages to travel on

   (D) make it easier to construct direct routes from one location to another

   (E) protect the underlying soil against the effects of rain, snow, and sleet

STOP

**IF YOU FINISH BEFORE TIME IS CALLED, YOU MAY CHECK YOUR WORK ON THIS SECTION ONLY.
DO NOT TURN TO ANY OTHER SECTION IN THE TEST.**

SECTION 3
60 Questions
30 Minutes

There are two types of questions in this section: synonyms and analogies.

Synonyms
Each question consists of one word in capital letters, followed by five answer choices. Select the answer choice consisting of the word or phrase closest in meaning to the word in capital letters.

Sample Question:

TORRID:

(A) mild
(B) painful
(C) pleasant
(D) hot
(E) sticky

Ⓐ Ⓑ Ⓒ ⬤ Ⓔ

1. HARMONIOUS:

   (A) clean
   (B) compatible
   (C) noisy
   (D) affectionate
   (E) argumentative

2. CORROBORATE:

   (A) validate
   (B) disagree
   (C) corrode
   (D) polish
   (E) fix

3. LOFTY:

   (A) comfortable
   (B) foamy
   (C) grand
   (D) hurtful
   (E) useless

4. ACRID:

   (A) tearful
   (B) sharp
   (C) lethal
   (D) lazy
   (E) jubilant

5. RELINQUISH:

   (A) conceal
   (B) injure
   (C) hide
   (D) cherish
   (E) surrender

6. DETER:

   (A) commingle
   (B) behave
   (C) surround
   (D) proceed
   (E) prevent

7. MATERIAL:

   (A) feeble
   (B) artificial
   (C) complex
   (D) gossamer
   (E) significant

8. FACILE:

   (A) doable
   (B) impossible
   (C) available
   (D) easy
   (E) plain

GO TO THE NEXT PAGE.

9. REVERBERATE:

(A) forget
(B) reverse
(C) deduce
(D) echo
(E) illuminate

10. GARRISON:

(A) admiral
(B) armada
(C) unification
(D) partition
(E) stronghold

11. INARTICULATE:

(A) illegible
(B) uncreative
(C) inspirational
(D) incoherent
(E) confident

12. SQUALID:

(A) filthy
(B) aquatic
(C) celestial
(D) squeamish
(E) traumatic

13. RAIMENT:

(A) sustenance
(B) apparel
(C) beverage
(D) lightning
(E) aroma

14. VICINITY:

(A) intensity
(B) length
(C) proximity
(D) viciousness
(E) connection

15. FACTION:

(A) story
(B) barricade
(C) stimulus
(D) portion
(E) group

16. POIGNANT:

(A) moving
(B) thorough
(C) irresistible
(D) repulsive
(E) uncertain

17. PROGNOSTICATE:

(A) diagnose
(B) prescribe
(C) assert
(D) prophesy
(E) examine

18. AVARICE:

(A) greed
(B) egotism
(C) wrath
(D) boredom
(E) ambition

19. UBIQUITOUS:

(A) scanty
(B) dispersed
(C) calm
(D) remote
(E) omnipresent

20. SCRUPULOUS:

(A) shoddy
(B) principled
(C) pristine
(D) impressive
(E) delicious

GO TO THE NEXT PAGE.

21. DEXTEROUS:

   (A) flexible
   (B) unmanageable
   (C) honorable
   (D) incapable
   (E) skillful

22. LETHARGIC:

   (A) rapid
   (B) sluggish
   (C) moderate
   (D) ingenious
   (E) puzzling

23. HIATUS:

   (A) surface
   (B) vacuum
   (C) break
   (D) tribe
   (E) bribe

24. FINITE:

   (A) finished
   (B) started
   (C) limited
   (D) incessant
   (E) unbounded

25. ENDEAVOR:

   (A) effort
   (B) trivia
   (C) coarseness
   (D) disposition
   (E) longevity

26. TERSE:

   (A) polite
   (B) rude
   (C) curt
   (D) nonsensical
   (E) wordy

27. WAYLAY:

   (A) pave
   (B) road
   (C) cobblestone
   (D) ambush
   (E) announce

28. JINGOISTIC:

   (A) bellicose
   (B) traitorous
   (C) jingly
   (D) narcissistic
   (E) pacifistic

29. DESTINATION:

   (A) path
   (B) juncture
   (C) solution
   (D) target
   (E) departure

30. FACULTY:

   (A) ability
   (B) building
   (C) crew
   (D) members
   (E) insight

GO TO THE NEXT PAGE.

Analogies

These questions will ask you to find the relationships between words. For each question, select the answer choice that best completes the analogy relationship.

Sample Question:

Glove is to hand as shoe is to

(A) mouth
(B) head
(C) finger
(D) foot
(E) sock

Ⓐ Ⓑ Ⓒ ● Ⓔ

---

31. Hide is to leather as

    (A) run is to whip
    (B) grape is to raisin
    (C) prune is to dried
    (D) mineral is to quartz
    (E) seek is to chain

32. Terrarium is to iguana as aviary is to

    (A) bird
    (B) chimpanzee
    (C) parakeet
    (D) lizard
    (E) wasp

33. Light is to dark as

    (A) delicious is to taste
    (B) bright is to sun
    (C) money is to destitute
    (D) wisdom is to immoral
    (E) wintry is to frosty

34. Student is to learn as

    (A) cop is to serve
    (B) fireman is to burn
    (C) logger is to wood
    (D) clergy is to scripture
    (E) counselor is to advise

35. Thorax is to abdomen as

    (A) trunk is to root
    (B) head is to arm
    (C) antenna is to mandible
    (D) vertebrate is to spine
    (E) magician is to wand

36. Aim is to accuracy as

    (A) exhale is to breath
    (B) stretch is to flexibility
    (C) reap is to crop
    (D) contaminate is to illness
    (E) pull is to push

37. Actor is to production as

    (A) patient is to operation
    (B) animal is to zoo
    (C) bird is to flock
    (D) inmate is to incarceration
    (E) soldier is to battle

38. Mouse is to rodent as

    (A) spider is to insect
    (B) poultry is to bird
    (C) centipede is to arachnid
    (D) gorilla is to primate
    (E) panda is to bear

GO TO THE NEXT PAGE.

39. Shade is to color as

    (A) decibel is to cacophony
    (B) scale is to weight
    (C) nuance is to word
    (D) candy is to juice
    (E) increment is to abstraction

40. Price is to invaluable as

    (A) caretaking is to inhumane
    (B) competence is to incapable
    (C) size is to immense
    (D) capacity is to calculable
    (E) supply is to infinitesimal

41. Trinket is to treasure as

    (A) tsunami is to earthquake
    (B) rock is to gem
    (C) jewel is to crown
    (D) speck is to dust
    (E) gale is to breeze

42. Diplomat is to emissary as

    (A) monarch is to constituency
    (B) delegate is to company
    (C) officer is to institution
    (D) country is to alliance
    (E) proxy is to agent

43. Palisade is to defense as

    (A) academy is to scholarship
    (B) corporation is to charity
    (C) palace is to nobility
    (D) museum is to tourism
    (E) warehouse is to bulk

44. Zeal is to phlegmatic as

    (A) punishment is to draconian
    (B) vagrant is to itinerant
    (C) gusto is to windy
    (D) opacity is to transparent
    (E) forethought is to considerate

45. Treatment is to remission as

    (A) analysis is to prescription
    (B) penalty is to penitentiary
    (C) sojourn is to domicile
    (D) supposition is to experimentation
    (E) therapy is to rehabilitation

46. Talkative is to withdrawn as

    (A) indecisive is to uncertain
    (B) flagrant is to inconspicuous
    (C) seriousness is to gravity
    (D) conniving is to scheming
    (E) idiosyncratic is to flattering

47. Dilapidated is to neglect as

    (A) disgruntled is to satisfy
    (B) rapacious is to deprive
    (C) desultory is to peruse
    (D) gnarled is to straighten
    (E) ascetic is to flatter

48. Admonish is to lambaste as

    (A) irk is to infuriate
    (B) hunch is to suspicion
    (C) injurious is to detrimental
    (D) charm is to charisma
    (E) recapitulate is to total defeat

49. Scapegoat is to hero as hedonist is to

    (A) glutton
    (B) egoist
    (C) barbarian
    (D) puritan
    (E) master

50. Intercept is to interference as

    (A) divulge is to revelation
    (B) inspire is to motivate
    (C) accept is to defeat
    (D) endeavor is to commitment
    (E) dethrone is to coronation

GO TO THE NEXT PAGE.

51. Shingle is to roof as

   (A) wall is to floor
   (B) epidermis is to skin
   (C) stomach is to digestion
   (D) nut is to wrench
   (E) ceiling is to room

52. Ballast is to buoyancy as

   (A) labyrinth is to exit
   (B) satellite is to orbit
   (C) dam is to waterfall
   (D) trough is to ditch
   (E) catalyst is to change

53. Zookeeper is to animal as

   (A) librarian is to book
   (B) nurse is to physician
   (C) ward is to charge
   (D) jailor is to prisoner
   (E) hunter is to victim

54. Longing is to nostalgia as

   (A) begging is to desperation
   (B) organizing is to grievance
   (C) bickering is to familiarity
   (D) chattering is to tranquility
   (E) flourishing is to mediocrity

55. Unorthodox is to traditional as

   (A) conscientious is to deliberate
   (B) apposite is to opposite
   (C) illustrious is to mundane
   (D) cautionary is to excessive
   (E) rotund is to bulbous

56. Speech is to extemporaneous as

   (A) denouement is to anticlimactic
   (B) result is to unexpected
   (C) decision is to whimsical
   (D) memoir is to unpublished
   (E) mystique is to clandestine

57. Pariah is to exile as

   (A) paragon is to admire
   (B) despot is to depose
   (C) gambler is to borrow
   (D) sick is to quarantine
   (E) philanderer is to worship

58. Genre is to category as

   (A) catalog is to item
   (B) mortgage is to credit
   (C) secular is to devout
   (D) robbery is to theft
   (E) sedan is to truck

59. Filial is to daughter as

   (A) equine is to offspring
   (B) fraternal is to cousin
   (C) avuncular is to aunt
   (D) parental is to father
   (E) childish is to nephew

60. Quarry is to stone as

   (A) marina is to boat
   (B) orchard is to fruit
   (C) shelter is to protection
   (D) cemetery is to grave
   (E) lumberyard is to wood

STOP

**IF YOU FINISH BEFORE TIME IS CALLED, YOU MAY CHECK YOUR WORK ON THIS SECTION ONLY.
DO NOT TURN TO ANY OTHER SECTION IN THE TEST.**

SECTION 4
25 Questions
30 Minutes

Work through each problem in this section. You may use the blank pace to the right of the page, if you need, to do your figuring. Then select the best one of the five suggested answer choices.

<u>Note</u>: Some of the problems are accompanied by figures, which are rendered as accurately as possible, EXCEPT when the problem explicitly states that its accompanying figure is not drawn to scale.

Sample Problem:

6,329	(A)	2,151
− 3,478	(B)	2,275
	(C)	2,807
	(D)	2,851
	(E)	2,951

Ⓐ Ⓑ Ⓒ ● Ⓔ

SPACE FOR FIGURING

1. When 74,706 is divided by 298, the result is closest to which of the following?

   (A) 2,500
   (B) 270
   (C) 255
   (D) 250
   (E) 25

---

2. $1.05 \times 24 = ?$

   (A) 36
   (B) 25.2
   (C) 25.12
   (D) 24.2
   (E) 24.24

---

3. $55\frac{5}{13} - 24\frac{10}{13} + 40\frac{15}{39} =$

   (A) 70

   (B) $70\frac{10}{13}$

   (C) 71

   (D) $71\frac{5}{13}$

   (E) $71\frac{20}{39}$

GO TO THE NEXT PAGE.

4. Evaluate: $2(2 + 5)^2 + (-18) \times 4 - 3 \div 3$

   (A) 25
   (B) 26
   (C) 27
   (D) 54
   (E) 319

5. 225 is 125 percent of

   (A) 100
   (B) 150
   (C) 156.25
   (D) 180
   (E) 200

6. If $15 - 2T = 4$, then $3T + 6 =$

   (A) 20
   (B) 20.5
   (C) 22
   (D) 22.5
   (E) 24

7. Calculate $3a^3 + 4b^4$ when $a = 3$ and $b = 2$.

   (A) 59
   (B) 65
   (C) 72
   (D) 80
   (E) 145

8. A rectangular plot of land has a perimeter of 50 meters. If the length of one of the sides is 10 meters, by what would percent would the area increase after all of the sides are each increased in length by 5 meters?

   (A) 25
   (B) 100
   (C) 150
   (D) 200
   (E) 300

GO TO THE NEXT PAGE.

SPACE FOR FIGURING

9. If x is divisible by 9 and y is divisible by 5, which of the following must be true?

   (A) 45 is the least common multiple of x and y.
   (B) xy is divisible by 15.
   (C) $x + y$ is 14.
   (D) 45 is the greatest common factor of x and y.
   (E) The result of $x - y$ is a multiple of 4.

10. If $x = 7$, what is the value of the expression $(x - 5)(x + 6)$?

   (A) $7^2 + 7 - 30$
   (B) $7^2 - 30$
   (C) $(7 \times \text{-}5) + (7 \times 6)$
   (D) $(7 - 5) + (7 + 6)$
   (E) $(7 \times (7 - 5))(7 \times (7 + 6))$

11. What is the sum of the values of the underlined digits?
    1,3<u>42</u>,6<u>17</u>.9<u>2</u>

   (A) 19
   (B) 469
   (C) 4,690
   (D) 40,600.90
   (E) 42,617.90

12. If rectangular field has a perimeter of 32 feet, which of the following represents the greatest area that the dimensions of the field could yield?

   (A) 60 ft^2
   (B) 63 ft^2
   (C) 64 ft^2
   (D) 68 ft^2
   (E) 69 ft^2

13. $5\frac{3}{7} + 3\frac{1}{14} + 2 =$

   (A) 10
   (B) 10.29
   (C) 10.5
   (D) 11.29
   (E) 11.5

GO TO THE NEXT PAGE.

SPACE FOR FIGURING

14. A train traveled from Washington, D.C. to New York, a distance of 500 miles, in 6 hours. Its rate of travel, in miles per hour, must have been between

(A) 70 and 75
(B) 75 and 80
(C) 80 and 85
(D) 85 and 90
(E) 90 and 100

15. Choose the inequality represented by the statement, "The difference of five times a number and six times another number is less than or equal to ten times the second number."

(A) $5x \leq 16y$
(B) $5x \geq 16y$
(C) $6x - 5y \leq 10y$
(D) $6x + 5y \geq 10y$
(E) $11(x - y) \leq 10y$

16. Seven equal pieces of string are cut from a larger piece of string that's 134 centimeters long. If the length in centimeters of every piece of string, including the leftover piece, if any, has an integer value, what could be the length of the leftover piece?

(A) 15 centimeters
(B) 16 centimeters
(C) 17 centimeters
(D) 18 centimeters
(E) There is no leftover piece.

17. There were 155 children and 104 parents at a carnival. Forty percent of the children bought cotton candy, and twenty-five percent of the adults bought popcorn. No one else bought any snacks. How many more people didn't buy any snacks than did buy snacks?

(A) 26
(B) 62
(C) 83
(D) 90
(E) 171

GO TO THE NEXT PAGE.

18. If x is a real number greater than 0, but less than 1, which of the following is greatest in value?

(A) $1 - x$

(B) $\dfrac{1}{x}$

(C) $\dfrac{1}{x^2}$

(D) x^4

(E) Cannot be determined from the given information

19. Cynthia can clean a pool in 2 hours. Cassie can clean the same pool in 3 hours. If they worked together to clean a pool that's double the size of the aforementioned pool, how long would it take them?

(A) 1 hour and 12 minutes
(B) 1 hour and 30 minutes
(C) 2 hours and 24 minutes
(D) 2 hours and 36 minutes
(E) 3 hours

20. Marla bought an eight-pack of 1-liter bottles of water for $11.20. Sandy bought a six-pack of 2-liter bottles of water for $15.60. Who got the better overall deal, per liter of water, and by how much per liter?

(A) Marla, by $1.20 per liter
(B) Marla, by $0.60 per liter
(C) Sandy, by $0.20 per liter
(D) Sandy, by $0.10 per liter
(E) They each paid the same amount per liter.

21. Rennie has 77 cents in his pocket. If he has some combination of only quarters, dimes, and pennies, and he doesn't have more than 10 of each type of coin, how many possible combinations of coins can he have in his pocket?

(A) 1
(B) 2
(C) 3
(D) 4
(E) 5 or more

GO TO THE NEXT PAGE.

SPACE FOR FIGURING

22. In a survey of 200 high school seniors, 99 expressed interest in math, 87 in English, and 47 were undecided. How many were interested in both math and English?

   (A) 24
   (B) 33
   (C) 50
   (D) 66
   (E) It cannot be determined from the information given.

23. Let b represent the base of a triangle. What is the area of the triangle, if the length of the height is four less than twice the length of the base?

   (A) $2b^2 - 4b$
   (B) $b^2 - 2b$
   (C) $2b - b^2$
   (D) $4b - 2b^2$
   (E) $2b^2$

24. Four people spend an average of $300.00 on food per person every month. If a fifth person joins the group, but eats double the average of everyone else, what would the average monthly cost of food be per person, for the five people?

   (A) $300.00
   (B) $330.00
   (C) $360.00
   (D) $390.00
   (E) $400.00

25. What percentage of the area of circle O is the area of the larger sector formed by radii OA and OB?

   (A) 40
   (B) 45
   (C) 50
   (D) 60
   (E) 65

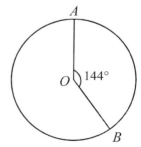

STOP

IF YOU FINISH BEFORE TIME IS CALLED, YOU MAY CHECK YOUR WORK ON THIS SECTION ONLY.
DO NOT TURN TO ANY OTHER SECTION IN THE TEST.

SSAT
UPPER LEVEL
Test 3

ANSWER SHEET

Make sure to completely fill in the bubbles corresponding to your answer choices.

Section 1

1	Ⓐ Ⓑ Ⓒ Ⓓ Ⓔ	6	Ⓐ Ⓑ Ⓒ Ⓓ Ⓔ	11	Ⓐ Ⓑ Ⓒ Ⓓ Ⓔ	16	Ⓐ Ⓑ Ⓒ Ⓓ Ⓔ	21	Ⓐ Ⓑ Ⓒ Ⓓ Ⓔ
2	Ⓐ Ⓑ Ⓒ Ⓓ Ⓔ	7	Ⓐ Ⓑ Ⓒ Ⓓ Ⓔ	12	Ⓐ Ⓑ Ⓒ Ⓓ Ⓔ	17	Ⓐ Ⓑ Ⓒ Ⓓ Ⓔ	22	Ⓐ Ⓑ Ⓒ Ⓓ Ⓔ
3	Ⓐ Ⓑ Ⓒ Ⓓ Ⓔ	8	Ⓐ Ⓑ Ⓒ Ⓓ Ⓔ	13	Ⓐ Ⓑ Ⓒ Ⓓ Ⓔ	18	Ⓐ Ⓑ Ⓒ Ⓓ Ⓔ	23	Ⓐ Ⓑ Ⓒ Ⓓ Ⓔ
4	Ⓐ Ⓑ Ⓒ Ⓓ Ⓔ	9	Ⓐ Ⓑ Ⓒ Ⓓ Ⓔ	14	Ⓐ Ⓑ Ⓒ Ⓓ Ⓔ	19	Ⓐ Ⓑ Ⓒ Ⓓ Ⓔ	24	Ⓐ Ⓑ Ⓒ Ⓓ Ⓔ
5	Ⓐ Ⓑ Ⓒ Ⓓ Ⓔ	10	Ⓐ Ⓑ Ⓒ Ⓓ Ⓔ	15	Ⓐ Ⓑ Ⓒ Ⓓ Ⓔ	20	Ⓐ Ⓑ Ⓒ Ⓓ Ⓔ	25	Ⓐ Ⓑ Ⓒ Ⓓ Ⓔ

Section 2

1	Ⓐ Ⓑ Ⓒ Ⓓ Ⓔ	9	Ⓐ Ⓑ Ⓒ Ⓓ Ⓔ	17	Ⓐ Ⓑ Ⓒ Ⓓ Ⓔ	25	Ⓐ Ⓑ Ⓒ Ⓓ Ⓔ	33	Ⓐ Ⓑ Ⓒ Ⓓ Ⓔ
2	Ⓐ Ⓑ Ⓒ Ⓓ Ⓔ	10	Ⓐ Ⓑ Ⓒ Ⓓ Ⓔ	18	Ⓐ Ⓑ Ⓒ Ⓓ Ⓔ	26	Ⓐ Ⓑ Ⓒ Ⓓ Ⓔ	34	Ⓐ Ⓑ Ⓒ Ⓓ Ⓔ
3	Ⓐ Ⓑ Ⓒ Ⓓ Ⓔ	11	Ⓐ Ⓑ Ⓒ Ⓓ Ⓔ	19	Ⓐ Ⓑ Ⓒ Ⓓ Ⓔ	27	Ⓐ Ⓑ Ⓒ Ⓓ Ⓔ	35	Ⓐ Ⓑ Ⓒ Ⓓ Ⓔ
4	Ⓐ Ⓑ Ⓒ Ⓓ Ⓔ	12	Ⓐ Ⓑ Ⓒ Ⓓ Ⓔ	20	Ⓐ Ⓑ Ⓒ Ⓓ Ⓔ	28	Ⓐ Ⓑ Ⓒ Ⓓ Ⓔ	36	Ⓐ Ⓑ Ⓒ Ⓓ Ⓔ
5	Ⓐ Ⓑ Ⓒ Ⓓ Ⓔ	13	Ⓐ Ⓑ Ⓒ Ⓓ Ⓔ	21	Ⓐ Ⓑ Ⓒ Ⓓ Ⓔ	29	Ⓐ Ⓑ Ⓒ Ⓓ Ⓔ	37	Ⓐ Ⓑ Ⓒ Ⓓ Ⓔ
6	Ⓐ Ⓑ Ⓒ Ⓓ Ⓔ	14	Ⓐ Ⓑ Ⓒ Ⓓ Ⓔ	22	Ⓐ Ⓑ Ⓒ Ⓓ Ⓔ	30	Ⓐ Ⓑ Ⓒ Ⓓ Ⓔ	38	Ⓐ Ⓑ Ⓒ Ⓓ Ⓔ
7	Ⓐ Ⓑ Ⓒ Ⓓ Ⓔ	15	Ⓐ Ⓑ Ⓒ Ⓓ Ⓔ	23	Ⓐ Ⓑ Ⓒ Ⓓ Ⓔ	31	Ⓐ Ⓑ Ⓒ Ⓓ Ⓔ	39	Ⓐ Ⓑ Ⓒ Ⓓ Ⓔ
8	Ⓐ Ⓑ Ⓒ Ⓓ Ⓔ	16	Ⓐ Ⓑ Ⓒ Ⓓ Ⓔ	24	Ⓐ Ⓑ Ⓒ Ⓓ Ⓔ	32	Ⓐ Ⓑ Ⓒ Ⓓ Ⓔ	40	Ⓐ Ⓑ Ⓒ Ⓓ Ⓔ

Section 3

1	Ⓐ Ⓑ Ⓒ Ⓓ Ⓔ	13	Ⓐ Ⓑ Ⓒ Ⓓ Ⓔ	25	Ⓐ Ⓑ Ⓒ Ⓓ Ⓔ	37	Ⓐ Ⓑ Ⓒ Ⓓ Ⓔ	49	Ⓐ Ⓑ Ⓒ Ⓓ Ⓔ
2	Ⓐ Ⓑ Ⓒ Ⓓ Ⓔ	14	Ⓐ Ⓑ Ⓒ Ⓓ Ⓔ	26	Ⓐ Ⓑ Ⓒ Ⓓ Ⓔ	38	Ⓐ Ⓑ Ⓒ Ⓓ Ⓔ	50	Ⓐ Ⓑ Ⓒ Ⓓ Ⓔ
3	Ⓐ Ⓑ Ⓒ Ⓓ Ⓔ	15	Ⓐ Ⓑ Ⓒ Ⓓ Ⓔ	27	Ⓐ Ⓑ Ⓒ Ⓓ Ⓔ	39	Ⓐ Ⓑ Ⓒ Ⓓ Ⓔ	51	Ⓐ Ⓑ Ⓒ Ⓓ Ⓔ
4	Ⓐ Ⓑ Ⓒ Ⓓ Ⓔ	16	Ⓐ Ⓑ Ⓒ Ⓓ Ⓔ	28	Ⓐ Ⓑ Ⓒ Ⓓ Ⓔ	40	Ⓐ Ⓑ Ⓒ Ⓓ Ⓔ	52	Ⓐ Ⓑ Ⓒ Ⓓ Ⓔ
5	Ⓐ Ⓑ Ⓒ Ⓓ Ⓔ	17	Ⓐ Ⓑ Ⓒ Ⓓ Ⓔ	29	Ⓐ Ⓑ Ⓒ Ⓓ Ⓔ	41	Ⓐ Ⓑ Ⓒ Ⓓ Ⓔ	53	Ⓐ Ⓑ Ⓒ Ⓓ Ⓔ
6	Ⓐ Ⓑ Ⓒ Ⓓ Ⓔ	18	Ⓐ Ⓑ Ⓒ Ⓓ Ⓔ	30	Ⓐ Ⓑ Ⓒ Ⓓ Ⓔ	42	Ⓐ Ⓑ Ⓒ Ⓓ Ⓔ	54	Ⓐ Ⓑ Ⓒ Ⓓ Ⓔ
7	Ⓐ Ⓑ Ⓒ Ⓓ Ⓔ	19	Ⓐ Ⓑ Ⓒ Ⓓ Ⓔ	31	Ⓐ Ⓑ Ⓒ Ⓓ Ⓔ	43	Ⓐ Ⓑ Ⓒ Ⓓ Ⓔ	55	Ⓐ Ⓑ Ⓒ Ⓓ Ⓔ
8	Ⓐ Ⓑ Ⓒ Ⓓ Ⓔ	20	Ⓐ Ⓑ Ⓒ Ⓓ Ⓔ	32	Ⓐ Ⓑ Ⓒ Ⓓ Ⓔ	44	Ⓐ Ⓑ Ⓒ Ⓓ Ⓔ	56	Ⓐ Ⓑ Ⓒ Ⓓ Ⓔ
9	Ⓐ Ⓑ Ⓒ Ⓓ Ⓔ	21	Ⓐ Ⓑ Ⓒ Ⓓ Ⓔ	33	Ⓐ Ⓑ Ⓒ Ⓓ Ⓔ	45	Ⓐ Ⓑ Ⓒ Ⓓ Ⓔ	57	Ⓐ Ⓑ Ⓒ Ⓓ Ⓔ
10	Ⓐ Ⓑ Ⓒ Ⓓ Ⓔ	22	Ⓐ Ⓑ Ⓒ Ⓓ Ⓔ	34	Ⓐ Ⓑ Ⓒ Ⓓ Ⓔ	46	Ⓐ Ⓑ Ⓒ Ⓓ Ⓔ	58	Ⓐ Ⓑ Ⓒ Ⓓ Ⓔ
11	Ⓐ Ⓑ Ⓒ Ⓓ Ⓔ	23	Ⓐ Ⓑ Ⓒ Ⓓ Ⓔ	35	Ⓐ Ⓑ Ⓒ Ⓓ Ⓔ	47	Ⓐ Ⓑ Ⓒ Ⓓ Ⓔ	59	Ⓐ Ⓑ Ⓒ Ⓓ Ⓔ
12	Ⓐ Ⓑ Ⓒ Ⓓ Ⓔ	24	Ⓐ Ⓑ Ⓒ Ⓓ Ⓔ	36	Ⓐ Ⓑ Ⓒ Ⓓ Ⓔ	48	Ⓐ Ⓑ Ⓒ Ⓓ Ⓔ	60	Ⓐ Ⓑ Ⓒ Ⓓ Ⓔ

Section 4

1	Ⓐ Ⓑ Ⓒ Ⓓ Ⓔ	6	Ⓐ Ⓑ Ⓒ Ⓓ Ⓔ	11	Ⓐ Ⓑ Ⓒ Ⓓ Ⓔ	16	Ⓐ Ⓑ Ⓒ Ⓓ Ⓔ	21	Ⓐ Ⓑ Ⓒ Ⓓ Ⓔ
2	Ⓐ Ⓑ Ⓒ Ⓓ Ⓔ	7	Ⓐ Ⓑ Ⓒ Ⓓ Ⓔ	12	Ⓐ Ⓑ Ⓒ Ⓓ Ⓔ	17	Ⓐ Ⓑ Ⓒ Ⓓ Ⓔ	22	Ⓐ Ⓑ Ⓒ Ⓓ Ⓔ
3	Ⓐ Ⓑ Ⓒ Ⓓ Ⓔ	8	Ⓐ Ⓑ Ⓒ Ⓓ Ⓔ	13	Ⓐ Ⓑ Ⓒ Ⓓ Ⓔ	18	Ⓐ Ⓑ Ⓒ Ⓓ Ⓔ	23	Ⓐ Ⓑ Ⓒ Ⓓ Ⓔ
4	Ⓐ Ⓑ Ⓒ Ⓓ Ⓔ	9	Ⓐ Ⓑ Ⓒ Ⓓ Ⓔ	14	Ⓐ Ⓑ Ⓒ Ⓓ Ⓔ	19	Ⓐ Ⓑ Ⓒ Ⓓ Ⓔ	24	Ⓐ Ⓑ Ⓒ Ⓓ Ⓔ
5	Ⓐ Ⓑ Ⓒ Ⓓ Ⓔ	10	Ⓐ Ⓑ Ⓒ Ⓓ Ⓔ	15	Ⓐ Ⓑ Ⓒ Ⓓ Ⓔ	20	Ⓐ Ⓑ Ⓒ Ⓓ Ⓔ	25	Ⓐ Ⓑ Ⓒ Ⓓ Ⓔ

Writing Sample

Select one of the two essay prompts below and write an essay or story to address or answer the prompt you selected. Your writing sample will help schools understand you better as an applicant.

A. How do you keep a positive attitude when you are going through difficult times?

B. When I saw it, my heart sank.

Use this page and the next to write your essay or story.

Continue on the next page.

SECTION I
25 Questions
30 minutes

Work through each problem in this section. You may use the blank pace to the right of the page, if you need, to do your figuring. Then select the best one of the five suggested answer choices.

Note: Some of the problems are accompanied by figures, which are rendered as accurately as possible, EXCEPT when the problem explicitly states that its accompanying figure is not drawn to scale.

Sample Problem:

6,329	(A)	2,151
− 3,478	(B)	2,275
	(C)	2,807
	(D)	2,851
	(E)	2,951

Ⓐ Ⓑ Ⓒ ● Ⓔ

SPACE FOR FIGURING

1. If $2P - 8 = 10 \div P$, then which of the following is a possible value of P?

   (A) -2
   (B) 0
   (C) 1
   (D) 4
   (E) 5

2. Which of the following numbers is not divisible by 17?

   (A) 41
   (B) 51
   (C) 85
   (D) 170
   (E) 340

3. Carla drives 15 miles. The first third of the drive takes her 10 minutes. The second third of the drive takes her 20 minutes. If the last third of the drive takes her 30 minutes, what was her overall speed for the entire drive?

   (A) 5 miles per hour
   (B) 7.5 miles per hour
   (C) 10 miles per hour
   (D) 12.5 miles per hour
   (E) 15 miles per hour

GO TO THE NEXT PAGE.

SPACE FOR FIGURING

4. If $0 < x + y < 1$, which of the following statements must be true?

    (A) The product of x and y is greater than 0.
    (B) If x is less than 0.5, y must be greater than 0.5.
    (C) If x is less than 0.5, y must be less than 0.5.
    (D) If x is greater than 0.5, y must be greater than 0.5.
    (E) If x is greater than 0.5, y must be less than 0.5.

---

5. What percent is the fraction $\dfrac{6}{11}$ closest in value to?

    (A) 0.5454%
    (B) 1.833%
    (C) 5.454%
    (D) 18.33%
    (E) 54.54%

---

6. To throw her sister a surprise birthday party, Sunnie buys a birthday cake, two cupcakes, and a large box of candles for $42.35. Later, her sister, feeling sorry for herself because everyone has apparently forgotten her birthday, goes to the same bakery and buys the same cake and three cupcakes for $42.66. How much more expensive is a cupcake than a box of candles?

    (A) $0.29
    (B) $0.31
    (C) $0.39
    (D) $0.61
    (E) $1.05

GO TO THE NEXT PAGE.

SPACE FOR FIGURING

7. x, y, and z are positive integers. Which of the following statements are valid, if $z^2 - y^2 = 2x^2$?

    I. x is odd.
    II. z can be less than or equal to y.
    III. If z is even, y is also even.

(A) I
(B) II
(C) III
(D) II and III
(E) I, II, and III

8. Which of the following is the value of the expression $\dfrac{5^4(5^3 + 5^2)}{125}$ divisible by?

(A) 9
(B) 15
(C) 24
(D) 45
(E) 60

9. Six squares, labeled 1-6, are arranged as shown in the figure. Folding squares 1, 3, 5, and 6 about square 2 and then folding square 4 over square 3 results in a cube. An isosceles right triangle can be removed from each of which of the following square corners to create a cube that is missing exactly one corner? (The positions of the square corners listed below are for the corners as they appear in the figure, not necessarily as they would appear after the figure is folded into a cube.)

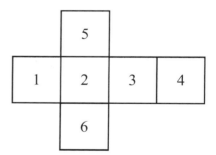

(A) <u>Square 1</u>: bottom left corner; <u>Square 4</u>: bottom left corner; <u>Square 6</u>: bottom right corner
(B) <u>Square 1</u>: bottom right corner; <u>Square 2</u>: bottom left corner; <u>Square 6</u>: top right corner
(C) <u>Square 1</u>: top left corner; <u>Square 4</u>: top left corner; <u>Square 5</u>: bottom right corner
(D) <u>Square 2</u>: bottom right corner; <u>Square 3</u>: bottom left corner; <u>Square 4</u>: top right corner
(E) <u>Square 3</u>: bottom right corner; <u>Square 4</u>: bottom left corner <u>Square 6</u>: bottom right corner

GO TO THE NEXT PAGE.

10. If $a - b = c \div d$, then which expression is equal to b?

   (A) $\dfrac{ad - c}{d}$

   (B) $\dfrac{c - a}{d}$

   (C) $\dfrac{c + a}{d}$

   (D) $\dfrac{cd + a}{d^2}$

   (E) $\dfrac{d^2 - ac}{d}$

11. If $x \,\textbf{.}\, y = (y + x)^2 - 2yx$, what is the value of m, if $m = 4 \,\textbf{.}\, 3$?

   (A) 1^2
   (B) 2^2
   (C) 3^2
   (D) 5^2
   (E) 7^2

12. Alexander took 4 tests. If his median score was 85 and his mean score was 87, what was the sum of his highest and lowest test scores?

   (A) 172
   (B) 174
   (C) 176
   (D) 178
   (E) 180

13. If the length of a diagonal of a square is 14 centimeters, what is the area of the square?

   (A) 49 cm^2
   (B) 56 cm^2
   (C) 98 cm^2
   (D) 112 cm^2
   (E) 196 cm^2

GO TO THE NEXT PAGE.

SPACE FOR FIGURING

14. Ronaldo has a box containing 10 blue marbles, 8 red marbles, 5 orange marbles, 4 green marbles, and 3 yellow marbles. On his first draw, he selects a yellow marble and does not return it to the box. He then draws a second marble. What is the probability that the second marble is yellow?

(A) $\dfrac{2}{29}$

(B) $\dfrac{3}{30}$

(C) $\dfrac{3}{30} \times \dfrac{3}{30}$

(D) $\dfrac{3}{30} \times \dfrac{2}{29}$

(E) $\dfrac{1}{30} \times \dfrac{2}{29}$

---

15. Which of the following expressions is equivalent to the expression $(x - 5)^2 - 3x + 11$?

(A) $(x - 6)^2 + x$
(B) $(x - 9)(x - 4)$
(C) $x^2 - 13x + 14$
(D) $x^2 - 7x - 14$
(E) $x^2 - 3x + 36$

---

16. Julianna is creating 2-letter passcodes in her introductory cryptography class. If she can choose from the letters A, B, C, D, E, and F, and the order of the letters matters (e.g., the passcode XY is different from the passcode YX), how many passcodes can Julianna create, if a letter cannot be used more than once per passcode?

(A) 10
(B) 15
(C) 20
(D) 30
(E) 60

GO TO THE NEXT PAGE.

Questions 17-18 refer to the table.

17. What is the difference between the mean and median of the selected y values displayed in the table?

(A) 0
(B) 0.2
(C) 0.35
(D) 0.55
(E) 0.7

Selected Values of x and y of an Unknown Graph	
x	y
-2.5	-5.25
-2	-3
-1.7	-1.89
-1.5	-1.25
-0.9	0.19

18. Which of the following equations could represent the graph from which the data points were selected?

(A) $y = x^2 + 1$
(B) $y = 1.5x - 1.5$
(C) $y = x^2 - 1$
(D) $y = -x^2 + 1$
(E) It cannot be determined from the information given.

19. Douglas has 2 six-sided dice. He rolls a 4 with the first die. What is the probability that he will roll a 4 with the second die?

(A) $\dfrac{1}{2}$

(B) $\dfrac{1}{4}$

(C) $\dfrac{1}{6}$

(D) $\dfrac{4}{6}$

(E) $\dfrac{1}{36}$

GO TO THE NEXT PAGE.

20. At noon, a car leaves Town M towards Town N at a rate of 70 miles per hour. At 1:30 pm, a bus also leaves Town M towards Town N at a rate of 90 miles per hour. At 2:00 pm, a van leaves Town N towards Town M at a rate of 65 miles per hour. If Towns M and N are 680 miles apart, how far is the bus from Town N when the car and van meet?

(A) 225 miles
(B) 250 miles
(C) 275 miles
(D) 300 miles
(E) 325 miles

21. On the x,y-coordinate plane, points A and B have coordinates of $(0, 3)$ and $(3, 0)$, respectively. If the coordinates of point C are $(0, -4)$, what is the area of triangle ABC?

(A) 1.5 units^2
(B) 3 units^2
(C) 7.5 units^2
(D) 10.5 units^2
(E) 21 units^2

22. What is the sum of the units digits of 28^3 and 37^4?

(A) 3
(B) 5
(C) 7
(D) 9
(E) 11

23. When Raymond calculates the expression $5^2 - 4 \times 3 + 7 \div 7$, he gets an answer of 10. By how much, if at all, is his answer off from the correct answer?

(A) 0
(B) 1
(C) 2
(D) 3
(E) 4

GO TO THE NEXT PAGE.

24. Curtis wants to build a rectangular garden that will have an area of 320 square feet. He will build a fence around his garden to prevent rabbits and deer from getting to his produce. To make measuring the dimensions of the fence less of a hassle, however, he will build the fence such that each side has an integer length of feet. Which of the following dimensions will minimize the amount of fencing Curtis will need?

(A) 8 feet by 40 feet
(B) 16 feet by 20 feet
(C) 32 feet by 10 feet
(D) 64 feet by 5 feet
(E) 80 feet by 4 feet

25. If angle BCD is an external angle of equilateral triangle ABC, which has side lengths of 6 inches, and segment CD also has length 6 inches, what is the area of triangle BCD (not shown)?

(A) 3 in.^{2}
(B) $3\sqrt{3}$ in.^{2}
(C) 6 in.^{2}
(D) $9\sqrt{3}$ in.^{2}
(E) 12 in.^{2}

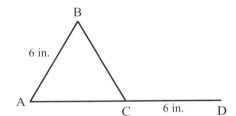

STOP

**IF YOU FINISH BEFORE TIME IS CALLED, YOU MAY CHECK YOUR WORK ON THIS SECTION ONLY.
DO NOT TURN TO ANY OTHER SECTION IN THE TEST.**

SECTION 2
40 Questions
40 Minutes

After reading each passage, answer its accompanying questions. Select your answers on the basis of the information presented in the passage only.

What do Bigfoot, the Loch Ness monster, and the Yeti have in common? They are creatures of lore, talked about by people and rumored to exist. Their existence is debated because scientifically valid evidence of their existence is not available, yet over the years many people have claimed to have seen them—some have even
Line 5   produced photographic or video "proof" that these creatures exist. Unfortunately, many of these pieces of evidence are either too blurry to be authenticated or just downright spurious. Thus, the debate rages on, and until the existence of these mythological creatures has either been definitively verified or debunked, they will continue to be referred to colloquially by many as "cryptids" and the pseudoscience
10   of cryptozoology will remain intact.

---

1. It can be inferred about Bigfoot, the Loch Ness monster, and Yeti that
   (A) they have each been seen by at least one person
   (B) photographic evidence of their existence has been validated
   (C) their existence will never be either proved or disproved
   (D) they have been discussed extensively
   (E) they are the figments of people's imaginations

2. "Cryptids" (line 10) can be defined as
   (A) animals whose existence has been debunked
   (B) creatures people have proved to exist
   (C) beasts of ancient mythology
   (D) animals whose presence has been underappreciated
   (E) creatures that may or may not be real

3. This passage would be most likely found in
   (A) a school report on cryptozoology
   (B) a dictionary entry for the word *cryptid*
   (C) a science fiction novel
   (D) an encyclopedia entry on hominids
   (E) a newspaper article about a cryptid sighting

4. Which of the following, if true, would best disprove the existence of the "creatures of lore" mentioned in the passage?
   (A) DNA obtained from what witnesses claim were creatures of lore turn out to be DNA from known species.
   (B) Satellite imagery reveals several potential creatures of lore, but further analysis reveals these "creatures" to be oddly shaped trees, foliage, or rock formations.
   (C) Decades of expeditions carried out by experts using the most advanced tracking and recording instruments have failed to yield evidence of any creature of lore.
   (D) Archaeologists uncover authentic diaries of ancient storytellers, and in the diaries, the storytellers detailed their plans to make up the creatures of lore in order to prevent kids from venturing too far from their tribes' camps or to compel good behavior.
   (E) The world's leading biologists publish their opinion that there is less than a 50% chance that the creatures of lore exist.

GO TO THE NEXT PAGE.

In 1997, the first mammal, Dolly the sheep, was successfully cloned. Dolly's clone's birth was a major milestone for the world of science and was the culmination of many technological breakthroughs. But more than that, it represented possibility—the possibility of cloning other animals and even of humans—and it
Line 5   was this possibility, which was an embodiment of the unknown, that proved to be terrifying. Ethics questions—the most prominent of which was whether it was ethical to clone humans—arose and a fierce debate raged on.

Since the late 1990s and early 2000s, the debate has lost momentum across the public forum, but the rate of the acquisition of scientific knowledge has not. In fact,
10   since then, geneticists were able to sequence the complete Neanderthal genome, which proved to contain more than 3 billion letters. It has also been speculated by some researchers that we would be capable of cloning a Neanderthal. But what would it be like for a clone of our distant ancestors to be born in the modern world, most likely to a group of scientists who want to observe and study it—or, more
15   accurately, him or her?

Though they probably went extinct nearly 30,000 years ago because of their inability to adapt to the competition they faced from the modern humans or to changes in the climate, Neanderthals were genetically close enough to humans to perform many of the same tasks that early modern humans did, such as using tools
20   and building fire. In fact, theories regarding the possibility that Neanderthals in some regions learned to use some of their tools from modern humans have been posited.

Given the similarities between modern humans and Neanderthals, it is not difficult to imagine that Neanderthals would have had many of the same feelings and emotions we do now. And if it goes without saying that a significant number of
25   people would decry the birth and containment of a human clone as unethical, how would people react to the study and observation of a Neanderthal clone in a laboratory setting? Moreover, even if the clone was not kept under close scientific scrutiny, what sort of public reception would the Neanderthal receive if scientists tried to integrate him or her into a modern human setting? Would it be fair for the
30   Neanderthal?

Let it be clear that Neanderthals are not modern humans. But does the fact that they are of a different species make it acceptable ethically to clone and study a Neanderthal? We do, after all, keep other species of animals, such as mice and other
35   small animals, in confinement to study, observe, and conduct experimentation on. So the question I pose to you today is, "Where do we draw the line of ethics?"

5. The following statements about Neanderthals are supported by the passage, except

(A) Neanderthals went extinct approximately 30,000 years ago
(B) Neanderthals knew how to use tools and build fire
(C) relatively speaking, Neanderthals were genetically very close to early modern humans
(D) Neanderthals knew how to perform all the same tasks that early modern humans could
(E) competition with modern humans drove the Neanderthals to extinction

6. The author wrote this passage to

(A) reveal new information about Neanderthals
(B) demand that all experiments on animals be ceased at once
(C) suggest that Neanderthals should be treated with dignity when they are cloned
(D) argue only against the cloning of higher order animals
(E) challenge the reader to think more carefully about questions of ethics

GO TO THE NEXT PAGE.

7. The birth of Dolly's clone instigated debates because

(A) society was worried about the consequences of having mindless bodies wandering around

(B) people were worried that human cloning would lead to widespread wars the world over

(C) of the ethics questions it raised with regard to human cloning

(D) it was understood that problems associated with overpopulation would become exacerbated

(E) no one had previously known how expensive, and consequently what a burden on taxpayers, cloning sheep would be

8. One potential concern raised by the author regarding the ethics of cloning a Neanderthal is

(A) the genetic compatibility of a Neanderthal fetus and modern human surrogate mother

(B) the fairness to the Neanderthal, regardless of who or which institution has governance, stewardship, and care of the Neanderthal

(C) the media frenzy that would inevitably ensue when people the Neanderthal's existence is made public

(D) the lack of practical knowledge of how to properly care for a Neanderthal in its childhood

(E) the immense funding needed to successfully clone a Neanderthal

9. The passage acknowledges that if a Neanderthal clone were brought into the modern era it would most likely

(A) not be capable of fending for itself against modern humans in a physical altercation

(B) face an immense language and communication barrier when trying to integrate itself into modern society

(C) lament having been brought into the modern world

(D) have emotions similar to those of modern humans

(E) have no way of understanding how to operate modern technology

GO TO THE NEXT PAGE.

Line 5

10

Have you ever used a rechargeable battery and wondered why the charge capacity of the battery diminishes over time? If you have used a portable electronic device, such as a tablet or phone, over the course of a year or two, or possibly longer, you may have noticed this phenomenon. More likely than not, your device is powered by a lithium-ion battery, and every time your device is charged and discharged, the lithium ions cause actual structural damage to the battery. Because of this gradual degradation in the structural integrity of the battery, the ability of the battery to hold charges diminishes. The problem is that in order to build more perfect batteries, scientists need to be able to see what types of damage the lithium ions cause at a nanoscopic level. Fortunately, however, a breakthrough in creating longer lasting rechargeable lithium-ion batteries may be nigh.

15

20

25

To address the problem of battery degradation, scientists from the Department of Energy started by collaborating to understand what was going on inside batteries at the atomic level. What they discovered by using advanced electron microscopy techniques was that the lithium-ion reactions erode the battery materials in a non-uniform pattern. That is, even though the consistency of the building materials may seem perfect from a large-scale perspective, at the atomic level, the consistency of the building materials was anything but. Because of these structural inconsistencies at the atomic level, the lithium ions exploit the weaker portions of the materials. (Conceptually, this is similar to the consistency found in asphalt roads. From a distance, they look perfectly smooth and flat, but when you peer in for a closer look, you can see that there are inconsistencies, i.e., pores, in the asphalt's texture. The porousness of asphalt roads are in part why potholes develop, especially during and after the winter season. When water seeps into the pores and freezes, the expanding ice crystals cause the asphalt to break apart where the asphalt is structurally the weakest.)

30

The goal, of course, of better understanding how lithium ions interact with the battery materials is to be able to adapt the current battery construction process to create batteries that are much better at holding higher levels of their original charges over longer periods of time. Whether scientists will be able to revise the current battery construction process, only time will tell, but at least they are one step closer.

10. Lithium ion batteries lose their ability to hold charges after a while due to
   (A) the charges wearing out over time
   (B) lithium's reactivity as an element; lithium bonds to the walls of the batteries with increased usage
   (C) the inability of engineers to develop batteries with perfectly contained electric charges
   (D) the poor construction of the hull of the batteries
   (E) the degradation of the batteries' structural integrity

11. The best title for the passage is
   (A) "Longer Lasting Batteries Coming Soon"
   (B) "Making Homemade Rechargeable Batteries"
   (C) "One Step Closer to Building Better Batteries"
   (D) "Making Batteries More Compatible with Latest Electronic Standards"
   (E) "The Dilemma with Batteries"

GO TO THE NEXT PAGE.

12. According to the passage, what causes potholes to form?

   (A) Cars that drive too aggressively cause chunks of asphalt to wear down and break apart, especially where the asphalt is the weakest.
   (B) Winter time causes the asphalt to get more brittle, so the combination of water erosion and friction generated by the contact of cars' tires wears down the asphalt more quickly.
   (C) The sun's heat and radiation causes the water molecules that have been trapped in the asphalt's nooks and crannies to expand vigorously, causing portions of the asphalt to break apart.
   (D) During winter, water that gets trapped in the pores and crevices of asphalt freezes and expands, causing the asphalt to break apart.
   (E) During the summer, when it is more humid out, atmospheric water vapor gets trapped underneath the asphalt, causing the ground mass to swell up even more, which then breaks apart the asphalt.

13. The degradation of lithium ion batteries is most analogous to

   (A) clothes wearing thin more slowly at the joints, even though the fabric at the joints is exposed to increased friction generated by the hardness of the bones and perpetual rubbing up against the fabric
   (B) an earthquake completely destroying both earthquake-resistant buildings and nonresistant buildings alike
   (C) water boiling faster when more pressure is applied to the cooking apparatus
   (D) a bully picking on the weakest kid in class for his lunch money
   (E) a predator stalking its prey before closing in on its victim

14. It can be inferred that the scientists of the Department of Energy were able to study what was happening inside batteries at the atomic level by using a(n)

   (A) high-powered optical microscope
   (B) nanoscopic telescope
   (C) x-ray generator
   (D) electron microscope
   (E) advanced spectroscope

15. The primary purpose of the second passage is to

   (A) compare and contrast lithium ion batteries with asphalt
   (B) suggest an alternative to the use of lithium ion batteries
   (C) shift the discussion topic away from lithium ion batteries to asphalt
   (D) explain what goes on inside a lithium ion battery at the atomic level
   (E) demonstrate the practicality of lithium ion batteries in a real-world setting

GO TO THE NEXT PAGE.

Line 5

10

15

The term "tractor beam" is a familiar science fiction term that was coined in 1931 by Edward Elmer Smith in his novel *Spacehounds of IPC*. Since then, the notion of the tractor beam has been employed by many works, most notably among which is the hit series *Star Trek*. The tractor beam, which is a device that can attract remote objects and draw them in towards it, has for many decades been confined to the realm of imagination and fantasy. Recent developments in ultrasound technology, though, may blur the lines of reality and fiction and eventually eradicate these lines altogether, at least with regard to the idea of the tractor beam.

Physicists at Dundee University were able to use ultrasound energy to attract a hollow triangle to the source of the energy. The concept of using ultrasound energy to move objects has been around for a while, but until now only particles at the molecular level could be moved. This latest "tractor beam" represents a major breakthrough in such technology because it can pull objects with a billion times more force than previous prototypes could. The technology is nowhere near ready to be deployed in the capacity the media has familiarized us with—the Dundee University team's beam is only currently capable of moving objects approximately 1 centimeter in size—but the dramatic improvement in technology is certainly promising.

16. The author believes that

(A) phenomena currently in the realm of fiction may one day become reality
(B) tractor operators will soon be able to transport trailers much more easily
(C) UFOs or other alien spacecraft are observing us remotely
(D) instantaneous teleportation of people will be possible in the future
(E) machinery used for lifting heavy objects will soon become obsolete

17. The latest "tractor beam" created by Dundee University physicists represented a breakthrough in that it

(A) used ultrasound energy, as opposed to tractor beam energy
(B) was able to pull objects with far more strength than previous models could
(C) was more compact than previous versions were, making it more portable
(D) could move particles at the molecular level
(E) used less energy to pull objects a billion times more massive than previous models could

18. It can be inferred that the hollow triangle mentioned in line 10 was

(A) extremely dense
(B) about the size of a molecule
(C) invisible to the naked eye
(D) moderately difficult for the average human to pick up without assistance
(E) about 1 centimeter big

19. The term "tractor beam" was first coined

(A) by Edward Elmer Smith in 1931
(B) in the hit series *Star Trek*
(C) when the first science fiction novel was published
(D) by Edward Smith in his 1913 book *Spacehounds of IPC*
(E) by a group of tractor manufacturers who also happened to be novelists

20. The tone of the author throughout the passage is

(A) incredulous
(B) bemused
(C) informative
(D) jaded
(E) ambivalent

GO TO THE NEXT PAGE.

Line 5

10

15

20

25

It had been eighteen harvests since he had acquired the plot of arable land. As he looked out the window of his home, the farmer saw healthy, robust crop. Pride and joy flooded his heart every time he saw the fruits of his labor. But, it had not always been this way.

Try as he might with his own two hands, the farmer could not yield the abundance of crops the farm had once enjoyed. Witnessing his own inadequacies drove the farmer into depression. As such, the land—his land—grew blacker and blacker with humus, dead and decaying produce covering more of his land with every passing year. There were, however, times in which miracles would be worked and hope would shine through the thunderheads of despair. In these scarce moments, renewed dedication and energy consumed the farmer. Inevitably, this newfound energy would quickly dematerialize.

"This year," he told himself, many a year, "I will rise up early every day and restore the beauty of my farm!" The moon rose and sank many evenings, and the sun rose and sank many days. As before, the farmer promised to do the same, to restore that shoddy field. But words are only words and empty promises are no promises at all.

Yet, one day, he woke up bright and early and stopped to pick up and throw away a rotting tomato. This led to him picking up another one and still another one after that. Before he knew it, he had cleaned up a large portion of his farm, and he remembered how sublime and awesome this plot of land had been when he first laid eyes on it; he remembered why he had acquired it. Starting from that day and on, the farmer woke up with the rise of every sun and restored his body, mind, and soul.

His hands toiled the ground until they were raw with blisters, until sweat cascaded down his back, until his hips bucked in pain. Every night he lay down on his bed with joy in his spirit, and prayed a prayer of thanksgiving. Now he looks out the window and relishes the sight of his hard-worked, verdant plot of arable land.

21. This passage is an extended metaphor for
(A) a typical farmer's life story
(B) an arrogant man's realization of the importance of humility
(C) a student's academic achievements and successes
(D) a son's story of rebellion against bad parents
(E) a perpetual failure's rediscovery of success

22. "The moon…many days" indicates that
(A) empty promises mean the same during the nights as they do during the days
(B) much time passed without the farmer making good on his promise to himself
(C) the farmer was keeping track of the lunar cycle very meticulously
(D) calendars did not exist then, so counting the days was critical
(E) days could only pass if nights also passed and vice versa

23. Which of the following questions is left unanswered by the passage?
(A) Approximately how much time passed from the time the farmer acquired the plot of land to the present day?
(B) Why did the farmer acquire the plot of land?
(C) What sorts of miracles gave the farmer brief spurts of renewed energy and dedication?
(D) What physical symptoms of exhaustion did the farmer experience and exhibit as he restored his field?
(E) What caused the farmer to fall into depression?

GO TO THE NEXT PAGE.

24. The farmer's final, committed restoration of his farm began with him
    (A) stopping to pick up a rotting tomato
    (B) cultivating his derelict farm
    (C) formulating a plan to restore his land
    (D) getting fed up with his own laziness
    (E) waking up early in order to clean up his field

25. It can be inferred that before the farmer acquired the farm,
    (A) the farmer's parents had done a much better job of operating the farm
    (B) the farm had yielded an abundance of crops
    (C) the farm was more fruitful than the farmer was able to make it in the end
    (D) the farm had regularly been covered by humus and detritus
    (E) the farmer had very little experience with farming

GO TO THE NEXT PAGE.

Line 5

10

15

20

25

30

The Beaufort Sea, spanning an area of 184,000 square miles north of both Alaska and Canada's Northwest Territories, has always been tranquil—that is, it has never displayed any significant wave activity—until relatively recently, when scientists detected 16-foot waves during a September 2012 storm in the region. This is because the Beaufort Sea has always had enough ice covering its waters to render wave formation impossible.

To clarify, sea ice is a natural phenomenon in Arctic bodies of water, especially during the winter months, when temperatures are the coldest; thus, it naturally follows that when summer comes and the temperatures are warmer, the ice thins out to some extent. In the case of the Beaufort Sea, the ice cover is at its thickest in April and at its thinnest in September. And even though the volume of ice fluctuates seasonally, the amount of seasonal ice loss in the Beaufort Sea had been relatively trivial thus far.

But when scientists detected waves in the Beaufort Sea for the first time in recorded history, renewed fears of climate change surfaced, adding more fuel to the fire that is the global warming debate. While waves in and of themselves are ordinarily no cause for alarm, in the case of the Beaufort Sea, their presence does give cause for alarm, as the size of the waves detected in the sea is expected to increase in the future, given current climate trends.

The size of waves is often determined by how much wind blows across the water's surface. The greater distances winds can blow over open water, the bigger the resultant waves will be. In the Beaufort Sea, as in many other bodies of water in the Arctic, these larger waves, which result when enough sea ice melts and yields more open water from which the waves can be formed, break up sea ice even more quickly and allow more sunlight to warm the water more quickly, triggering a self-perpetuating cycle of sea ice loss, which itself is a problem whose ramifications extend beyond the stress people feel from the fear they experience.

With a greater surface area of open water available, the rate and balance of carbon dioxide exchange between the water and atmosphere could become skewed because of the increased likelihood of an increased output of greenhouse gases into the atmosphere, leading a to a litany of other problems, shoreline erosion being just one of them.

26. According to the passage, the size of waves is in part determined by
(A) how fast winds blow
(B) the depth of the body of water
(C) how much open water is available for winds to blow over
(D) the amount of pollution present
(E) the moon's gravitational pull

27. Between the months of April and September, the Beaufort Sea
(A) freezes over
(B) cools down
(C) thaws somewhat
(D) melts completely
(E) experiences no detectable change in climate

28. If the passage were continued or extended, the following paragraph would most logically be about
(A) the impact factories have on oceanic carbon dioxide levels
(B) the economic impact global warming has on nations and industries
(C) the importance of the plants play in carbon dioxide absorption
(D) the ramifications of shoreline erosion
(E) the amount of greenhouse gases that have been released into the atmosphere in the past three decades by the greater availability of open waters

GO TO THE NEXT PAGE.

29. The passage lists all but which of the following as a fact about the Beaufort Sea?

    (A) It spans184,000 square miles.
    (B) It is north of Alaska.
    (C) It is the northernmost arctic sea in North America.
    (D) It is north of Canada's Northwest Territories.
    (E) It has not displayed any significant wave activity until 2012.

30. It can be inferred that the self-perpetuating cycle of sea ice loss

    (A) is most heavily impacted by sunlight
    (B) tends to naturally accelerate with every cycle, until the cycle is stopped
    (C) is irreversible
    (D) is the result of temperatures not being low enough in the winter to cause sea ice formation
    (E) will lead to larger waves in all bodies of sea water throughout the world, not just in arctic seas

GO TO THE NEXT PAGE.

Line 5

10

15

When we think of burglaries, we think of men clad in black picking a lock or disabling an alarm system and then sneaking into the target establishment to perpetrate a theft. We think of burglars as thieves who plan their crimes months in advance and who would get away with the crime if not for some small, unforeseeable wrench that gets thrown into their plans.

But in the case of Alphonse Warner*, a 27-year-old man from Minnesota, the wrench was provided by none other than Warner himself. Rather stupidly, Warner logged into his Facebook account at the home he burgled. But to top it off, he forgot to sign out before absconding with the stolen goods, which included cash, credit cards, a watch, and a checkbook, among other things.

Unsurprisingly, the police did not have much difficulty tracking down and apprehending Warner, whom they found to have the stolen possessions. It seems that the moral of the story is: Steer clear of crime because "crime doesn't pay," as the saying goes, but when you shoot yourself in the foot in the perpetration of the crime, you can be sure that you will—pay, that is.

*Name changed to protect the author against lawsuits.

31. The author makes the assumption that
   (A) it is a common perception that burglars are very careful in planning and executing their crimes
   (B) burglars always get caught by the police, no matter how careful they were in planning the burglary
   (C) Hollywood has glamorized criminal antiheros so much that we expect all criminals to be elite criminal masterminds
   (D) it is common for criminals to leave blatant traces that they were there at crime scenes
   (E) burglars will likely log into their social media websites at the crime scenes and then forget to log out afterwards

32. The author's view of Alphonse Warner can best be described as
   (A) respectful
   (B) objective
   (C) contemptuous
   (D) sympathetic
   (E) horrified

33. The moral of the passage is best expressed as:
   (A) commit crimes intelligently
   (B) think things through before doing them
   (C) log into your Facebook account when you're committing a crime
   (D) get into the habit of cleaning up after yourself
   (E) don't do things just because everyone else is doing them

34. Which of the following was not specifically included on the list of things in Warner's possession when the police apprehended him?
   (A) a watch
   (B) jewelry
   (C) cash
   (D) credit cards
   (E) checkbook

35. In context, the word *wrench* (lines 5 and 7) most nearly means
   (A) a tool for gripping and turning or twisting
   (B) a physically painful, sudden twist
   (C) emotional discomfort
   (D) a hindrance
   (E) a twisted interpretation of

GO TO THE NEXT PAGE.

Line 5

10

15

20

25

If you're anything like I was when I was a kid, you probably had an extensive list of foods that you were "allergic" to. So it was terribly unfortunate that, though you wanted to eat these foods, you were simply unable to. Of course, this list never included unhealthy, but delicious, junk foods, such as pizza, hamburgers, and French fries; it only included the foods that looked a little too funny, were a little too green, or tasted a little too healthy, even if they were scrumptious. But your parents, being that they're, well, parents, would try to cajole you, often unsuccessfully, into eating these nutritious abominations by telling you about how healthy they are. As kids, why would we want to reject eating foods that are both delicious and healthy?

Two researchers tried to answer this question by studying and evaluating the eating habits of children who were three to five years old. To do this, the researchers associated a positive message with each of a variety of foods. For example, some foods were associated with better vision, while others were associated with increased strength, and so on and so forth. What the researchers found was that, compared to the kids in the control group, the kids who were offered foods that were associated with a positive message more readily rated the foods as less tasty, planned to eat less of the foods, and in fact did eat less of the foods when made available to them.

One possible explanation for these findings has emerged: perhaps young children's brains are not sufficiently developed enough to realize and accept that foods can serve multiple purposes. Instead, the children reason that everything can only serve a single purpose. Thus, if a food item is good for their health, then it cannot also be good for their taste buds simultaneously. Does this mean we have to change our approach to how we present food to young children? It may be too early to tell as of now, but the researchers' findings are certainly worth taking into consideration.

36. The author's tone in the first paragraph is

(A) metaphorical
(B) satirical
(C) appreciative
(D) disinterested
(E) histrionic

37. The researchers found that associating a positive message with foods

(A) caused young children to enjoy those foods more
(B) caused young children to be more aware of the health implications of unhealthy foods
(C) caused young children to avoid those foods altogether
(D) caused young children to prefer those foods less
(E) caused no change in the dietary preferences of young children

38. It is hypothesized that young children

(A) naturally dislike healthy foods because healthy foods tend to taste worse
(B) seek out healthier foods because their bodies crave healthier foods more
(C) shun healthier foods because healthier foods tend to have a lower fat content, and it is important for babies to have a proper amount of fats in reserve
(D) cannot properly process the idea that foods can serve multiple purposes
(E) will eat foods more eagerly if only the health benefit of the food is conveyed and the tastiness of the food is not mentioned at all

GO TO THE NEXT PAGE.

39. It can be inferred that the young children in the control group
    (A) were not told the healthy foods were healthy
    (B) were told the healthy foods were extra healthy
    (C) thought the other kids were eating less appetizing foods
    (D) believed they were eating very expensive foods
    (E) were instructed to say that the healthier foods tasted better

40. The researchers' findings can be considered
    (A) as we find new ways to make unhealthy foods less appetizing
    (B) as we convince young children that healthy foods are, in fact, more delicious than junk foods
    (C) before we tell children directly about the positive benefits of healthy foods
    (D) while biologists invent new ways of making healthy foods taste better without sacrificing or negating their health benefits
    (E) when nutritionists devise new charts that deemphasize the health benefits of healthy foods

STOP

IF YOU FINISH BEFORE TIME IS CALLED, YOU MAY CHECK YOUR WORK ON THIS SECTION ONLY.
DO NOT TURN TO ANY OTHER SECTION IN THE TEST.

SECTION 3
60 Questions
30 Minutes

There are two types of questions in this section: synonyms and analogies.

Synonyms
Each question consists of one word in capital letters, followed by five answer choices. Select the answer choice consisting of the word or phrase closest in meaning to the word in capital letters.

Sample Question:

TORRID:

(A) mild
(B) painful
(C) pleasant
(D) hot
(E) sticky

Ⓐ Ⓑ Ⓒ ● Ⓔ

1. RAMBUNCTIOUS:

   (A) craven
   (B) savage
   (C) boisterous
   (D) playful
   (E) serene

2. UNKEMPT:

   (A) illogical
   (B) luxurious
   (C) orderly
   (D) disheveled
   (E) insensitive

3. ADAMANT:

   (A) stubborn
   (B) metallic
   (C) sharp
   (D) ferocious
   (E) glorious

4. CONDONE:

   (A) start
   (B) cooperate
   (C) finish
   (D) scavenge
   (E) permit

5. PROVOKE:

   (A) destroy
   (B) configure
   (C) pursue
   (D) promise
   (E) excite

6. IMPARTIAL:

   (A) unbiased
   (B) whole
   (C) miniscule
   (D) fractional
   (E) redeemable

7. SOPORIFIC:

   (A) thinking irrationally
   (B) inducing sleep
   (C) scattering freely
   (D) releasing spores
   (E) sputtering incoherently

8. JUBILATION:

   (A) depression
   (B) exultation
   (C) confrontation
   (D) debilitation
   (E) amusement

GO TO THE NEXT PAGE.

9. UTOPIA:
   (A) citadel
   (B) stockade
   (C) paradise
   (D) pasture
   (E) dormitory

10. INNUENDO:
    (A) explicit message
    (B) revelation
    (C) suggestion
    (D) staccato
    (E) gradual increase

11. ABERRATION:
    (A) oddity
    (B) beast
    (C) pet
    (D) modality
    (E) defect

12. ANTITHESIS:
    (A) ally
    (B) stupidity
    (C) antipode
    (D) hypothesis
    (E) nemesis

13. COUNTENANCE:
    (A) scale
    (B) relationship
    (C) measure
    (D) appearance
    (E) scar

14. BEREFT:
    (A) psychic
    (B) deprived
    (C) melancholy
    (D) bounteous
    (E) laden

15. GOSSAMER:
    (A) thin
    (B) goose-like
    (C) quirky
    (D) regenerative
    (E) allegorical

16. FALLOW:
    (A) sickly
    (B) deniable
    (C) inactive
    (D) intolerable
    (E) shallow

17. ICONOCLAST:
    (A) legend
    (B) heretic
    (C) sculptor
    (D) follower
    (E) leader

18. PLATITUDE:
    (A) inventive thought
    (B) high altitude
    (C) optimistic approach
    (D) flat terrain
    (E) trite remark

19. MYOPIC:
    (A) blind
    (B) shortsighted
    (C) profound
    (D) insincere
    (E) cagey

20. RENDEZVOUS:
    (A) French bread
    (B) mission
    (C) assignment
    (D) meeting
    (E) secret

GO TO THE NEXT PAGE.

21. WIZENED:

   (A) intelligent
   (B) magical
   (C) undeserving
   (D) shriveled
   (E) antique

22. RECANT:

   (A) restate
   (B) censure
   (C) amble
   (D) reinforce
   (E) withdraw

23. PRECOCIOUS:

   (A) developmental
   (B) advanced
   (C) unblemished
   (D) drab
   (E) insistent

24. CONCUR:

   (A) agree with
   (B) defer to
   (C) negotiate with
   (D) cooperate with
   (E) accept tacitly

25. GERMANE:

   (A) technological
   (B) cognizant
   (C) pertinent
   (D) obvious
   (E) theatrical

26. DUPLICITY:

   (A) double
   (B) conundrum
   (C) virtue
   (D) copycat
   (E) deceit

27. ECLECTIC:

   (A) shocking
   (B) strange
   (C) banal
   (D) diverse
   (E) homogenous

28. SUBLIME:

   (A) sour
   (B) holy
   (C) meaningful
   (D) affable
   (E) impressive

29. CATHARSIS:

   (A) religious obligation
   (B) meditative expedition
   (C) emotional purgation
   (D) comprehensive evaluation
   (E) chemical reaction

30. BEQUEATH:

   (A) belie
   (B) disparage
   (C) relegate to
   (D) chase after
   (E) pass down

GO TO THE NEXT PAGE.

Analogies

These questions will ask you to find the relationships between words. For each question, select the answer choice that best completes the analogy relationship.

Sample Question:

> Glove is to hand as shoe is to
>
> (A) mouth
> (B) head
> (C) finger
> (D) foot
> (E) sock
>
> Ⓐ Ⓑ Ⓒ ● Ⓔ

31. Waiter is to food as

   (A) coroner is to cadaver
   (B) referee is to violation
   (C) engineer is to innovation
   (D) ferry is to passenger
   (E) messenger is to missive

32. Chicken is to omelet as

   (A) cow is to hamburger
   (B) pig is to pork
   (C) fish is to caviar
   (D) crab is to lobster
   (E) veal is to venison

33. Walk is to trot as

   (A) scurry is to amble
   (B) canter is to gallop
   (C) saunter is to gait
   (D) skip is to pedal
   (E) hop is to bounce

34. Batter is to cake as

   (A) cement is to concrete
   (B) grind is to flour
   (C) potato is to salad
   (D) rice is to grain
   (E) cotton is to cloth

35. Ring is to marriage as

   (A) trophy is to success
   (B) tax is to obligation
   (C) monument is to statue
   (D) law is to rule
   (E) badge is to identification

36. Gamble is to invest as

   (A) guess is to derive
   (B) imitate is to copy
   (C) strike is to hit
   (D) imbibe is to food
   (E) throw is to bat

37. Doctrine is to tenet as

   (A) pedestrian is to eccentric
   (B) archaic is to obsolete
   (C) stallion is to mare
   (D) morality is to philosophy
   (E) rationale is to effect

38. Ledger is to transaction as

   (A) handbook is to manual
   (B) candle is to age
   (C) binder is to paper
   (D) annal is to event
   (E) collage is to project

GO TO THE NEXT PAGE.

39. Seawater is to briny as

   (A) shrimp is to scrumptious
   (B) freshwater is to murky
   (C) desert is to mirage
   (D) facsimile is to image
   (E) tundra is to arctic

40. Tire is to rim as

   (A) scarf is to neck
   (B) wheel is to bus
   (C) coat is to warmth
   (D) briefcase is to documents
   (E) barrette is to hair

41. Filament is to bulb as

   (A) postage is to stamp
   (B) cheese is to dairy
   (C) top is to lid
   (D) bristle is to brush
   (E) hook is to fishing rod

42. Debonair is to sophisticated as

   (A) extravagant is to cavalier
   (B) simple is to accessible
   (C) boorish is to rustic
   (D) casual is to mainstream
   (E) paltry is to sustainable

43. Proton is to atom as

   (A) desk is to furniture
   (B) computer is to microchip
   (C) chromosome is to cell
   (D) shell is to artillery
   (E) ignition is to switch

44. Squalor is to sanitation as

   (A) indifference is to concern
   (B) tolerance is to acceptance
   (C) magnitude is to size
   (D) premonition is to oracle
   (E) immorality is to punishment

45. Founder is to establishment as

   (A) mechanic is to repair
   (B) inventor is to gadget
   (C) governor is to state
   (D) pioneer is to exploration
   (E) compass is to navigation

46. Merchandise is to tax as

   (A) export is to outside
   (B) barter is to trade
   (C) airport is to border
   (D) import is to tariff
   (E) highway is to speed

47. Operating is to machinery as

   (A) planning is to luck
   (B) dictating is to transcription
   (C) inspecting is to home
   (D) enacting is to law
   (E) directing is to film

48. Red is to violet as

   (A) green is to envy
   (B) communism is to fascism
   (C) theocracy is to religion
   (D) dependence is to necessity
   (E) legitimacy is to validity

49. Gourmand is to chef as

   (A) masochist is to sadist
   (B) locksmith is to vault
   (C) hobbyist is to enthusiast
   (D) chauffeur is to limousine
   (E) rancher is to cowboy

50. Perimeter is to triangle as

   (A) circumference is to circle
   (B) edge is to polygon
   (C) length is to rectangle
   (D) vertex is to angle
   (E) transversal is to parallel lines

GO TO THE NEXT PAGE.

51. Inkling is to theory as
    (A) belief is to doubt
    (B) likelihood is to improbability
    (C) mule is to donkey
    (D) suspect is to convict
    (E) cause is to effect

52. Ostentatious is to modesty as
    (A) austere is to restriction
    (B) infamous is to fame
    (C) amorphous is to shape
    (D) vapid is to complexion
    (E) diffident is to tenacity

53. Pulchritude is to beauty as compunction is to
    (A) remorse
    (B) precision
    (C) joy
    (D) punctuality
    (E) devotion

54. Dissonance is to melodious as
    (A) boorishness is to elegant
    (B) gluttony is to reluctant
    (C) dedication is to diligent
    (D) consternation is to repulsive
    (E) heterogeneity is to diverse

55. Handcuffs is to gavel as
    (A) ambulance is to firefighter
    (B) water is to hydrant
    (C) sickle is to millstone
    (D) airplane is to shuttle
    (E) bandage is to tape

56. Business is to tycoon as
    (A) literature is to author
    (B) ruler is to emperor
    (C) field is to laureate
    (D) school is to salutatorian
    (E) critic is to connoisseur

57. Affidavit is to declaration as
    (A) receipt is to product
    (B) hieroglyph is to cuneiform
    (C) scroll is to papyrus
    (D) facsimile is to coincidence
    (E) contract is to agreement

58. Guerrilla is to highwayman as
    (A) arena is to gladiator
    (B) entourage is to group
    (C) vendor is to customer
    (D) soldier is to bandit
    (E) yeoman is to supervisor

59. Destitution is to penury as
    (A) soliloquy is to monologue
    (B) euphemism is to insult
    (C) libel is to fact
    (D) query is to answer
    (E) qualm is to squabble

60. Bewilderment is to obfuscation as
    (A) equality is to legality
    (B) incoherence is to eloquence
    (C) anxiety is to stress
    (D) gratification is to pity
    (E) friction is to static

STOP

**IF YOU FINISH BEFORE TIME IS CALLED, YOU MAY CHECK YOUR WORK ON THIS SECTION ONLY.
DO NOT TURN TO ANY OTHER SECTION IN THE TEST.**

SECTION 4
25 Questions
30 Minutes

Work through each problem in this section. You may use the blank pace to the right of the page, if you need, to do your figuring. Then select the best one of the five suggested answer choices.

Note: Some of the problems are accompanied by figures, which are rendered as accurately as possible, EXCEPT when the problem explicitly states that its accompanying figure is not drawn to scale.

Sample Problem:

6,329	(A)	2,151
− 3,478	(B)	2,275
	(C)	2,807
	(D)	2,851
	(E)	2,951 Ⓐ Ⓑ Ⓒ ● Ⓔ

SPACE FOR FIGURING

1. If V and W are real numbers such that V is greater than W, which of the following statements must be true?

    (A) $V^2 > W^2$
    (B) $V^3 > W^2$
    (C) $V^4 > W^2$
    (D) $V + W > 0$
    (E) $V - W > 0$

---

2. After Beverly gives Chuck half of her candies, she has 7 more than twice the number of candies he originally started with. If Chuck started with 2 candies, how many did Beverly start with?

    (A) 4
    (B) 7
    (C) 14
    (D) 18
    (E) 22

---

3. $0.91 \times \dfrac{10}{7} =$

    (A) 0.13
    (B) 0.637
    (C) 1
    (D) 1.3
    (E) 6.37

GO TO THE NEXT PAGE.

4. If the radius of a circle is decreased by 40%, what is the net percent decrease in the area of the resulting circle?

   (A) 64%
   (B) 60%
   (C) 56%
   (D) 40%
   (E) 36%

5. Which of the following represents the solution for the absolute value inequality $2|x + 3| \leq 10$?

   (A)

   (B)

   (C)

   (D)

   (E)

6. A shirt is on sale at a store for 75% of its original price. Jo is a club member of the store, so she gets an additional 20% off the discounted price. If she pays $36.00 for the shirt, what was the original price of the shirt?

   (A) $180.00
   (B) $80.00
   (C) $72.00
   (D) $60.00
   (E) $54.00

GO TO THE NEXT PAGE.

SPACE FOR FIGURING

7. If S is a positive square integer, which of the following could be the value of P, to satisfy the equation $5P + 4S = 3(S - P)$?

    (A) -4
    (B) -2
    (C) -1
    (D) 0
    (E) 2

8. Karen and Trevor are training for a math competition. Karen solves 13 problems a day, while Trevor solves 8 problems a day. How many more problems will Karen have solved than Trevor after 27 days?

    (A) 126
    (B) 135
    (C) 216
    (D) 351
    (E) 567

9. The figure shows a check from a restaurant called Yummy Creations. The order amount is the cost of the food items ordered. The tax is 5% percent of the order amount. The subtotal is the sum of the order amount and the tax. The tip is an amount determined by the diner, but it is customarily a percentage of the order amount. The total is the sum of the subtotal and the tip. If the diner mistakenly applied a 20% tip to the subtotal amount and not the order amount, how much more will the diner have spent in total than he intended?

    (A) $0.25
    (B) $0.30
    (C) $0.35
    (D) $0.40
    (E) The total cost would be the same.

| Thank You for Choosing |
| Yummy Creations |

Order #: 00001

| 1 | Salad Appetizer | $5.00 |
| 2 | Steak w/Fries | $25.00 |

Order Amount: $_____.____
Tax (5%): $_____.____
Subtotal: $_____.____

Tip: $_____.____

Total: $_____.____

10. If a, b, and c are all positive integers in the equation $ax^2 + bx + c = 4(x + 2)^2$, what is the value of $a + b + c$?

    (A) 6
    (B) 9
    (C) 12
    (D) 27
    (E) 36

GO TO THE NEXT PAGE.

SPACE FOR FIGURING

11. The stem-and-leaf plot shows Mr. Tabor's 30 students' scores on his most recent test. A new student joins the class afterwards and makes up the test. After entering in the new student's score to the class's test results, Mr. Tabor finds that the class's new median, and mode scores remained the same as before. What is the new student's test score?

    (A) 77
    (B) 78
    (C) 79
    (D) 80
    (E) 81

Test Scores Stem-and-Leaf	
5	1 7
6	4 4 4 5 6 8
7	2 2 3 3 7 7 7 9
8	3 4 4 6 6 7 8 8
9	1 2 3 5 5
10	0

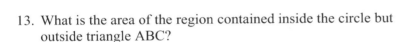

Questions 12-14 refer to the figure.

12. Isosceles right triangle ABC is inscribed in a circle whose diameter is $10\sqrt{2}$ units. If point D (not shown) is the midpoint of $\overline{AC}$, what is the length of the $\overline{BD}$?

    (A) 5 units
    (B) $5\sqrt{2}$ units
    (C) 10 units
    (D) $5\sqrt{5}$ units
    (E) $7\sqrt{3}$ units

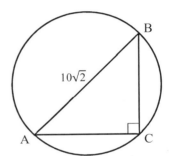

13. What is the area of the region contained inside the circle but outside triangle ABC?

    (A) $50(\pi - 1)$ square units
    (B) $50(4\pi - 1)$ square units
    (C) $100(\pi - 2)$ square units
    (D) $100(2\pi - 1)$ square units
    (E) $200(\pi - 1)$ square units

14. Which of the following expression could be used to determine how much greater the circumference of the circle is than the perimeter of triangle ABC?

    (A) $\pi - 20$
    (B) $20\pi\sqrt{2} - 20 - 10\sqrt{2}$
    (C) $20\pi\sqrt{2} + 20$
    (D) $10\pi\sqrt{2} - (10\sqrt{2} + 20)$
    (E) $10\pi\sqrt{2} + 20 - 20\sqrt{2}$

GO TO THE NEXT PAGE.

SPACE FOR FIGURING

15. The chart shows how Connor spends his allowance by percent. If his weekly allowance is $15, then approximately how much more money would he save per year, if he instead saved the money he has allotted for games?

(A) $120
(B) $135
(C) $150
(D) $270
(E) $420

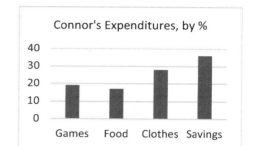

16. What is the least common multiple of 8, 15, and 36?

(A) 240
(B) 360
(C) 720
(D) 2160
(E) 4320

Set X = {2, 4, 5, 6}
Set Y = {3, 6}

17. If one number is selected at random from each set, what is the probability that the number chosen from set Y will be greater than the number chosen from set X?

(A) $\dfrac{1}{6}$

(B) $\dfrac{3}{8}$

(C) $\dfrac{1}{2}$

(D) $\dfrac{5}{8}$

(E) $\dfrac{3}{4}$

GO TO THE NEXT PAGE.

18. For his school project, Herbert is studying a local pond fish species. He drags a net through the pond at random and catches 59 males and 66 females. Assuming his catch is representative of the overall fish population, which is estimated to be 5,000, about how many more females are there than males in the pond?

    (A) 35
    (B) 70
    (C) 210
    (D) 280
    (E) 350

19. Jennie picked three numbers at random. The second number she picked was 6 more than twice the first number, and the third number was 3 less than half the second. Which expression correctly represents the sum of the three numbers?

    (A) $x + (2x + 6) + (x - 3)$
    (B) $x + 2(x + 6) + (x + 3)$
    (C) $x + 2(x + 6) + (x - 3)$
    (D) $x + (2x + 6) + x$
    (E) $x + 2(x + 6) - 3$

20. A cake recipe calls for 3 cups of flour, 1 cup of butter, 5 cups of sugar, and 1 cup of vanilla extract. Mildred realizes she only has 0.25 cups of flour but enough of the other ingredients. If she bakes the largest cake she can, using the same proportions of ingredients, what is the total volume of the ingredients she will use, including the flour, to the nearest hundredth of a cup?

    (A) 3.33 cups
    (B) 2.5 cups
    (C) 1.67 cups
    (D) 0.83 cups
    (E) 0.33 cups

21. Blair drove 15 miles east, 35 miles north, and then 3 miles west to reach his destination. If he had driven in a straight line to his destination, how many fewer miles would he have driven?

    (A) 13
    (B) 16
    (C) 18
    (D) 37
    (E) 40

GO TO THE NEXT PAGE.

SPACE FOR FIGURING

22. Simplify the expression $\dfrac{bx - ax}{ab}\left[\left(\dfrac{b}{x}\right)\left(\dfrac{a^2}{b-a}\right)\right]$,
    where $a \neq 0$, $b \neq 0$, $a \neq b$, and $x \neq 0$.

    (A) a
    (B) b
    (C) ab
    (D) $x(b^2 - a^2)$
    (E) $x(b - a^2)$

23. If the pattern of shading was continued in the figure, which of the following squares would be shaded?

    (A) 125th
    (B) 233rd
    (C) 342nd
    (D) 444th
    (E) 576th

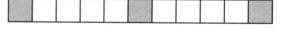

24. Solve for w, when $r = 25$ and $s = 24$: $\dfrac{r^2 - s^2}{w} = w$

    (A) 1
    (B) 7
    (C) 25
    (D) 36
    (E) 49

25. The partially shaded figure shows square ABCD, which is comprised of 36 smaller, equally sized right triangles. How many more of these triangles must be shaded in order to make the shaded pattern symmetrical about diagonal $\overline{AC}$?

    (A) 4
    (B) 5
    (C) 6
    (D) 7
    (E) 8

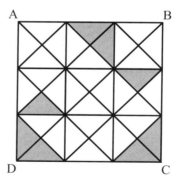

STOP

IF YOU FINISH BEFORE TIME IS CALLED, YOU MAY CHECK YOUR WORK ON THIS SECTION ONLY.
DO NOT TURN TO ANY OTHER SECTION IN THE TEST.

ANSWERS & EXPLANATIONS

SSAT
UPPER LEVEL
TEST KEY 1

Sections 1 & 4: Quantitative Reasoning

Directions: For each question, record your answer in the column where it says "Your Answer", next to the number of the question. If your answer does not match the correct answer, mark an 'X' in the column labeled "X|O". If you omitted the question, leave the space blank and mark 'O' in the "X|O" column.

Section 1

#	Correct Answer	Your Answer	X|O	Concepts Tested
1	D			ARO
2	A			AG
3	B			ARO
4	E			GM
5	A			SP
6	C			ARO
7	E			GM
8	D			DSP
9	B			AG
10	E			AG
11	C			AG
12	A			AG
13	C			DSP
14	A			DSP
15	B			ARO
16	E			NT
17	D			ARO
18	B			AG
19	B			AG
20	D			SP
21	C			GM
22	A			AG
23	C			FG
24	B			AG
25	D			SP

Section 4

#	Correct Answer	Your Answer	X|O	Concepts Tested
1	A			NT
2	C			AG
3	E			ARO
4	D			ARO
5	C			NT
6	E			AG
7	C			ARO
8	B			AG
9	A			DSP
10	D			ARO
11	D			ARO
12	E			AG
13	C			NT
14	A			ARO
15	B			AG
16	B			AG
17	D			ARO
18	B			DSP
19	D			ARO
20	A			GM
21	E			AG
22	D			GM
23	A			GM
24	E			DSP
25	C			DSP

CONCEPTS TESTED LEGEND

ARO – Arithmetic Operations
AG – Algebra

FG – Functions & Graphs
SP – Spatial Perception
NT – Number Theory

GM – Geometry & Measurement
DSP – Data Analysis, Statistics, & Probability

SCORING

Total Omitted (TO): _____

Total Incorrect (TI): _____

Total Missed (TM): _____
(TO + TI)

Raw Score: 50 – **TM** – 0.25 × **TI**

50 – _____ – 0.25 × _____ =

[_____]

Rounded Raw Score: _____
(Round to the nearest integer value.)

Section 2: Reading Comprehension

Directions: For each question, record your answer in the column where it says "Your Answer", next to the number of the question. If your answer does not match the correct answer, mark an 'X' in the column labeled "X|O". If you omitted the question, leave the space blank and mark 'O' in the "X|O" column.

#	Correct Answer	Your Answer	X|O	Concepts Tested
1	D			ID
2	C			MIP
3	E			ID
4	B			ID
5	C			INF
6	B			INF
7	D			INF
8	A			ID
9	E			MIP
10	A			AT
11	C			ID
12	B			INF
13	E			INF
14	D			MIP
15	B			MIP
16	B			ID
17	E			ID
18	D			INF
19	D			INF
20	D			MIP

#	Correct Answer	Your Answer	X|O	Concepts Tested
21	A			ID
22	C			INF
23	B			INF
24	A			ID
25	E			ID
26	E			AT
27	D			ID
28	C			DEF
29	D			INF
30	D			MIP
31	A			ID
32	B			INF
33	E			INF
34	D			ID
35	A			AT
36	C			ID
37	E			INF
38	B			ID
39	A			ID
40	C			ID

CONCEPTS TESTED LEGEND

ID – Identifying Details   INF – Inference & Assumption   DEF – Definition in Context
MIP – Main Idea or Purpose   AT – Author's Tone

SCORING

Total Omitted (TO): _____

Total Incorrect (TI): _____

Total Missed (TM): _____
(TO + TI)

Raw Score: $40 - \text{TM} - 0.25 \times \text{TI}$

$40 - \underline{\hspace{1cm}} - 0.25 \times \underline{\hspace{1cm}} =$

$\boxed{}$

Rounded Raw Score: _____
(Round to the nearest integer value.)

Section 3: Verbal Reasoning

Directions: For each question, record your answer in the column where it says "Your Answer", next to the number of the question. If your answer does not match the correct answer, mark an 'X' in the column labeled "X|O". If you omitted the question, leave the space blank and mark 'O' in the "X|O" column.

#	Correct Answer	Your Answer	X|O	Concepts Tested
1	D			SYN
2	B			SYN
3	B			SYN
4	A			SYN
5	C			SYN
6	C			SYN
7	A			SYN
8	D			SYN
9	A			SYN
10	B			SYN
11	A			SYN
12	D			SYN
13	B			SYN
14	A			SYN
15	D			SYN
16	D			SYN
17	D			SYN
18	E			SYN
19	A			SYN
20	A			SYN
21	B			SYN
22	B			SYN
23	E			SYN
24	B			SYN
25	A			SYN
26	B			SYN
27	A			SYN
28	E			SYN
29	C			SYN
30	B			SYN

#	Correct Answer	Your Answer	X|O	Concepts Tested
31	E			AN
32	E			AN
33	B			AN
34	C			AN
35	B			AN
36	C			AN
37	D			AN
38	C			AN
39	A			AN
40	A			AN
41	B			AN
42	D			AN
43	A			AN
44	C			AN
45	D			AN
46	E			AN
47	C			AN
48	A			AN
49	B			AN
50	D			AN
51	E			AN
52	D			AN
53	B			AN
54	A			AN
55	E			AN
56	A			AN
57	C			AN
58	D			AN
59	C			AN
60	B			AN

SCORING

Total Omitted (TO): _____

Total Incorrect (TI): _____

Total Missed (TM): _____
(TO + TI)

Raw Score: $60 - \text{TM} - 0.25 \times \text{TI}$

$60 - \underline{\hspace{1cm}} - 0.25 \times \underline{\hspace{1cm}} =$

$\boxed{}$

Rounded Raw Score: _____
(Round to the nearest integer value.)

133

Section 1: Quantitative Reasoning

1. **(D)** Since there will be 29 people at the party, if Arnie wants to make sure everyone can drink two sodas, he needs 58. Since sodas come in cases of 12, he needs to buy at least 5 cases, for a total of 60 sodas, which would be enough.

2. **(A)** Ronnie has 3 stickers, so Janie has $3x$ stickers. To find how many more stickers Janie has, subtract 3 from $3x$ to get $3x - 3$. Factor 3 from each term of the expression to get $3(x - 1)$.

3. **(B)** Let x be the number. 35% of x is $0.35x = 147$. To find x, divide both sides by 0.35:

$$\frac{147}{0.35} = \frac{14700}{35} \xrightarrow[\div 7]{\div 7} \frac{2100}{5} = 420 = x$$

18% of 420 = $0.18 \times 420 = 75.6$

4. **(E)** The volume of the rectangular prism is 2 in × 3 in × 4 in = 24 in³. The volume of a cube whose sides measure 2 feet is, in cubic inches, 24^3 in³. To see how many rectangular prisms would fit in the cube, divide 24^3 in³ by 24 in³ to get $24^2 = 24 \times 24 = 576$.

   Note: Dividing works simply in this case because each dimension of the rectangular prism is a factor of the side length, in inches, of the cube.

5. **(A)** The best approach is to try tracing each figure. It should become apparent after several attempts with each figure that the shape in (A) is the only one that can be drawn without retracing or lifting your pencil or pen.

6. **(C)** Divide 93,249 by 6,070 to get approximately 15.36. Rounding to the nearest whole number yields 15.

   Another way to approach this problem is to round 93,249 to 90,000 and 6,070 to 6,000. 90,000 ÷ 6,000 = 15. This will eliminate (A), (B), and (E). To see if 16 or 15 is closer, multiply 6,070 by 16 and 6,070 by 15 to see which is closer. 6,070 × 16 = 97,120, whereas 6,070 × 15 = 91,050, which is closer to 93,249.

7. **(E)** $N = 24$ cm, and the measure of segment $AC = N + 4N = 5N = 24 \times 5 = 120$ cm.

8. **(D)** Let x be the smallest integer. The 6 integers can then be represented as:

   $x, x + 2, x + 4, x + 6, x + 8, x + 10$

   To find the average of these numbers, first find their sum and then divide the sum by 6. The sum of the numbers is $6x + 30$. The average is 4, which means:

   $$\frac{6x + 30}{6} = 4 \quad \rightarrow \quad x + 5 = 4 \quad \rightarrow \quad x = -1$$

   The largest integer is $-1 + 10 = 9$.

9. **(B)** Solve this using a system of equations by first making one of the coefficients of a variable in an equation match the coefficient of the same variable in the other equation by multiplication, such as:

   $3X + 4Y = 55$
   $(2X + 2Y = 35) \times 2$

   This leads to:

   $4X + 4Y = 70$
   $3X + 4Y = 55$

   Subtract the bottom equation from the top equation to get: $X = 15$

   Substitute 15 for X into one of the original equations, as such:

   $2(15) + 2Y = 35$
   $30 + 2Y = 35$
   $2Y = 5, Y = 2.5$

   Thus, $X + Y = 15 + 2.5 = 17.5$

10. **(E)** To find the value of m, square root both sides of the equation to get:

$$\sqrt[3]{m} = 8$$

Then cube both sides to get: $m = 8^3 = 8 \times 8 \times 8 = 512$.

11. **(C)** 130% of $w = 1.3w = 6.5$. Divide both sides by 1.3 to get $w = 5$. $4w = 20$, and 70% of 20 = $0.7 \times 20 = 14$.

12. **(A)** Rearrange the inequality $2 - X > 3X + 4$ to: $2 > 4X + 4$, which can be further rewritten as: $4X < -2$. Solving for X, we get $X < -0.5$. Since X is less than -0.5, the only choice that works is (A).

13. **(C)** The chart indicates that about 45% of criminal law attorneys were working in the public sector. About 50% of them were working in the private sector, since those working in the private sector are represented by the portion of the bar from 45% to about 95%. This leaves about 5% in the international sector.

    45% of 15,000 is $0.45 \times 15,000 = 6750$
    5% of 15,000 is $0.05 \times 15,000 = 750$

    The difference then is $6750 - 750 = 6000$.

14. **(A)** The percent of contract law attorneys in the private sector is: 80% - 15% = 65%. 65% as a decimal is 0.65, which can be converted as follows:

$$0.65 = \frac{65}{100} \xrightarrow[\div 5]{\div 5} \frac{13}{20}$$

15. **(B)** On the first day, Lucius collected 1 stamp ($0.001). On the second day, he collected 3 stamps ($0.003). On the third day, he collected 9 stamps ($0.009). On the fourth day, he collected 27 stamps ($0.027). On the fifth day, he collected 81 stamps ($0.081). On the sixth day, he collected 243 stamps ($0.243).

    Find the sum total: $0.001 + $0.003 + $0.009 + $0.027 + $0.081 + $0.243 = $0.364 or $0.36, rounded to the nearest cent.

16. **(E)** The positive prime integers less than 44 are: 2, 3, 5, 7, 11, 13, 17, 19, 23, 29, 31, 37, 41, and 43, for a total of 14. 8 of them are less than 22. Thus, the probability that x is less than 22 is 8 out of 14 or, when simplified, 4 out of 7.

17. **(D)** Ramon's base wage is $1,800 ÷ 40 hours = $45 per hour. To find how much he makes in 50 hours, multiply the rate by the number of hours: $45/hr × 50 hrs = $2,250.

18. **(B)** Set up a system of equations, as such:

    $3A + 2P = 100$
    $4A + 5P = 187$

    There are two ways to approach this problem:

    Method 1

    Multiply the equations by the necessary constants to equalize the coefficient of one of the variables, so we can eliminate one variable. If we want to equalize the coefficient of P, we can do the following:

    $$(3A + 2P = 100) \times 5 \quad \rightarrow \quad 15A + 10P = 500$$
    $$(4A + 5P = 187) \times 2 \quad \rightarrow \quad 8A + 10P = 374$$

    Subtract the bottom equation from the top:

    $$7A = 126 \quad \rightarrow \quad A = 18$$

    Substitute 18 for A in one of the original equations, as such:

    $3(18) + 2P = 100$
    $54 + 2P = 100$
    $2P = 46, P = 23$

    Thus, $A + P = 41$. Since the bag weighs 2 oz., the total weight of the bag, one apple, and one pear is $41 + 2 = 43$ oz.

    Method 2 (Easier Method)

    Add the systems of equations together as follows:

3A + 2P = 100
4A + 5P = 187
7A + 7P = 287

Divide each side of the resulting equation by 7 to get the following equation:

A + P = 41

Thus, the weight of the fruits and the bag is 41 + 2 = 43 oz.

19. **(B)** Kevin originally had 62 games. If he sells 30, then he's left with 32. If he buys 18 more, then he has 50.

The ratio of games he has now to the ratio of games he originally had is thus 50 to 62, which simplifies to 25 to 31.

20. **(D)** One quick way of simplifying this problem is by recognizing that the block to the right is comprised of 4 squares.

The figure presented in choice (A) has 12 squares, which is a multiple of 4. However, because the figure is also a perfect rectangle, it must be able to accommodate 2 L-shaped blocks placed together to make a 2 × 4 rectangular block, as such:

Such a block cannot be fit into the shape in (A), however, because only the top 2 rows would be covered. The same is true of (C), which has 24 squares but does not satisfy the row requirement.

The figure presented in choice (B) has 18 squares, which is not a multiple of 4, so this can be eliminated.

The figure presented in (E) doesn't work. The top two rows of squares can be perfectly occupied by 2 × 4 blocks. Then a 2 × 4 block can be placed vertically below the top two rows, so that the entire right two rows are also occupied. Immediately below the top two rows, a 2 × 4 block can be placed, to cover the 3rd and 4th rows from the top. However, this

leaves 4 blocks in a straight line that cannot be occupied by an L-shaped block.

(D) can be solved as follows:

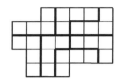

21. **(C)** Let A be the area of the isosceles right triangle and the square.

The area of an isosceles right triangle is given by ½ × s^2, where s is the length of one of the non-hypotenuse sides. Furthermore, in an isosceles right triangle, the hypotenuse is always $s\sqrt{2}$.

The perimeter of the isosceles right triangle is: $s + s + s\sqrt{2} = 2s + s\sqrt{2}$.

The area of a square is given by x^2, where x is the side length of the square.

Thus, ½ × $s^2 = x^2$
$s^2 = 2x^2$
$s = x\sqrt{2}$

The perimeter of the square is $4x$. Thus, the ratio of the perimeter of the triangle to that of the square is given by:

$2s + s\sqrt{2} : 4x$

Substituting $x\sqrt{2}$ for s, we get:

$2x\sqrt{2} + 2x : 4x$
$2x(\sqrt{2} + 1) : 4x$, which can be simplified to:

$\sqrt{2} + 1 : 2$

22. **(A)** The total number of apples that fell is $33 + 42 + 35 + 49 + x = y$. Simplifying the expression results in $159 + x = y$. To find x in terms of y, subtract 159 from both sides to isolate x by itself:

$x = y - 159$

23. **(C)** To find the value of a, we must first find the slope of the line, as follows:

$$m = \frac{9-(-4)}{2-3} = \frac{13}{-1} = -13$$

We now have the linear equation $y = -13x + b$. To find b, plug in the x and y values from a coordinate, such as:

$9 = -13(2) + b$
$9 = -26 + b$
$b = 9 + 26 = 35$

Thus the full equation is $y = -13x + 35$. To find a, substitute 0 for x and a for y:

$a = -13(0) + 35 = 35$

24. **(B)** To find the number of customers Jack and Jill need to continue earning the same rate as before, it is important to find the number of customers they had originally. To do so, divide $6,600 by $120 per customer to get 55 customers.

At the reduced rate, Jack and Jill are earning a profit of $120 - $40 = $80 per customer. To find how many customers they'd need to make the same profit as before, divide $6,600 by $80 to get 82.5 customers.
Because they can't get half of a customer, they need to get 83 customers in total to make at least the same profit as before.

To answer the question of how many more customers they'd need, do $83 - 55 = 28$.

25. **(D)** This problem can be solved by trial and error. But in case it proves difficult, still, follow along with the explanation to make more sense of it:

Label the dot in the lowermost left corner as '4', the dot in the uppermost right corner as '5', and the dot in the lowermost right corner as '6'.

(A) can be drawn without lifting the pencil or retracing any part of the figure by going from the points in the following order:

$1 \to 2 \to 3 \to 1 \to 4 \to 6 \to 3$ OR
$1 \to 2 \to 3 \to 6 \to 4 \to 1 \to 3$

(B) can be drawn without lifting the pencil or retracing any part of the figure by going from the points in the following order:

$1 \to 2 \to 3 \to 1 \to 4 \to 3$ OR
$1 \to 2 \to 3 \to 4 \to 1 \to 3$

(C) can be drawn without lifting the pencil or retracing any part of the figure by going from the points in the following order:

$1 \to 2 \to 3 \to 6 \to 5 \to 1$

(E) can be drawn without lifting the pencil or retracing any part of the figure by going from the points in the following order:

$1 \to 2 \to 3 \to 6 \to 4 \to 1 \to 5 \to 2$ OR
$1 \to 2 \to 3 \to 1 \to 4 \to 6 \to 3 \to 5 \to 2$

(D) can't be drawn without lifting the pencil or retracing any part of the figure because after 1, 2, 3, you must go to 4. From 4, you can go to either 1 or 2. If you go to 1, you have to retrace the segment from 1 to 2 or from 1 to 4. If you go to 2 from 4, you have to retrace the segment from 1 to 2 or from 4 to 2.

Section 2: Reading Comprehension

Parasitic Control

1. **(D)** Line 13 explicitly states that the Nematomorph hairworm controls its host by altering its host's brain's biochemistry. (A) is incorrect because the Nematomorph hairworm does not control its host by compelling its host to try to find food underwater. It does cause the host to dive into water and commit suicide, but there is not mention of it compelling the host underwater to find food. (B) is incorrect because nowhere does it say that the Nematomorph hairworm feeds off its host's body. It is perfectly logical to say that the Nematomorph hairworm needs to eat, but 1) we don't know if the Nematomorph hairworm is feeding off the host's source of nutrients or if it is actually eating the body, and more importantly 2) there is nothing in the passage to suggest that the Nematomorph hairworm controls its host's body by feeding off it. (C) is incorrect because there is no mention of panic and subsequent loss of control. (E) is incorrect nothing suggests that the Nematomorph hairworm eats away at its host's brain.

2. **(C)** Lines 1-4 indicate that society has been fascinated by the idea of zombies for a long time and how widespread that said fascination is. *The Walking Dead* is mentioned to support the notion that society is fascinated with zombies. (A) is incorrect because the author is not trying to cause the reader to be scared of zombies. (B) is incorrect because there is no evidence to suggest that *The Walking Dead* is the author's favorite show. Furthermore, if the passage were about promoting the author's favorite show, there should be some encouragement for readers to watch it. (D) is incorrect because the passage does not discuss how much of an impact zombies have on popular media. (E) is incorrect because the author does not suggest that zombies will eventually become real.

3. **(E)** Line 16 states that once the Nematomorph hairworm leaves its host, it swims away to find a mate. (A) is incorrect because the passage does not mention the Nematomorph hairworm trying to find a host for its eggs. (B) is incorrect because there is no mention of the Nematomorph

hairworm eating its host's dead body. (C) is incorrect because there is no mention of the Nematomorph hairworm finding dry ground to find a mate. (D) is incorrect because the passage does not mention an aquatic shelter.

4. **(B)** Line 5 indicate that phytoplasma can convert their host plants' flowers into leafy shoots that are unable to produce offspring. Thus, the plants are rendered infertile. (A) is incorrect because there is no mention of the phytoplasma affecting insects' ability to spread pollen. (C) is a tempting choice, but it is incorrect because the phytoplasma convert the plants' flowers into leafy shoots, not damage the plants' leafy shoots. (D) is incorrect because it insinuates that the insects voluntarily choose what they want to distribute. (E) is incorrect because the phytoplasma interferes with the dissemination of pollen, not cause delays in its dissemination.

Keyboard Memorization

5. **(C)** It's possible to infer that the Vanderbilt researchers were at least somewhat surprised by the results. Lines 4-7 indicate that researchers wanted to see how many letters on the keyboard were instantly recognizable and identifiable. Lines 13-14 indicate that the experiment brought to light new questions about people's cognitive learning skills. (A) is incorrect because if the researchers had not been surprised new questions would not have been brought to light. (B) is incorrect because there's no indication that doubt existed as to the validity of the results. (D) is incorrect because there's no comparison of typing speeds between the typists and the researchers. (E) is incorrect because there's nothing to indicate that the researchers could not correctly identify the placement of the keys.

6. **(B)** Lines 1-2 indicate that most people would correctly recognize that the letters QWERTY represent the first 6 letters of a keyboard. Thus, it is possible to infer that the they are among the most recognizable letters of a keyboard, in terms of placement. (A) is incorrect because it is directly refuted by the passage in lines 1-2. (C) is incorrect because it's overstating things. While

those letters are among the most recognized ones, the passage does not indicate that everyone recognizes them absolutely. (D) is incorrect because keyboards cannot be arranged freely. (E) is incorrect because nothing in the passage indicates optimality of key placement.

7. **(D)** The answer is found in lines 8-14. The experiments involved bringing in typists who could type at 72 words per minute with an average of a 94% accuracy level. Yet, when tested, they could not correctly identify the letters of a keyboard with the same degree of accuracy. Thus, the passage indicates there is a disconnect between our active memory and passive memory. (A) is incorrect because it is possible that accurate typing is possible to achieve at slower speeds. (B) is incorrect because the passage doesn't indicate that accurate typing happens faster when keys aren't memorized; at some level, the keys must be memorized to ensure faster and more accurate typing. (C) is incorrect because the passage does not draw a comparison between typing and handwriting. (E) is incorrect because the effects of the observation of third parties is not documented in this passage.

8. **(A)** Lines 8-12 indicate that in the first experiment the typists had to correctly identify the placement of keys on a standard keyboard. In the second, a blank key lit up, and the typists had to identify which letter that key represented. (B) is incorrect because time was not involved in the second experiment. (C) is incorrect because the first experiment did not involve identifying 15 out of 26 keys; it just happened to be that the typists ended up being able to identify 15 out of the 26 letters on a keyboard. Moreover, the second experiment did not involve time. (D) is incorrect because typing speeds and accuracy were not measured in the experiments—only letter identification was. (E) is incorrect because the first experiment did not involve memorizing letters of a scrambled keyboard.

9. **(E)** Lines 13-14 indicate that the research findings introduced more questions about our cognitive learning process, so that implies there is more to cognitive learning skills than was previously understood. (A) is incorrect because the author was not trying to dissuade readers

from memorizing things. (B) is incorrect because the passage does not indicate that the author was trying to figure out the most efficient way to type. (C) is incorrect because the history of keyboards is not at issue in the passage. (D) is incorrect because it is not on point enough. Although the passage does mention passive learning, it is not a focal point.

First Monkeys in Space

10. **(A)** Lines 9-10 state that the Kármán line establishes the boundaries of outer space at 100 kilometers above the Earth's surface. Albert I's rocket only took him 63 kilometers above the surface of the Earth. Thus, all of the other choices are incorrect. (B), for instance, is incorrect because it is not known at what stage of the flight Albert I died, so it is not supported by the passage. (C) is incorrect because there is nothing to indicate that the Kármán line changes occasionally. (D) is incorrect because it cannot be gleaned from the passage whether the technology was available or not to go higher than 100 kilometers above Earth's surface at the time Albert I took flight. (E) is incorrect because it doesn't matter if Albert II's rocket flew higher.

11. **(C)** Yorick was the first to survive the entirety of the trip, as lines 14-16 state. This means that both Albert I and Albert II died during the trips to space. And since no other monkeys are mentioned in the passage, it can be inferred that at least 2 died.

12. **(B)** The passage is purely informational, so out of the answer choices, a reference book makes the most sense for this passage to be found in. (A) is incorrect because the tone is too objective and informational for a science fiction novel. (C) is incorrect because a bibliography is a list of works cited. (D) is incorrect because the passage is not in the first person and not about the events of the author's life. (E) is incorrect because such information would be too technical to put all in one place in a movie script.

13. **(E)** As mentioned in lines 14-16, Yorick was the first monkey to survive outer space flight. Since that is the only noteworthy fact that is presented about Yorick, it can be inferred that's why his flight was important. (A) is incorrect because the

logic is unsound. While Yorick had done something only previously mice had done, according to (A), as long as Yorick did anything that previously only mice had achieved, then his accomplishment would have been momentous. (B) is incorrect because the time frame of the scientists was not what made Yorick's flight momentous, although this could be a tempting answer; it's reading too much into the passage, however. (C) is incorrect because the passage does not indicate that Yorick's survival meant everything had been perfected for human sustainability in a rocket. (D) is incorrect because Yorick's genetic superiority is not discussed. Moreover, other reasons could have been at play for the other monkeys' deaths.

14. **(D)** This passage is about what happened before Neil Armstrong became the first man to set foot on the moon, so "Behind the Scenes of the First Step on the Moon" makes the most sense as the title. (A) is incorrect because it focuses too narrowly on Yorick. (B) is incorrect because it is too narrow and also three monkeys are discussed in this passage. (C) is incorrect because it focuses too narrowly on the Kármán line. (E) is incorrect because this passage is not about the importance of sacrifices, although sacrifices had been made to better understand space flight.

Genghis Khan

15. **(B)** Lines 1-5 discuss how much land Genghis Khan conquered. The mention of the surface area of the United States is there to serve as a comparison basis. (A) is incorrect because there is no comment about the enormity of the land mass of the United States. (C) is incorrect because there is nothing to indicate nationalistic pride. (D) is incorrect because the passage does not mention that the United States should expand its borders. (E) is incorrect because the information is provided as a comparison point. Thus, it is not irrelevant.

16. **(B)** Lines 6-7 describe Genghis Khan's empire expansion as ruthless because it left scores of millions dead in its wake. (A) is incorrect because lines 7-12 indicate ways in which Genghis Khan was levelheaded and not at all barbaric. (C) is incorrect; while it can be inferred that he was power hungry and ultra ambitious,

that's not why his empire expansion could be described as merciless. Having extreme greed and ambition does not necessarily lead to mercilessness. (D) is incorrect because there is no mention in the passage that he slaughtered people just for the sake of slaughtering them. (E) is incorrect because the feelings of his soldiers is not mention in the passage.

17. **(E)** *Glib* means smooth or flowing easily, as with words and speech. There is no indication in the passage that Genghis Khan operated easily or smoothly. (A) is incorrect because Genghis Khan could be said to be unrelenting for the tenacity with which he pursued the expansion of his empire. (B) and (C) are incorrect because he was willing to be amenable to peaceful methods and even offered talented enemy soldiers positions within his own military. (D) is incorrect because he was ruthless in his empire expansion and being responsible for the deaths of millions.

18. **(D)** It is most surprising that Genghis Khan was ruthless but still open to peaceful acquisitions of other societies and kingdoms. The word "intriguingly" (line 7) most directly suggests the surprising nature of Genghis Khan. But also the descriptions of Genghis Khan's actions make it apparent that he acted in ways that seemed contrary to how he should seem. (A) is incorrect because the passage does not indicate that Genghis Khan wanted to take over the world. (B) is incorrect because it is not stated or suggested that Genghis Khan offered worthy adversaries quick and painless deaths. (C) is incorrect because the pace of his expansion is not discussed. (E) is incorrect because there's no mention in the passage about what he did to people after conquering them.

19. **(D)** In lines 1-2, the passage states that no one in the history of the world conquered as much territory as Genghis Khan had. (A) is incorrect because the passage does not compared Genghis Khan to anyone other conqueror, in terms of ruthlessness and deaths; it is not proper to assume that vastest empire equates to most deaths caused. (B) is incorrect because it is not known how many foreign empires and societies he assimilated or if he assimilated more than anyone else in history did. (C) is incorrect because the fairness of his terms of condition of

surrender are not discussed. (E) is incorrect because it is not known how friendly, if at all, he was towards his opponents.

Phalanxes and Democracy

20. **(D)** The passage is about democracy and how the role of the phalanx in Ancient Greek militaries may have helped to foster the mindset the people needed to adopt a democratic form of governance. (A) is incorrect because the fact that phalanxes were essential to Greek poleis is only a small facet of the passage. (B) The passage does not indicate that Cleisthenes drove out the tyrant Hippias. (C) is incorrect. It is not suggested in the passage that the reason or primary reason phalanxes were effective were the armor and weapons the soldiers wore and bore. One major aspect of the phalanx's success is the unity the soldiers had with each other. (E) is incorrect because it is only briefly mentioned.

21. **(A)** Lines 14-16 describe the armor the hoplites wore. The shields were designed to protect each warrior's left right and the right side of the man standing to his left. Thus, the facts in (A) are wrong, which makes (A) the right choice. (B) is incorrect because lines 12-14 indicate that phalanxes were comprised of rows of soldiers. (C) is incorrect because the passage does say in lines 16-19 that the phalanxes, when moving, were armed and impenetrable barriers that advanced on their enemies. (D) is incorrect because lines 14-15 indicate that the hoplite soldiers wore heavy armor and carried spears and swords. (E) is incorrect because lines 20-22 indicate the importance of synchronicity.

22. **(C)** Lines 11-12 indicate that the Greek fixation on war led to the rise of the phalanx as the centerpiece of Greek militaries. (A) is incorrect because it assumes too much. While the phalanx was critical to the success of Greek militaries, it is not known whether victory was impossible for a Greek military without at least one phalanx. (B) is incorrect for the opposite reason (A) is incorrect. If anything, phalanxes were required for the sustainability of Greek militaries. (D) is incorrect because the passage does not mention if Greek militaries did not use phalanxes. Furthermore, there is no mention of cavalry and chariots in the passage. (E) is incorrect because it

is possible, and even likely, that democracy would eventually have been adopted in Athens.

23. **(B)** Lines 20-25 describe what was required for the phalanx to be successful. There had to be a complete homogeneity of effort, and as such each soldier depended on the other around him; this codependency fostered the mindset that everyone was equal when fighting in a phalanx. (A) is not supported. There is no suggestion by the passage that phalanxes were behind Hippias's ouster. (C) is a tempting choice, but it is not on point because of the phrase "frustrations and hardships", which is reading too much into what's presented by the passage. (D) is incorrect because it is not on point. First, the fact that 20 to 40 percent of free males of every polis served as hoplites does not necessarily mean freedom was prioritized; a significant number of free men could mean that freedom was not a concern, since they already had their freedom. (E) is incorrect because the passage does strongly suggest a connection between phalanxes and the adoption of democracy, as discussed earlier.

24. **(A)** The only question left unanswered is why Hipparchus was assassinated. (B) is incorrect because Cleisthenes was the one who ushered in the acceptance of democracy as a form of governance. (C) is incorrect because the passage states that Hippias became an increasingly repressive tyrant after his brother Hipparchus was assassinated. (D) is incorrect because we know that 6 to 8 lines of soldiers made up the typical phalanx. (E) is incorrect because it is stated in lines 27-28 that there is convincing evidence that the hoplite phalanx played a nontrivial in the history of Athenian democracy.

25. **(E)** Lines 9-11 indicate that Greece was comprised of hundreds of city-states, or poleis, during 7th century B.C. (A), (B), and (D) are incorrect because we don't know if there was a national government. (C) is incorrect because no information is provided on how much chaos and anarchy was present.

Horror Paradox

26. **(E)** The author's tone is objective and informative. The author presents information

about fear and why we are interested in it; he does not present a commentary or his opinion on the matter. (A) is incorrect because ignorant means unaware of. The author does not appear ignorant or illogical. (B) Analytical works, but biased doesn't because the author is reporting the facts. (C) is incorrect because the author is not shocked or offended. The author may be surprised people enjoy being scared, but he is not offended. (D) is incorrect because the author is not agitated, even if the author is amused by the fact that people love being scared so much.

27. **(D)** Lines 11-14 indicate that people experience increased heartbeats, sweaty palms, a decrease in skin temperature, muscle tension, and increased blood pressure. Rashes are not mentioned.

28. **(C)** Lines 6-10 describe the horror paradox. Despite our fears, we continue to allow ourselves to be audiences for tales of nighttime horrors. It's a paradox because it is illogical to want to continue listening to or watching things that are terrifying. (A) is incorrect because it is describing a possible explanation for the fact that people seem to enjoy being scared, but it is not defining what the horror paradox is. (B) is incorrect because the brain's ability to adapt to new technology of movies has nothing to do with why we continue to let ourselves be scared. (D) is incorrect because it is not mentioned or suggested in the passage that scary phenomena are more likely to happen during the day. (E) is incorrect because the movie industry's ability to generate revenues in excess of $100 million has does not explain why we enjoy being scared.

29. **(D)** It can be inferred from the passage that the author believes $100 million in box office sales to be at least fairly successful for a movie. Line 20 indicates that a significant number of people enjoy being scared. Lines 24-27 state the movie box office sales figure to support the notion that many people enjoy being scared. (A) is incorrect because the passage does not suggest that every person enjoys the horror genre; thus it is overstating things. (B) is incorrect because it is possible that ghouls, ghosts, and the like can scare people in the daytime. (C) is incorrect because it is not stated or suggested in the passage that only a terrifying ordeal can serve as a rite of passage. (E) is incorrect because the

passage only lists Diane Ackerman as a writer. Not enough context is given to indicate whether she is an expert on human psychology.

30. **(D)** The author wrote this passage to explain what causes fear and why people continue to embrace the horror genre. (A) is incorrect because the passage does not even once recommend watching horror movies as a rite of passage. (B) is incorrect because the profitability of the horror genre is stated to show how much people seem to enjoy being scared. (C) and (E) are incorrect because explaining why people are vulnerable at night and consequently afraid of the dark is only a small component of the function of the passage.

31. **(A)** Lines 1-5 indicate that we are accustomed to mastering our world by day, so at night we feel even more vulnerable, and this is where our fear comes from: the acute vulnerability we feel. (B) is incorrect because the passage does not indicate whether drops in temperature cause us to experience more fear. The passage indicates that skin temperature dropping is a consequence of experiencing fear, but not the other way around. (C) is incorrect because there is no mention or suggestion of brainwashing in the passage. (D) is incorrect because feeling safe indoors at night could more naturally lead us not to feel vulnerable at night. (E) is incorrect because the logic is incorrect. If we understand that horror stories and tales are for the most part fictional, we should feel less vulnerable at night.

Moral Lessons

32. **(B)** Line 10 indicates that some situations call for, or even require, dishonesty and deception. (A) is incorrect because it is not logical to conclude that the author believes lying is always good and perfectly acceptable from the statement that certain situations call for lying. (C) is incorrect for a similar reason. While fables and moral lessons may teach overly broad principles, they are not necessarily always impractical. (D) The passage does not suggest that white lies are always permissible. (E) is incorrect because the author indicates some situations permit lying.

33. **(E)** Lines 5-7 posit that few would argue the lessons taught by fables are erroneous because it

is easier to imagine how dishonesty can result in disaster and, as a consequence, simpler and safer to teach young children that lying is absolutely bad. Because it is easier, simpler, and safer to teach these lessons about honesty, these lessons are taught out of convenience. Ignorance, obligation, regret, and hesitation are not mentioned in the passage as reasons few people would argue against the lessons taught by fables, thus the other choices are incorrect.

34. **(D)** Lines 11-12 indicate that moral struggle is generally good because it keeps us anchored and helps us to better understand ourselves. (A) is incorrect because understanding others is not mentioned in the passage at all. (B) is incorrect because too much moral struggle can lead to becoming counterproductive, as is mentioned in lines 13-14. (C) is incorrect because moral struggle does lead to some measure of regret and remorse, but it is not readily ascertainable from the passage that it allows us to feel less regret and remorse in the future. Furthermore, in the future moral struggle may lead to more regret. (E) is incorrect because there is no mention in the passage that moral struggle helps us finds the most morally effective solutions.

35. **(A)** The author is opinionated and practical. The author does not believe that teaching absolute honesty is the most practical solution in the long run because real-life situations can be complex. (B) is incorrect because the author sounds emphatic possibly, but aggressive is incorrect. And he is not objective. (C) is incorrect because the author is not scornful. He does not look down on others who hold a different opinion. In fact, in lines 5-7, the passage indicates that the author understands why other people hold different opinions. (D) is incorrect because the author is not appreciative or passive. He takes a very active tone. (E) is incorrect because the author does not take an impractical tone.

Bodily Humors

36. **(C)** Lines 11-13 indicate that Hippocrates believed the four humors of the body to be: blood, phlegm, yellow bile, and black bile. Cartilage is not in the list, so (C) is correct.

37. **(E)** Lines 17-20 indicate that accidental deaths due to bloodletting were not uncommon, yet the practice continued to thrive for an extended time. Moreover, in line 9, it is stated that the practice of bloodletting reached its peak in the 19th century. This implies that the benefits of bloodletting were thought to outweigh the risks. (A) and (B) are incorrect because it is logically incorrect to infer from the passage that other humors would be purged if one humor was thought to be in excess. Only the humor that was in excess would be purged. (C) is incorrect because there is no indication that the deficient humor would be obtained from someone else. (D) is incorrect because there is no mention in the passage of what modern medicine has discovered in relation to the human body. If anything, modern medicine has discovered that the four humors theory to be false.

38. **(B)** Lines 2-3 indicate that many illnesses could be treated by phlebotomy. (A) is incorrect because even if leeches were particularly effective at drawing out blood that would have no bearing on how common of a practice phlebotomy was, if there was no perceived need for phlebotomy. (C) is incorrect because convenience is not discussed. If anything, bloodletting was seen as a necessity. (D) is incorrect because the motives of doctors is not discussed in the passage. (E) is incorrect because the relief people experienced is not discussed.

39. **(A)** Lines 13-14 indicate that it was believed that illnesses resulted when the humors were out of balance. The other choices aren't discussed in the passage. There is no mention of accidental incisions, sanitation, spending time around others who were will, and bacteria and viruses.

40. **(C)** Lines 7-8 indicate that the practice of bloodletting probably originated some 3,000 years ago with the ancient Egyptians or Sumerians. (A) is incorrect because the practice of bloodletting continued with the Greeks and Romans, but probably did not originate with them. (B) is incorrect because bloodletting probably reached its peak during the Renaissance but did not originate during then; the same is true for why (D) is incorrect. (E) is incorrect because the very first instance that led to the adoption of bloodletting is not discussed.

Section 3: Verbal Reasoning

Synonyms

1. **(D)** VIVID (adj.) means very clear, bright, or noticeable. Striking also means noticeable.

2. **(B)** MUTINY (v.) means to revolt or rebel against authority.

3. **(B)** THRIFTY (adj.) means careful with money or resources, as does economical.

4. **(A)** JARGON (n.) means the language specific to a particular trade, craft, or profession. It can also mean unintelligible speech or writing—in other words, gibberish.

5. **(C)** FUNDAMENTAL (adj.) means basic or necessary. Essential also means necessary.

6. **(C)** PARCH (v.) means to make extremely dry. Desiccate means to completely dry out.

7. **(A)** HUMILITY (n.) is the quality or state of being humble and modest. Meekness is the state of being humble and patient or submissive.

   Moderation is the act or process of showing restraint or avoiding the extremes, so it is not the best answer.

8. **(D)** AGGRAVATE (v.) means to worsen a situation or condition that is already bad or suboptimal.

9. **(A)** COMMENCE (v.) means to start an activity.

10. **(B)** MELLOW (adj.) means pleasant and agreeable. Thus, the best choice here is relaxed because it means free from stress and tension.

11. **(A)** POSTERITY (n.) means descendants or future generations.

12. **(D)** CONTRITE (adj.) means remorseful, sorrowful, or repentant.

13. **(B)** EFFICACY (n.) means effectiveness.

14. **(A)** TENUOUS (adj.) means weak, unsound, or flimsy.

15. **(D)** NEOPHYTE (n.) means beginner or novice. An amateur is someone who participates in an activity recreationally, as opposed to professionally, or is inexperienced in that activity.

16. **(D)** VORACIOUS (adj.) means desiring or eating a lot of food. It can also mean extremely eager. Ravenous means extremely hungry.

17. **(D)** DEPLETE (v.) means to reduce the numbers of a good or resource, to the point the good or resource is used up entirely or almost so. Exhaust means to tire out or use up the energy of. It can also mean to use up completely.

18. **(E)** ATROPHY (n.) means deterioration due to lack of use. It is used frequently in the context of muscle degeneration from lack of use, such as when one breaks a bone and must avoid using that limb.

19. **(A)** HACKNEYED (adj.) means commonplace, overused or overplayed, or ordinary.

20. **(A)** EXTRANEOUS (adj.) means external or foreign—essentially, not coming from within. It can also mean irrelevant. Thus, unnecessary is the best choice. If something is unnecessary, it can be viewed as irrelevant.

21. **(B)** BLASPHEMY (n.) means extremely disrespectful speech or behavior, going against that which is considered sacred. Sacrilege means violation of something considered sacred.

22. **(B)** PERFUNCTORY (adj.) means done hastily or superficially, out of necessity. It can also mean not caring or showing enthusiasm.

23. **(E)** FORTUITOUS (adj.) means happening accidentally or coincidentally. It can also mean fortunate. Serendipitous means happening accidentally; it can also mean good or favorable.

24. **(B)** COERCE (v.) means to force someone or something to behave in a certain way or to take a certain action.

25. **(A)** VIRULENT (adj.) means very toxic or poisonous. It can also mean very hostile. Noxious means harmful.

26. **(B)** INDEFATIGABLE (adj.) means incapable of getting tired out. Tireless means not getting tired.

27. **(A)** REMINISCE (v.) means to think about the past, especially fondly.

28. **(E)** FLUMMOX (v.) means to confuse or bewilder. Confound means to confuse.

29. **(C)** GAFFE (n.) means mistake, particularly one made in a social setting. A misstep is an error in conduct or behavior.

30. **(B)** ABLUTION (n.) means cleansing by washing.

Analogies

31. **(E)** A chicken has 2 legs and a pig has 4. A penguin also has 2 legs and a moose has 4. Furthermore, a chicken is a bird, while a pig is a mammal. A penguin is a bird, while a moose is a mammal.

32. **(E)** A baker makes bread, and a sculptor makes statues. It could be said that a woman makes babies, but a baker's job is to make bread, and a sculptor's job is to make statues. A woman's job is not to make babies. Neither does a waiter make food nor a bank teller make money.

33. **(B)** A galaxy is comprised of stars. An album is comprised of photographs. None of the other choices indicate a "member to group" relationship.

34. **(C)** A whine is a cry or sound of complaint or unease. A tantrum is a violent demonstration of anger or frustration. It is a matter of degree, going from less intense to more intense. A squeak is a smaller sound than a roar is, which follows the pattern of going from less intense to more intense.

35. **(B)** A program is a guide or schedule of events to a performance. An itinerary is a plan for a journey.

36. **(C)** A glove is a piece of equipment that a pugilist uses for his sport. (A pugilist is a boxer.) A bow is a piece of equipment that an archer uses for his sport.

37. **(D)** An odometer measures distance traveled, while a barometer measures atmospheric pressure. The relationship is thing to purpose or function. An altimeter measures height, a scale measures weight, and a thermometer measures temperature, so (B), (C), and (E) are incorrect.

38. **(C)** A pacemaker is used to help the heart keep beating properly. Cardiac is the adjective meaning "of or relating to the heart." A hearing aid is used to help with hearing. Auditory is the adjective meaning "of or related to the sense of hearing."

39. **(A)** Walk and ambulate are synonyms, with ambulate meaning to "walk or move about." Plod and trudge are also synonyms, meaning "to walk or move slowly with heavy steps." The other choices are the opposites of plod.

40. **(A)** An oaf is a stupid, mentally cumbersome person. Thus, an oaf lacks acumen. A novice is a beginner, so a novice lacks experience.

41. **(B)** A curator is someone who manages or maintains a museum or art gallery. An editor is someone who manages a newspaper or magazine.

42. **(D)** Defoliate means to strip the leaves off a tree or bush. To peel an orange is to take the skin off the orange. Both involve removing a component of the object.

43. **(A)** Omnipotent means being all-powerful—in other words, having unlimited or absolute power. Omniscient means all-knowing or having absolute or complete knowledge of everything.

44. **(C)** A doctor provides prescriptions, which the apothecary, which is another word for pharmacist, fulfills. In other words, the apothecary is the person who comes after the

doctor in the treatment process. An architect designs a building, and an engineer advises the architect what materials to use in the construction of the building. In other words, the engineer is the person who comes after the architect in the building construction process.

45. **(D)** A barn is a structure you'd find almost exclusively on a farm or in a rural area. A skyscraper is a structure you'd find almost exclusively in an urban or metropolitan area.

46. **(E)** Quash means to quell or suppress, so it is the opposite of incite, which means to stir up or initiate. Animus means hatred or animosity, which is the opposite of affection, which means fondness for or attachment to.

47. **(C)** Infantile and puerile both mean childish, so they are synonyms. Juvenile and adolescent both mean related to youth and can mean lacking maturity, so they are synonyms as well.

48. **(A)** A toady is someone who behaves servilely towards another. To lionize is to treat someone as a celebrity or to idolize that person. Thus, a toady is someone who lionizes another. A misanthrope is someone who hates. To loathe is to hate. Thus, a misanthrope is someone who hates. The relationship is a type of person and what what behavior he displays.

49. **(B)** Descent is the process of moving downwards, as in elevation or status. Plummet means to drop down or descend rapidly. Ascent is the process of increasing in elevation or status. Skyrocket means to go up or increase rapidly.

50. **(D)** A census is a survey to measure the size of a population. An inventory is a survey to see how much stock there is. A survey does not measure how many questions there are, and a poll's purpose is not to measure the number of voters there are. A poll determines the opinions of the people participating in the poll.

51. **(E)** To enervate is to weaken, while to energize is to strengthen or invigorate. Thus, they are opposites. To deny is to claim no knowledge of while to admit is to claim knowledge of.

52. **(D)** Pulverization is the destruction of something forcefully. To erode is to wear something, as a surface, down gradually and more gently. Compulsion is the act of forcing someone or something take action. To cajole is to persuade someone or something to take action through gentleness and flattery.

53. **(B)** Keys unlock locks. Clues unlock mysteries.

54. **(A)** Agility is a trait that acrobats must possess. Fairness is a trait that arbiters must have. An arbiter is someone who decides issues.

55. **(E)** An appendage is something that's added on or supplemental. It is not a vital or core component. Auxiliary means helpful, additional, or supplemental. An appendage is thus seen as auxiliary. A core is something that's vital or necessary, so it is essential.

56. **(A)** A telephone transmits or carries voices. A car carries passengers, even if the passenger is the driver himself.

57. **(C)** Frugal means to be careful with money or resources. A spendthrift is one who spends extravagantly or wastefully. Thus, a spendthrift is not frugal. Pious means religiously devout. An atheist is someone who does not believe in the existence of God or any other supreme being and is thus not religious. Thus, an atheist is not pious.

58. **(D)** An acre is as unit of measurement that would be appropriate for measuring the area of a field. An hour is a unit of measurement that would be appropriate for measuring the length of time needed for a flight. (A) is incorrect because a second and a year are both units of measurement. (B) is incorrect because they are also both units of measurement, with a kilowatt equal to a thousand watts. (C) is incorrect; a millimeter is a unit of measurement of size, but size is an abstract concept. (E) is incorrect because magnitude is an abstract concept.

59. **(C)** Shots are administered by needles, and incisions are administered by scalpels.

60. **(B)** Favorable and propitious are synonyms, as are auspicious and opportune.

Section 4: Quantitative Reasoning

1. **(A)** If q is a positive real number less than 1, that means that the range of values for q can be expressed as: $0 < q < 1$, which means that q is a positive decimal number.

    When a positive decimal number is squared, the result is less than the original decimal number. Thus, $q > q^2$. For example, if q is 0.9, then q^2 is 0.81. Thus, I works.

    II doesn't work because q cannot be negative, since it is stated in the question that q is positive.

    III doesn't work because q is a positive decimal number. Continuing with the example from before, if $q = 0.9$, and $q^2 = 0.81$, then $q^3 = 0.729$, which is less than 0.81.

2. **(C)** Divide the equation $25B^2 = 9$ by 25 on both sides to isolate B:

$$B^2 = \frac{9}{25} \rightarrow B = \pm\sqrt{\frac{9}{25}} \rightarrow B = \pm\frac{3}{5}$$

    Because $B + C = 1$, $C = 1 - B$. Substitute to get:

$$C = 1 - \pm\frac{3}{5} \rightarrow C = 1 + \frac{3}{5} = \frac{8}{5} \text{ OR}$$

$$C = 1 - \frac{3}{5} = \frac{2}{5}$$

    $\frac{8}{5}$ isn't an answer choice, so the answer is $\frac{2}{5}$.

3. **(E)** Because $\frac{8}{17}$ is smaller than $\frac{12}{17}$, it is necessary to borrow 1 from the whole number in 355. The result is as such: $355\frac{8}{17} = 354\frac{25}{17}$.

    Do the subtraction to get:
$$354\frac{25}{17} - 196\frac{12}{17} = 158\frac{13}{17}.$$

4. **(D)** $1.675 \div 10^{-3} = 1.675 \times 10^3 = 1.675 \times 1,000 = 1,675$

5. **(C)** First, find the least common multiple of two of the numbers. Find the least common multiple of 32 and 36:

    Prime factorization of 32: $2 \times 2 \times 2 \times 2 \times 2$
    Prime factorization of 36: $2 \times 2 \times 3 \times 3$

    Since both contain 2×2, we find the least common multiple by using 4 as the common element and multiplying that by 8 and 9. $4 \times 8 \times 9 = 288$.

    Now, find the least common multiple of 288 and 40. To do so, first find the prime factorization of 40: $2 \times 2 \times 2 \times 5 = 8 \times 5$.

    Since both 288 and 40 share 8, the least common multiple is $8 \times 4 \times 9 \times 5 = 72 \times 20 = 1,440$.

6. **(E)** Let x be the smallest of the three integers. The average of these is 17, which means:

$$\frac{x + (x+1) + (x+2)}{3} = 17 \rightarrow \frac{3x+3}{3} = 17$$
$$x + 1 = 17, x = 16$$

    The largest integer is therefore $16 + 2 = 18$. The integer following that is $18 + 1 = 19$. Thus, $18 + 19 = 37$.

7. **(C)** To cut the three log pieces into 6 equal-sized smaller pieces, three cuts have to be made, one for each log piece. Since 3 cuts are required, the time it would take to make all 3 cuts is $3 \times (3$ minutes and 45 seconds) = 9 minutes and 135 seconds. Since 135 seconds = 2 minutes (120 seconds) and 15 seconds, add that to 9 minutes: 9 minutes + 2 minutes and 15 seconds = 11 minutes and 15 seconds.

8. **(B)** $\dfrac{92a^3b^{-2}c^4d}{23a^2b^3d^{-1}} = \dfrac{4\cancel{92}a^{\cancel{3}1}c^4d^2}{\cancel{23}\,\cancel{a^2}(b^3 \times b^2)} = \dfrac{4ac^4d^2}{b^5}$

Remember: When dealing with rational expressions, negative powers are equivalent to positive powers on the other end of the fraction. In other words, a negative power in the numerator is equivalent to having a positive power of the same magnitude in the denominator and vice versa.

9. **(A)** The total weight of the 3 watermelons is 3 × 8.8 pounds = 26.4 pounds. The total weight of the 5 pumpkins is 5 × 6.4 pounds = 32 pounds. The total weight of all 8 produce items is 58.4 pounds. The average of all 8 is therefore 58.4 pounds ÷ 8 = 7.3 pounds.

10. **(D)** To solve this, calculate the value of each choice:

The value of (A) is 1: $\cancel{3} \times \frac{7}{2\cancel{1}7} = 1$.

The value of (B) is 1: $\frac{\cancel{8}}{1\cancel{7}} \times \frac{5\cancel{1}3}{\cancel{24}3} = 1$

The value of (C) is 1: $1\frac{3}{10} \times \frac{20}{26} = \frac{1\cancel{3}}{\cancel{10}} \times \frac{20}{2\cancel{6}2} = 1$

The value of (D) is $\frac{5}{6}$: $5 \times \frac{2\cancel{5}}{\cancel{150}6} = \frac{5}{6}$

The value of (E) is 1: $\frac{1\cancel{9}}{\cancel{2}} \times \frac{\cancel{4}2}{\cancel{38}2} = 1$

11. **(D)** 50 pennies weigh 50 × 2.50 grams = 125 grams. The roll paper weighs 1.5 grams, so the total weight would be 125 + 1.5 grams = 126.5 grams.

12. **(E)** Combine like powers: $6x^4 - x^4 = 5x4$, $0 - (-4x^3) = 4x^3$; $-5x^2 - 0 = -5x^2$; $9x - (-7x) = 16x$; 1

Put the terms together to form a polynomial: $5x^4 + 4x^3 - 5x^2 + 16x + 1$

13. **(C)** $2M + 5 < 22$, so $2M < 17$. This means $M < 8.5$. Since M is a positive integer, the maximum value of M is 8. This means that $5M + 19$ has a maximum value of $5(8) + 19 = 59$.

14. **(A)** Convert $15\frac{2}{3}$ feet to inches by multiplying 15 by 12 and $\frac{2}{3}$ by 12. $15 \times 12 = 180$ and $\frac{2}{3} \times 12$

= 8 inches, for a total of 188 inches. Divide 188 by 4 to find the number of barbs that need to be placed. $188 \div 4 = 47$. We need to add one more, however, to account for the barb placed at the very beginning of the fence. $47 + 1 = 48$.

15. **(B)** Both x and y must be 0 because it is impossible for any number to be negative when it is raised to the fourth power.

16. **(B)** For 5 consecutive even integers, let x be the smallest. The list of integers would thus be: x, $x + 2$, $x + 4$, $x + 6$, and $x + 8$. The smallest integer is one-third of the largest:

$$x = \frac{1}{3} \times (x + 8)$$

$3x = x + 8$, which means $2x = 8$, $x = 4$

The second smallest integer is $x + 2 = 4 + 2 = 6$.

17. **(D)** To find the cost per hectare (ha), first convert 10 hectares to square meters. Since 1 hectare = 10,000 square meters, 10 hectare = 100,000 square meters.

The cost per square meter is therefore $560,000 ÷ 100,000 square meters = $560 ÷ 100 square meters = $5.60 per square meter.

18. **(B)** The sum of 550 and 420 is 970, which is larger than the number of people surveyed. As such, there must be overlaps. To determine how much of an overlap there is, let's say that x is the number of people who own both cats and dogs. This means $550 - x$ is the number of people who own only dogs and $420 - x$ is the number of people who own only cats. The number of people surveyed must be the sum of the number of just dog owners, just cat owners, and both pet owners. Perform the following operation:

$(550 - x) + (420 - x) + x = 900$
$970 - x = 900$, $x = 70$

Thus, the number of people who own both at least one dog and one cat is 70.

19. **(D)** Break 4,265 into its component values: $4,000 + 200 + 60 + 5$. Thus, $9 \times 4,265 = 9 \times$

(4,000 + 200 + 60 + 5). Distribute 9 to each term to get $9 \times 4{,}000 + 9 \times 200 + 9 \times 60 + 9 \times 5$.

20. **(A)** We are looking for the radii of the spheres in order to see how far the centers of the spheres are from one another.

The radius of the smaller sphere can be found by using the volume formula provided:

$36\pi = 4\pi r^3 \div 3 \rightarrow 36 = 4r^3 \div 3$
$r^3 \div 3 = 9 \rightarrow r^3 = 27$
$r = 3$ in.

The radius of the larger sphere can be found by following the same process:

$288\pi = 4\pi r^3 \div 3 \rightarrow 288 = 4r^3 \div 3$
$r^3 \div 3 = 72 \rightarrow r^3 = 216$
$r = 6$ in.

Since the smaller sphere has a radius of 3 in., and the larger sphere has a radius of 6 in., the distance between the centers is 9 in.

21. **(E)** The value of $23p$ pennies is $23p$ cents (try substituting in a value for p to see that this is true), and the value of $47d$ dimes is $47d \times 10 = 470d$ cents, since a dime is worth 10 cents (again, try using substitution). Thus, her total is $23p + 470d$ cents.

22. **(D)** If the measure of $\angle AOC$ is $x°$, and the measure of $\angle AOD$ is double, then the measure of $\angle AOD$ is $2x°$. The sum of x and $2x$ is 180, since the angles are supplementary. x is thus 60. The measure of $\angle COB$ is $120°$ because it is the vertical angle of $\angle AOD$. The area of sector COB is one-third of the area of the circle. The area of a circle is πr^2. Since the area of this circle is $15^2\pi$ or 225π. $225 \div 3 = 75$, so the area of sector COB is 75π cm^2.

23. **(A)** The box containing the 200 snow globes has a volume of 120 ft^3. To find the volume of a box that can accommodate 450 snow globes, set up a proportion, as follows:

$$\frac{x \text{ ft}^3}{450 \text{ globes}} = \frac{120 \text{ ft}^3}{200 \text{ globes}}$$

Multiply both sides by 450 to get:

$$x = \frac{120}{200} \times 450 = \frac{6}{10} \times 450 = 6 \times 45 = 270.$$

(A) is the only choice that represents 270 ft^3. (B) multiplies to 216 ft^3, so it's too small. (C) multiplies to 1,152 ft^3, which is too big. (D) multiplies to 360 ft^3, which is too big. (E) multiplies to 960 ft^3, which is also too big.

24. **(E)** First find x. To do so, set up the following equation: $25 + 10 + 40 + x + x = 100$, since the sum of the percentages must be 100. We therefore get $75 + 2x = 100$. Rewrite the equation to isolate and solve for x:

$2x = 100 - 75 = 25$
$x = 25 \div 2 = 12.5$

Since she saves $x\%$, which is 12.5%, we can find how much she saves by performing the following calculation: $0.125 \times \$8{,}000 = \$1{,}000$.

But remember that this is per month. To find how much she saves a year, multiply $1,000 by 12 to get $12,000.

25. **(C)** Mallory's budget is $8,000 per month. In 3 months, her budget is $24,000.

In 3 months, spends $0.4 \times \$24{,}000 = \$9{,}600$ on rent and $0.25 \times \$24{,}000 = \$6{,}000$ on utilities. She therefore spends $\$9{,}600 - \$6{,}000 = \$3{,}600$ more on rent than utilities in 3 months.

SSAT
UPPER LEVEL
TEST KEY 2

Sections 1 & 4: Quantitative Reasoning

Directions: For each question, record your answer in the column where it says "Your Answer", next to the number of the question. If your answer does not match the correct answer, mark an 'X' in the column labeled "X|O". If you omitted the question, leave the space blank and mark 'O' in the "X|O" column.

<table>
<tr><td colspan="5" align="center">**Section 1**</td></tr>
<tr><td>#</td><td>Correct Answer</td><td>Your Answer</td><td>X|O</td><td>Concepts Tested</td></tr>
<tr><td>1</td><td>C</td><td></td><td></td><td>GM</td></tr>
<tr><td>2</td><td>A</td><td></td><td></td><td>ARO</td></tr>
<tr><td>3</td><td>A</td><td></td><td></td><td>GM</td></tr>
<tr><td>4</td><td>D</td><td></td><td></td><td>ARO</td></tr>
<tr><td>5</td><td>D</td><td></td><td></td><td>ARO</td></tr>
<tr><td>6</td><td>D</td><td></td><td></td><td>ARO</td></tr>
<tr><td>7</td><td>E</td><td></td><td></td><td>AG</td></tr>
<tr><td>8</td><td>B</td><td></td><td></td><td>GM</td></tr>
<tr><td>9</td><td>E</td><td></td><td></td><td>DSP</td></tr>
<tr><td>10</td><td>A</td><td></td><td></td><td>AG</td></tr>
<tr><td>11</td><td>D</td><td></td><td></td><td>GM</td></tr>
<tr><td>12</td><td>A</td><td></td><td></td><td>AG</td></tr>
<tr><td>13</td><td>E</td><td></td><td></td><td>GM</td></tr>
<tr><td>14</td><td>D</td><td></td><td></td><td>ARO</td></tr>
<tr><td>15</td><td>C</td><td></td><td></td><td>AG</td></tr>
<tr><td>16</td><td>E</td><td></td><td></td><td>GM</td></tr>
<tr><td>17</td><td>E</td><td></td><td></td><td>AG</td></tr>
<tr><td>18</td><td>B</td><td></td><td></td><td>ARO</td></tr>
<tr><td>19</td><td>C</td><td></td><td></td><td>AG</td></tr>
<tr><td>20</td><td>D</td><td></td><td></td><td>AG</td></tr>
<tr><td>21</td><td>C</td><td></td><td></td><td>ARO</td></tr>
<tr><td>22</td><td>A</td><td></td><td></td><td>GM</td></tr>
<tr><td>23</td><td>A</td><td></td><td></td><td>DSP</td></tr>
<tr><td>24</td><td>E</td><td></td><td></td><td>ARO</td></tr>
<tr><td>25</td><td>A</td><td></td><td></td><td>GM</td></tr>
</table>

<table>
<tr><td colspan="5" align="center">**Section 4**</td></tr>
<tr><td>#</td><td>Correct Answer</td><td>Your Answer</td><td>X|O</td><td>Concepts Tested</td></tr>
<tr><td>1</td><td>D</td><td></td><td></td><td>ARO</td></tr>
<tr><td>2</td><td>B</td><td></td><td></td><td>ARO</td></tr>
<tr><td>3</td><td>C</td><td></td><td></td><td>ARO</td></tr>
<tr><td>4</td><td>A</td><td></td><td></td><td>ARO</td></tr>
<tr><td>5</td><td>D</td><td></td><td></td><td>ARO</td></tr>
<tr><td>6</td><td>D</td><td></td><td></td><td>AG</td></tr>
<tr><td>7</td><td>E</td><td></td><td></td><td>AG</td></tr>
<tr><td>8</td><td>B</td><td></td><td></td><td>GM</td></tr>
<tr><td>9</td><td>B</td><td></td><td></td><td>NT</td></tr>
<tr><td>10</td><td>A</td><td></td><td></td><td>AG</td></tr>
<tr><td>11</td><td>D</td><td></td><td></td><td>ARO</td></tr>
<tr><td>12</td><td>C</td><td></td><td></td><td>GM</td></tr>
<tr><td>13</td><td>C</td><td></td><td></td><td>ARO</td></tr>
<tr><td>14</td><td>C</td><td></td><td></td><td>ARO</td></tr>
<tr><td>15</td><td>A</td><td></td><td></td><td>AG</td></tr>
<tr><td>16</td><td>A</td><td></td><td></td><td>NT</td></tr>
<tr><td>17</td><td>C</td><td></td><td></td><td>AG</td></tr>
<tr><td>18</td><td>C</td><td></td><td></td><td>NT</td></tr>
<tr><td>19</td><td>C</td><td></td><td></td><td>AG</td></tr>
<tr><td>20</td><td>D</td><td></td><td></td><td>ARO</td></tr>
<tr><td>21</td><td>D</td><td></td><td></td><td>NT</td></tr>
<tr><td>22</td><td>B</td><td></td><td></td><td>DSP</td></tr>
<tr><td>23</td><td>B</td><td></td><td></td><td>GM</td></tr>
<tr><td>24</td><td>C</td><td></td><td></td><td>DSP</td></tr>
<tr><td>25</td><td>D</td><td></td><td></td><td>GM</td></tr>
</table>

CONCEPTS TESTED LEGEND

ARO – Arithmetic Operations
AG – Algebra

FG – Functions & Graphs
SP – Spatial Perception
NT – Number Theory

GM – Geometry & Measurement
DSP – Data Analysis, Statistics, & Probability

SCORING

Total Omitted (TO): _____

Total Incorrect (TI): _____

Total Missed (TM): _____
(TO + TI)

Raw Score: $50 - \mathbf{TM} - 0.25 \times \mathbf{TI}$

$50 - \underline{\quad\quad} - 0.25 \times \underline{\quad\quad} =$

$\boxed{}$

Rounded Raw Score: _____
(Round to the nearest integer value.)

Section 2: Reading Comprehension

Directions: For each question, record your answer in the column where it says "Your Answer", next to the number of the question. If your answer does not match the correct answer, mark an 'X' in the column labeled "X|O". If you omitted the question, leave the space blank and mark 'O' in the "X|O" column.

#	Correct Answer	Your Answer	X|O	Concepts Tested
1	C			ID
2	D			INF
3	A			INF
4	E			AT
5	B			MIP
6	E			ID
7	B			ID
8	A			INF
9	E			INF
10	C			ID
11	B			INF
12	E			DEF
13	C			INF
14	A			ID
15	B			ID
16	A			INF
17	B			INF
18	C			MIP
19	E			INF
20	B			INF

#	Correct Answer	Your Answer	X|O	Concepts Tested
21	C			AT
22	C			INF
23	D			INF
24	A			INF
25	E			INF
26	D			MIP
27	B			DEF
28	C			ID
29	D			INF
30	C			ID
31	C			ID
32	B			ID
33	A			ID
34	A			INF
35	D			MIP
36	A			INF
37	E			INF
38	D			MIP
39	A			ID
40	B			ID

CONCEPTS TESTED LEGEND

ID – Identifying Details   INF – Inference & Assumption   DEF – Definition in Context
MIP – Main Idea or Purpose   AT – Author's Tone

SCORING

Total Omitted (TO): _____

Total Incorrect (TI): _____

Total Missed (TM): _____
(TO + TI)

Raw Score: $40 - \text{TM} - 0.25 \times \text{TI}$

$40 - \underline{\hspace{1cm}} - 0.25 \times \underline{\hspace{1cm}} =$

$\boxed{}$

Rounded Raw Score: _____
(Round to the nearest integer value.)

Section 3: Verbal Reasoning

Directions: For each question, record your answer in the column where it says "Your Answer", next to the number of the question. If your answer does not match the correct answer, mark an 'X' in the column labeled "X|O". If you omitted the question, leave the space blank and mark 'O' in the "X|O" column.

#	Correct Answer	Your Answer	X|O	Concepts Tested
1	B			SYN
2	A			SYN
3	C			SYN
4	B			SYN
5	E			SYN
6	E			SYN
7	E			SYN
8	D			SYN
9	D			SYN
10	E			SYN
11	D			SYN
12	A			SYN
13	B			SYN
14	C			SYN
15	E			SYN
16	A			SYN
17	D			SYN
18	A			SYN
19	E			SYN
20	B			SYN
21	E			SYN
22	B			SYN
23	C			SYN
24	C			SYN
25	A			SYN
26	C			SYN
27	D			SYN
28	A			SYN
29	D			SYN
30	A			SYN

#	Correct Answer	Your Answer	X|O	Concepts Tested
31	B			AN
32	C			AN
33	C			AN
34	E			AN
35	A			AN
36	B			AN
37	E			AN
38	D			AN
39	C			AN
40	C			AN
41	B			AN
42	E			AN
43	A			AN
44	D			AN
45	E			AN
46	B			AN
47	B			AN
48	A			AN
49	D			AN
50	A			AN
51	B			AN
52	E			AN
53	D			AN
54	A			AN
55	C			AN
56	C			AN
57	A			AN
58	D			AN
59	D			AN
60	B			AN

SCORING

Total Omitted (TO): _____

Total Incorrect (TI): _____

Total Missed (TM): _____
(TO + TI)

Raw Score: $60 - \text{TM} - 0.25 \times \text{TI}$

$60 - \underline{\hspace{1cm}} - 0.25 \times \underline{\hspace{1cm}} =$

$\boxed{}$

Rounded Raw Score: _____
(Round to the nearest integer value.

Section 1: Quantitative Reasoning

1. **(C)** In a right triangle, the longest side is the hypotenuse. The hypotenuse can be calculated according to the Pythagorean Theorem: $a^2 + b^2 = c^2$. By applying the Pythagorean Theorem to the answer choices, we can eliminate the incorrect choices.

    For (A): $2^2 + 2^2 = 8 = \left(2\sqrt{2}\right)^2$, so the dimensions listed in A can represent a right triangle.

    For (B): $\left(\sqrt{3}\right)^2 + 3^2 = 3 + 9 = 12 = \left(2\sqrt{3}\right)^2$, so the dimensions listed in B can represent a right triangle.

    For (C): $10^2 + 24^2 = 100 + 576 = 676 \neq 25^2$; $25^2 = 625$, so the dimensions listed in C cannot represent a right triangle.

    For (D): $7^2 + 24^2 = 49 + 576 = 625 = 25^2$, so the dimensions listed in D can represent a right triangle.

    For (E): $15^2 + 20^2 = 225 + 400 = 625 = 25^2$, so the dimensions listed in E can represent a right triangle.

2. **(A)** Ernest has $600 - 54 = 546$ marbles left. To find what percent this is, divide 546 by 600 to get 0.91 or 91%.

    Another way to approach this problem is to recognize that 6 is 1% of 600. 54 is 6×9, so it represents 9%. If Ernest gives away 9%, then he will have $100\% - 9\% = 91\%$ left.

3. **(A)** If the length of a side of triangle B is 45 cm, and the length of the corresponding side of similar triangle A is 9 cm, the ratio of the side lengths of triangles A to B is 9 to 45 or 1 to 5. That means that the ratio of the areas is 1 to 25. (This is because both the base and the height of triangle A is 5 times smaller than those of triangle B. Thus, the area, which is calculated by $\frac{1}{2}bh$, of triangle A will be 25 times less than that of triangle B.)

4. **(D)** If Dillon gives out the same number of comic books to all of his friends, the most he can give out is 3 copies to each. That is $3 \times 15 = 45$. He will have $51 - 45 = 6$ comic books left over.

5. **(D)** $\left(-\dfrac{6}{7}\right)^3 \div \left(\dfrac{6}{7}\right)^2 =$

    $\left(-\dfrac{6}{7}\right)^3 \times \left(\dfrac{7}{6}\right)^2 =$

    $-\dfrac{6 \times 6 \times 6 \times 7 \times 7}{7 \times 7 \times 7 \times 6 \times 6} = -\dfrac{6}{7}$

6. **(D)** Round 99,346 to 100,000 and 4,013 to 4,000. $100,000 \div 4,000 = 100 \div 4 = 25$. Thus, (A), (B), and (E) can be eliminated. However, even if we round 99,346 to 99,000 and divide that by 4,000, we would still get 24.75, which rounds to 25.

7. **(E)** $C + D = 7$ and $E + D = 18$. $D = 7 - C$. Substituting $7 - C$ for D, we get $E - C + 7 = 18$ and $E - C = 11$. Beyond that, it is impossible to determine what the values of E and C are.

    Note: As a general rule, when there are two equations and more than two variables, it is not possible to solve for the variables.

8. **(B)** The area of semicircle A is 18π in^2, which means that the area of the entire circle (had it been drawn) would be 36π in^2. Because the area of a circle is figured by the formula $A = \pi r^2$, $r^2 = 36$, after dividing both sides by π. This means $r = 6$ and $d = 12$. Since the diameter of the circle and the top base of the trapezoid coincide, the length of the top base of the trapezoid is 12 in.

    Because the bottom base of the trapezoid has a length of 1.5 times the top base's length, the bottom base has a length of $12 \times 1.5 = 18$ in. Thus, the area of the trapezoid can now be determined: $A = \frac{1}{2} \times (12 + 18) \times 3 = \frac{1}{2} \times 30 \times 3 = 15 \times 3 = 45$ in^2.

9. **(E)** The average is found by taking the sum of the scores and dividing the sum by the number of scores. The sum of the scores of Karl's tests is $55 + 63 + 57 + 72 + 81 = 328$. $328 \div 5 = 65.6$.

10. **(A)** $0.65 \times 4x = 2.6x = 5.2$. Solve for x by dividing both sides by 2.6. $5.2 \div 2.6 = 2$, so $x = 2$. $0.3 \times 0.5 \times 2 = 0.3$.

11. **(D)** The length of AB is a multiple of 3, since the length of AB is $s + 2s$, and s is a whole number. To get the correct answer, try multiplying the answer choices by 2 to see if the result is a multiple of 3.

    Multiplying 23 by 2 gives 46, which is not a multiple of 3, so (A) is incorrect. Multiplying 23.5 by 2 gives 47, which is not a multiple of 3, so (B) is incorrect. Multiplying 25 by 2 gives 50, which is not a multiple of 3, so (C) is incorrect. Multiplying 25.5 by 2 gives 51, which is a multiple of 3 (3×17), so (D) is correct. Multiplying 28 by 2 gives 56, which is not a multiple of 3, so (E) is incorrect.

12. **(A)** Multiply both sides of the inequality by 2 to get rid of the 0.5. This leaves us with $T + 3 < 8$. Subtract 3 from both sides to get $T < 5$. Thus, (A) is the only possible choice. (B) can't work because T must be less than 5, not less than or equal to 5.

13. **(E)** Since the measure of $\angle ABC$ is 40° more than that of $\angle BAC$, and $\angle ABC$ measures 75°, the measure of $\angle BAC$ is $(75 - 40)° = 35°$. This means that $\angle BCA$ measures $180° - (35 + 75)° = 70°$. $\angle BCD$ is supplementary to $\angle BCA$, so the measure is $180° - 70° = 110°$.

14. **(D)** The sale price of the coat is $100\% - 45\% = 55\%$ of the original price. Thus, the sale price is $0.55 \times \$185.00 = \$101.75$.

15. **(C)** Let $7x$ and $5x$ represent the lengths of the longer road and shorter road, respectively. If the shorter road's length is increased by 20 miles, it will still be 20 miles shorter than the longer road. Write an equation and solve for x:

    $5x + 20 = 7x - 20$
    $5x + 40 = 7x$
    $2x = 40, x = 20$

    Since we're solving for the length of the longer road, multiply x by 7 to get: $7x = 140$.

16. **(E)** The distance from Roald's house to Porter's house cannot be determined because Porter could either live $15 - 14 = 1$ mile away from Roald, if they live on the same side of the school, or $15 + 14 = 19$ miles away, if they live on opposite sides of the school.

17. **(E)** The average of A and B is equal to the sum of C and D, so the whole system can be expressed as:

    $$\frac{A + B}{2} = C + D.$$

    To isolate C, subtract D from both sides:
    $C = \frac{A + B}{2} - D$, which can be written as
    $C = (A + B) \div 2 - D$.

18. **(B)** If Tracy orders one pair of shoes for each member, he would order 165 pairs, which would cost: $165 \times \$50.00 = \$8,250.00$. If he ordered two pairs for each member, he would order 330 pairs. Because this is greater than 200 pairs, he would receive a discount of 45%. Thus, his total order before the discount would be $330 \times \$50.00 = \$16,500.00$. After applying the 45% discount, the cost would be $\$16,500 - \$16,500 \times 0.45 = \$9,075.00$. The difference in price between ordering one pair and two pairs per student is: $\$9,075.00 - \$8,250 = \$825.00$.

19. **(C)** Let W represent the weight of a watermelon and A that of an apple: $3W = 40A$. The weight of a watermelon, in relation to the weight of an apple is:

    $$1W = \frac{40A}{3}$$

    To find the weight of 7 watermelons, multiply each side by 7 to get:

    $$7W = \frac{280A}{3}$$

Because $\dfrac{280}{3} = 93\frac{1}{3}$, the weight of 7 watermelons can most accurately be approximated to that of 93 apples.

20. **(D)** On each day of Christmas, Nick gives each child one more gift than he did on the previous day. If he gave each child 1 gift on the 1st day, that means he gave each child 2 gifts on the 2nd day, 3 gifts on the 3rd day, 4 on the 4th day, 5 on the 5th day, and 6 on the 6th day.

    This means that in 6 days, each child received 1 + 2 + 3 + 4 + 5 + 6 = 21 gifts. Since there are 13 children, Nick gave a total of 21 × 13 = 273 gifts in 6 days.

21. **(C)** Use elimination to arrive at the correct answer.

    If the values of (A) are used, we get 4821 + 4181 = 9002, which is incongruous with 8402.

    If the values of (B) are used, we get 3721 + 3171 = 6892, which is incongruous with 7402.

    If the values of (C) are used, we get 3726 + 3676 = 7402, which is congruous with 7402.

    If the values of (D) are used, we get 4726 + 4676 = 9402, which is incongruous with 7402.

22. **(A)** The radius of the third circle is equal to the diameter of the two congruent circles. If r is the radius of the congruent circles, then $2r$ is the radius of the larger, third circle. Thus, the area of the third circle will be $\pi(2r)^2 = 4\pi r^2$, which is 4 times the area of each of the congruent circles. Thus, the ratio of the area of the larger circle to one of the first two circles is $4\pi r^2$ to πr^2 or 4 : 1.

23. **(A)** From March to April, crude oil production increased 6 million barrels, for a gain of 50%

    $$\left(\frac{18-12}{12} \times 100\%\right).$$

    From April to May, crude oil production increased 7 million barrels, for a gain of 38.89%

    $$\left(\frac{25-18}{18} \times 100\%\right).$$

From May to June, crude oil production increased 10 million barrels, for a gain of 40%

$$\left(\frac{35-25}{25} \times 100\%\right).$$

From June to July, crude oil production increased 5 million barrels, for a gain of 14.29%

$$\left(\frac{40-35}{35} \times 100\%\right).$$

From July to August, crude oil production increased 17 million barrels, for a gain of 42.5%

$$\left(\frac{57-40}{40} \times 100\%\right).$$

Thus, April saw the greatest percent gains over the previous month.

24. **(E)** Ordinarily, before the bundle, the store's revenue was: $75.00 × 100 + $55.00 × 200 = $7,500.00 + $11,000 = $18,500.00. To find how many bundles need to be sold, divide $18,500.00 by $120.00 to get 154.167. Since selling 154 bundles would equate to revenues of less than $18,500 (154 × $120.00 = $18,480.00, to be exact), at least 155 bundles must be sold.

25. **(A)** Let a, b, and c represent the areas of the three regions of unknown areas, with a being the largest of these three, b the second largest, and c the smallest. (Note, however, that b and c must still be larger than 15 km², since 15 km² is the area of the smallest region.) The sum of the areas can be expressed as $a + b + c + 15 + 59 = 163$. Thus, $a + b + c = 163 - 74 = 89$. To find the greatest possible value of b, make a and c as small as possible.

    If a is 16, then $b + c = 89 - 16 = 73$. Since we are trying to make b as large as possible, while still making c larger than b, we need to make b and c as close to each other in value as possible. Thus, if we say $c = b + 1$, then we can write the above equation as $b + (b + 1) = 73$ or $2b + 1 = 73$. This means $2b = 72$, and $b = 36$.

Section 2: Reading Comprehension

Lesula Discovery

1. **(C)** Lines 9-13 indicate that the discovery of the lesula is significant because it was just the second monkey species discovered in 28 years. The discovery is further significant because it promises the possibility of more animal species in the future. (A) is incorrect because the lesula had not been a known species to the scientific community. (B) is incorrect because there is no mention of the relation of the two species. (D) is incorrect because it is not relevant to the significance of the discovery of the lesula. It wouldn't have mattered where the lesula was found. (E) is incorrect because there is no mention that the lesula had mythological or legend status.

2. **(D)** Lines 1-4 indicate that with our modern technology and innumerable nature documentaries, it is easy to believe that we have discovered every animal species. This means that technology is an integral part of the discovery of animals. Further, this means that our technology is advanced enough for us to discover most, if not all, species. (A) is incorrect because the author is optimistic for the hope of discovery of other species of animals in the future. (B) is incorrect because it is not a logically sound conclusion. Just because the rate of technological advancement increases does not mean the rate of animal discovery will also increase. If there comes a time where no more animals are left to be discovered, it would be impossible for the rate of animal discovery to increase, even if the rate of technological advancement increased. (C) is incorrect because luck is not mentioned or discussed in the passage. (E) is incorrect because it is not a valid logical conclusion. The passage states that the sun-tailed monkey was discovered 28 years before the lesula was, but that does not mean that new species of mammals will be discovered every 28 years. A more logical conclusion would be to compare the date of the discovery of the kipunji to that of the lesula, since the kipunji was discovered immediately before the lesula was.

3. **(A)** Lines 4-9 indicate that the lesula was discovered in 2007, yet it was not until 2012 that the lesula's existence was made public. The gap of 4-5 years indicates that some time is needed before an animal species can be officially announced. (B) is incorrect because it is not logically supported by the passage, though it may make sense; it is too absolute of a statement. (C) is incorrect because it, too, is logically invalid; the chance of finding animals in other parts of the world is not discussed by the passage. (D) is incorrect because the prestige of *PLOS ONE* is not discussed. (E) is incorrect because it is not known what people thought about the discoverability of new monkey species, once the sun-tailed monkey was discovered.

4. **(E)** The author expresses his fascination when he uses language such as "it is easy to believe we have discovered every species alive… [y]et, in the June of 2007…" (lines 2-4). The author expresses his optimism when he writes, "…because it promises the possibility of the discovery of more animal species in the future" (lines 12-13). (A) is incorrect because there is nothing to indicate that the interest the author displays is feigned or faked. (B) is incorrect because the author's enthusiasm is not forced, and the author does not used veiled sarcasm. (C) is incorrect because the author show no derision for anyone or anything. Furthermore, the author shows optimism, not doubt. (D) is incorrect because the author does not show scorn, which is almost synonymous with derision.

Tort Law

5. **(B)** The passage is to discuss what torts are and how they are approached in a court of law. (A) is incorrect. While the passage does discuss the etymology of the word *tort*, it is not a primary focal point of the passage; rather it is a lead or hook to the passage. (C) is incorrect because the author's main point of the passage is not to caution against engaging in lawsuits. Furthermore, there is nothing to suggest that the author is against lawsuits when they are warranted. (D) is incorrect. While the author briefly outlines the steps needed for a tort action,

he does not go into too many details. Furthermore, even if it can be construed as the author having gone into much detail, that is not the primary purpose of the passage. (E) is not correct because the passage focuses more on providing an overview of the process of a tort suit, not the process of getting out of one.

6. **(E)** The author does not discourage litigation if it is the only option available. The author does discourage litigation because it is expensive, time consuming, emotionally harrowing, and not as glamorous as the media makes it out to be, as indicated in lines 28-31. Thus, choices (A) to (D) are incorrect.

7. **(B)** Lines 19-20 list some of the common defenses that a defendant might raise: assumption of risk, consent, self-defense, and defense of others. Negligence is not listed as one (making the other choices incorrect), though it could very well be one in the real world, if the plaintiff's own negligence resulted in the tort.

8. **(A)** Lines 11-12 discuss summary judgments and directed verdicts; when the plaintiff is unable to satisfy the elements of the tort claim. Lines 20-22 discuss summary judgments and directed verdicts when the defendant cannot properly raise a defense. Furthermore, lines 12-14 state "With several different ways for the defendant to win almost automatically," which implies that directed verdicts and summary judgments are used when the plaintiff has failed to properly his case. (B) is incorrect because the passage states that the plaintiff can obtain a summary judgment or directed verdict as well. (C) is incorrect because the frequency of summary judgments and directed verdicts is not discussed. (D) is incorrect because the ability to bring the case back to trial is not discussed. (E) is incorrect because it is not logically supported, based on the passage, although there is enough evidence to suggest that they are likely among the quickest methods of deciding a case.

9. **(E)** Use elimination to arrive at the correct answer. (A) is incorrect because that would be a valid defense for the defendant to raise. If the plaintiff gave the defendant keys to a tractor, knowing that the defendant doesn't know how to drive a tractor, then the defendant can claim that the plaintiff assumed the risk of something going wrong by giving the defendant the keys. (B) is incorrect because that would be a valid defense. If the plaintiff instructs the defendant to hit him to see how strong the defendant is, and the defendant hits him, then the plaintiff has assumed the risk of injury. (C) is wrong because it involves self-defense, and self-defense is a valid torts defense. (D) is wrong because it is a valid tort defense to step in for another person's defense. (E) is correct because it presents the least valid defense situation the defendant can raise, compared to the other choices. Name calling is not enough of a reason to prompt the defendant to steal and then total the plaintiff's car.

10. **(C)** Lines 15-19 indicate that, in order to establish a prima facie case, the plaintiff must satisfy every element of the tort claim he is trying to assert. (A) is not correct because the plaintiff does not necessarily need to present an airtight case the defendant cannot refute. If that were the case, then the passage would not have discussed the possible defenses the defendant might raise. (B) is incorrect because reasonable doubt is not discussed. (D) and (E) are incorrect because the plaintiff must satisfy all of the elements of the tort he is asserting.

Best Musicians

11. **(B)** Lines 9-16 discuss the sales success that the Beatles have enjoyed and indirectly relates it to being history's all-time best musical performers. (A) is incorrect because the passage does not suggest that audiences would willingly listen to an artist's music, if they don't enjoy the genre. (C) is incorrect. While it may seem true, there may be other factors that prevent one from making money. (D) is incorrect because it is assumed that others will always buy an album. (E) is incorrect because musical brilliance and the invention of new genres is not discussed.

12. **(E)** The word relative is used to show a figurative comparison. The phrase "a handful" is figurative language, meaning a small or graspable amount or number. But the number of successful musicians over the years is quite large, so applying the phrase "a handful" more literally, while still within the context of

figurative speech, would mean fewer than 5 musicians or bands have been successful. The use of the word relative indicates that the number of successful musicians and bands, while possibly still a large number, is a very small number compared to the total number of musicians and bands that have come and gone.

13. **(C)** Lines 5-6 list Whitney Houston, Elvis Presley, Bob Dylan, and Michael Jackson, as being among the all-time greats, so (A), (B), (D), and (E) are incorrect. Mariah Carey is not listed.

14. **(A)** Lines 12-16 list the Beatles' achievements. Nowhere in the passage does it indicate or suggest that the Beatles composed thousands of songs. Thus, (B) to (E) are incorrect.

Rent Seeking

15. **(B)** Lines 21-23 indicate that the real problem is that the industries receive less than what society pays for and that this is a form of economic waste. Lines 23-27 further delineate why waste leads to inefficiency. Though (A) is a tempting choice, it is incorrect because the amount the tax payers have to pay for rent seeking is not in itself considered economic waste. Economic waste is the imperfect transfer of resources, as discussed in lines 23-24. (C) is incorrect because how much the lower income families have to pay is not discussed in the passage. (D) is incorrect economic waste is not bad because it encourages selfishness. (E) is incorrect because how people feel about not being able to perfectly transfer resources is not discussed.

16. **(A)** Economic waste results when there is an imperfect transfer of resources. If there is a perfect transfer of resources, that is, without loss, it can be inferred that there is no economic waste. (B) is incorrect because the passage does suggest that lobbying efforts do produce economic waste. (C) is incorrect because economic waste and being wasteful are not synonymous. It is possible to produce economic waste without being wasteful. Wasteful is a person's state of mind and how lax with his resources or money he is. (D) is incorrect because a loss of jobs is not discussed. (E) is incorrect because the passage indicates that the practice of rent seeking will probably never end.

17. **(B)** Rent seeking is defined as the attempt of an individual or party to increase the amount of rent it makes. That is, rent seeking is the attempt to get more than what one is willing to work for. Thus, an employee who seeks a raise of $50,000, even though he is content with where he is and is not interested in working elsewhere, is said to be seeking rent. Choices (A), (C), (D), and (E) are incorrect because they do not illustrate a rent being sought. (A) is incorrect because the employee is not looking to benefit himself directly. (C) is not an example of rent seeking because the employee is looking for increased compensation to make it worth his staying at his current job. (D) is not an example of rent seeking because it does not involve the employee asking for more than he is willing to work for. (E) is incorrect because he's merely asking for an exchange of equivalent resources.

18. **(C)** Very generally, the passage is about rent seeking and why it can be bad. (A) is incorrect because this passage is not seeking to demand industries to cease their wasteful and rent seeking efforts. The passage does not use language that would indicate the author's desire for industries to cease and desist what they're doing. (B) is incorrect because the discussion of Gordon Tullock is only in the context of rent seeking. The main purpose of the passage is not to credit Gordon Tullock. (D) is incorrect because rent seeking is already a common practice. (E) is incorrect because the author does acknowledge that there is nothing wrong with wanting to make more money, in lines 9-10.

19. **(E)** The author makes it known that rent seeking is bad because it leads to inefficiencies. Thus, the author would probably agree that the resources that get wasted could be used productively if they were invested in other things. (A) is incorrect. Just because Gordon Tullock's idea of rent seeking was the only thing discussed here, that doesn't mean rent seeking was the only contribution he made to the field of economics. (B) is incorrect because this passage is not about apartment or building rent. (C) The author criticizes economic waste, but there's nothing to support the idea that the author believes rent seeking to be a jailable or criminal offense. (D) is incorrect because it is not logically correct. If

the government always agreed to the financial benefits that companies sought, that might not necessarily eradicate rent seeking and could possibly cause a litany of other problems for the government.

Secrets Poem

20. **(B)** "Steel fortress" is used in the context of the protagonist resolving to never reveal certain secrets because if he does there will be serious consequences. The best choice here is thus sturdy determination. (A) is incorrect because the steel fortress is built around the heart, so it is not a literal defense against people or things. (C) is incorrect because the steel fortress is figurative and metaphorical, not literal. (D) is incorrect because it reads too much into the poem. There's nothing to indicate that the secrets are about crimes. Further, the steel fortress is more directly about not revealing secrets. (E) is incorrect because the steel fortress is not an obstacle, per se. While it could be seen as one, in the sense that it is interfering with the protagonist's pursuit of relief and freedom, it is seen more of as a protective device that the protagonist voluntarily accepted for himself.

21. **(C)** The overall tone of the passage is one of anguish or sadness and desperation. (A) is incorrect because it is not enthusiastic. (B) is incorrect because it is not unconscionable. (D) is incorrect because it is not capricious, which means unpredictable or erratic. (E) is incorrect. Onerous means burdensome or oppressive. That might work. Redemptive means pertaining or relating to redemption or salvation. The tone of the passage is not optimistic at all.

22. **(C)** "Lady Liberty" is used in the context of freedom from the anguish and angst that the protagonist is experiencing. He is keeping the burden of certain secrets, and he wants to be free of them. Unfortunately, doing so means risking danger and treachery of some sort. (A) is incorrect because the passage is not dealing with literal prisoners. (B) is incorrect because it is the protagonist himself that is preventing the secrets from being released. It is not known whether he is being denied his freedom of speech and press. (D) and (E) are incorrect because this passage is

not about literal confinement or inability to make one's own decisions.

23. **(D)** The "liquid gold barley" helps the "rigid heart sailor" find solace by flowing melodiously through his veins to a pleasant rhythm. Thus, it probably helps him feel more relaxed. (A) is incorrect because nothing indicates that the liquid gold barley will erase the protagonist's memories. (B) is incorrect because the protagonist's heart rate is not discussed. (C) is incorrect because it is not possible to know if the liquid gold barley will help the protagonist view his past differently. (E) is incorrect because there is no mention of overcoming fears.

24. **(A)** "Prisoners" refers to the secrets that are being kept by the protagonist. They long to get out but can't. The prisoners are trapped in the prison, and the secrets are locked in the box. Thus, they mean the same thing. (B) is incorrect because dungeon cells are not trying to get out. (C) is incorrect because grave circumstances would be the consequence of the prisoners or secrets getting out, but they do not allude to the prisoners or secrets. (D) is incorrect because best friend is being used to refer to the swashings (swashing means splashing) of the liquid gold barley. (E) is incorrect because the prisoners would face treachery; treachery itself is not being used to allude to prisoners.

Mendelian Genetics

25. **(E)** The blending theory proposed that inherited traits blended together from generation to generation. Thus, if the size of the offspring was always the average of the sizes of its parents, then the blending theory would be best supported. (A) doesn't work because the offspring of two curly-haired parents should have curly hair, according to the blending theory. (B) doesn't work because a serious injury isn't inherited, so the blending theory wouldn't apply here. (C) doesn't work because the offspring of two animals should have the average of their parents' strength, according to the blending theory. (D) is incorrect because, according to the blending theory, all of the offspring of a white flower and red flower should be pink.

26. **(D)** This passage is about the remarkable work Mendel did and how they were rediscovered by other scientists. (A) is incorrect because it is too narrow. The passage is not just about describing genetic engineering. (B) is incorrect because, while factually accurate, it is too narrow. (C) is incorrect because it is not necessarily a true statement. While Mendel did choose the pea plant out of convenience, we don't know if it was the easiest plant to choose. Moreover, even if they were the easiest plants that could have been chosen, it's still not the main idea of the passage. (E) is incorrect because Mendel's work did not impact those of de Vries's and Korrens's.

27. **(B)** Lines 17-18 provide a definition of *phenotype*: physical characteristics. However, the context also establishes phenotype as being a physical characteristic that is passed down. For instance, the passage discusses the phenotypes of the plants Mendel bred and how the phenotypes of the offspring related to the phenotypes of the parents. Thus, it is possible to conclude that a phenotype is physical characteristic that is passed down from the parents. (A) is incorrect because it is overly broad. Anything could mean inheritances, as well, but those are certainly not phenotypes. (C) is incorrect because there are many genetic traits, but not all of them are expressed physically. (D) is incorrect because the passage suggests that phenotypes must be genetically inherited and thus acquired. (E) is incorrect because phenotypes are only physical traits that have been inherited, not the collective of all physical traits.

28. **(C)** Lines 4-8 discuss artificial selection. Early breeders only permitted crops and animals with desirable traits to reproduce, so that these traits would show up in the offspring, but at least some of the time the offspring would show traits that had not been predicted or were not predictable. Because of this phenomenon, artificial selection was not a perfect process and was therefore a limitation. (A) is incorrect because artificial selection was not limiting in the number of traits that could be bred. (B) is incorrect because the amount of time it took is not cited as a limitation. (D) is incorrect because different species weren't born occasionally. Look carefully at the wording. (E) is incorrect because infertility is not mentioned as a limitation.

29. **(D)** Mendel published his findings in 1866, but it wasn't until 1901, some 35 years later, that his work was rediscovered and republished. Had his work been appreciated, it is possible and likely that others could have and would have built on his research. (A) is incorrect because the author doesn't express doubt about Mendel's findings. (B) is incorrect because the author clearly does not believe artificial selection and genetic engineering are the same things. Lines 1-8 describe the differences between genetic engineering and artificial selection. (C) is incorrect because it is possible that Mendel's work would have been rediscovered eventually, even without de Vries. (E) is incorrect because other people, such as de Vries and Korrens, would have developed the study of genetics.

30. **(C)** Lines 23-27 indicate that Mendel's work allowed him to refute the "blending theory," which was the leading theory of inheritance at the time. (A) is incorrect because Mendel actually proved that traits are passed down in specific, patterned ratios. (B) is incorrect because Mendel proved that traits are passed down independently of other traits. Lines 18-22 show why (A) and (B) are incorrect. (D) is incorrect because lines 25-26 indicate that some traits are more dominantly expressed than others are, so Mendel did not disprove this at all. (E) is incorrect because lines 24-25 indicate that Mendel did find that each parent only contributes half of its genetic material to its offspring; thus, he did not disprove the statement made in (E).

About Pencils

31. **(C)** A misnomer is an inappropriate name for something. Pencil lead is because it contains no lead whatsoever. (A), (B), (D), and (E) are all incorrect because none of them indicate why "pencil lead" is a misnomer.

32. **(B)** Lines 6-7 indicate graphite was discovered sometime between 1564 and 1565, which is the mid-1560s, not the early 1560s or late 1560s, as (A) and (C) indicate. (D) is incorrect because the 15th century is the 1400s. Early 16th century would be early in the 1500s, which the 1560s is clearly not, so (E) is incorrect.

33. **(A)** Lines 9-12 indicate that graphite was too soft and brittle to be properly used as a writing material, so it required a holder of some sort. (B) is an overstatement. Though graphite is described as being soft and brittle, we don't know if it was as free-flowing as a liquid would be. (C) is incorrect. While it may have been too messy to hold in one's hand, the messiness is not the reason a holder was needed. (D) is incorrect because it is not supported that graphite evaporates. (E) is incorrect because the atomic stability of graphite is not discussed.

34. **(A)** Lines 2-5 state that the more graphite there is (and, as a result, less clay) in pencil lead, the darker the color the pencil lead will produce. The less graphite there is (and, as a result, more clay) in pencil lead, the lighter the color the pencil lead will produce. Thus, (A) is correct. (B) is incorrect because it states the opposite of what's correct. (C) is incorrect because the color of pencil lead without graphite cannot be inferred, as graphite is a critical component of pencil lead. (D) is incorrect because colored pencils are not discussed at all. (E) is incorrect because it is not mentioned in the passage that clay provides the lead with greater structural integrity. It might be the clay is used for coloration purposes, though it is possible that clay does provide pencil lead with greater structural integrity. There's simply not enough information.

35. **(D)** This passage is about what pencil lead is comprised of and how its primary material, graphite, was discovered and implemented as a writing material. Thus, (D) best reflects this. (A) is incorrect because only "pencil lead" is listed as a misnomer. (B) The consistency of pencil lead is not the main idea of the passage. (C) is incorrect because it is overly broad. The passage does not discuss any other writing implement other than the pencil. (E) is incorrect because graphite's comparison to coal is only a very minor aspect of the passage.

Roman Roads

36. **(A)** Lines 4-6 indicate that the Roman Empire's vast network of highways was a major reason Rome achieved the success it enjoyed. (B) is incorrect because the passage does not compare the extensiveness of Rome's roads with those of other ancient empires. (C) is incorrect because it is not implied by the passage that the Roman Empire was razed to the ground at all or that enemy invaders would have done so earlier, if Rome hadn't had its vast network of roads. (D) is incorrect because the words permanently and severely are overstating things. (E) is incorrect because travel for leisure is not discussed.

37. **(E)** Lines 19-21 indicate that the stone pillars that punctuated the sides of Roman roads relayed important and relevant information to the traveler, such as the distance to the nearest town. Modern highway signs tell drivers how many miles there are to the nearest exits and which exits lie ahead.

38. **(D)** The primary purpose of the passage is to discuss how roads were critical to the Roman Empire's success and how they were engineered. (A) is incorrect because the passage is not about the ramifications the invention of cars had on our society. (B) is incorrect because the passage is not an essay on the value roads provide in the transport of supplies and people. (C) is incorrect because the engineering principles of modern roads are not discussed. (E) is incorrect because the passage does not provide a hypothesis on the most efficient way of constructing roads.

39. **(A)** Lines 13-16 indicate that before roads were constructed in Rome surveyors would use sighting poles to plot the most direct route from one location to another. There is nothing to indicate that the surveyors used the sighting poles to measure the distance from one point to another, so (C) is incorrect. (B), (D), and (E) are incorrect because they introduce "facts" that weren't discussed or suggested.

40. **(B)** Lines 16-19 indicate that roads in ancient Rome consisted of multiple layers in order to ensure flatness and durability, to maximize traveling effectiveness and efficiency. (A) is incorrect because there is no mention of making the roads softer for easier travel. (C) is incorrect because there is not mention of making the roads harder for easier travel. (D) is incorrect because the multiple layers of roads have no bearing on constructing direct routes from one place to another. (E) is incorrect because the concern of the underlying soil is not discussed.

Section 3: Verbal Reasoning

Synonyms

1. **(B)** HARMONIOUS (adj.) means pleasant or agreeable. COMPATIBLE means capable of existing together in harmony.

    Affectionate means showing tenderness and fondness. It may be a tempting choice, but being affectionate is still more removed from the definition of harmonious than compatible is.

2. **(A)** CORROBORATE (v.) means to affirm or confirm. VALIDATE means to verify the authenticity of, so it is most similar in meaning to corroborate.

3. **(C)** LOFTY (adj.) means high up, as in the air or height. It can also mean elevated in rank or stature, as degree of accomplishment or achievement. GRAND means impressive in size, impression, or impact. It can also mean splendid.

4. **(B)** ACRID (adj.) means SHARP or biting, as in taste or smell. It can also be used when describing one's remarks.

5. **(E)** RELINQUISH (v.) means to give up or SURRENDER, as in giving up a position.

6. **(E)** DETER (v.) means to discourage, hinder, or PREVENT.

7. **(E)** MATERIAL (adj.) means relevant or important, of much consequence. SIGNIFICANT means important.

8. **(D)** FACILE (adj.) means performed or done with ease. Thus, EASY is the best choice.

9. **(D)** REVERBERATE (v.) means to ECHO or resonate.

10. **(E)** GARRISON (n.) means group of soldiers stationed in a fortified location or the fortified location itself. STRONGHOLD means well-fortified place.

11. **(D)** INARTICULATE (adj.) means unable to express clearly or coherently—in other words, it means INCOHERENT.

12. **(A)** SQUALID (adj.) means FILTHY or repulsive, as from a lack of hygiene or care.

13. **(B)** RAIMENT (n.) means clothing or attire. APPAREL means clothing, especially outer wear.

14. **(C)** VICINITY (n.) means surrounding area, distance, or range of some place. It also means being near or close to something. PROXIMITY is the nearness or closeness to something or some place.

15. **(E)** FACTION (n.) means a GROUP or clique within an organization.

16. **(A)** POIGNANT (adj.) means intensely emotionally or mentally touching or MOVING.

17. **(D)** PROGNOSTICATE (v.) means to foretell or predict. PROPHESY means the same.

18. **(A)** AVARICE (n.) means extreme or insatiable GREED or desire.

19. **(E)** UBIQUITOUS (adj.) means existing or present universally. It can also mean widespread. OMNIPRESENT means present everywhere.

20. **(B)** SCRUPULOUS (adj.) means having and abiding by a strong set of principles—being very PRINCIPLED.

21. **(E)** DEXTEROUS (adj.) means SKILLFUL or adroit.

22. **(B)** LETHARGIC (adj.) means slow or lazy. SLUGGISH means lazy or lacking energy, so lethargic and sluggish are rather synonymous.

23. **(C)** HIATUS (n.) means gap or BREAK between events or timeframes.

24. **(C)** FINITE (adj.) means having, existing, or operating within boundaries; in other words, it means LIMITED.

25. **(A)** ENDEAVOR (n.) means attempt or EFFORT.

26. **(C)** TERSE (adj.) means concise and short, often in a cold or rude way. CURT means rudely brief in speech.

27. **(D)** WAYLAY (v.) means to intercept suddenly and unexpectedly, usually for the purpose of assaulting or robbing. AMBUSH means to wait in hiding or secret for, to attack or assault.

28. **(A)** JINGOISTIC (adj.) means supporting or being in favor of war, usually out of patriotic zeal. BELLICOSE means eager to fight or aggressive and hostile.

29. **(D)** DESTINATION (n.) means the point or place of arrival—in other words, the end point of a travel or journey. TARGET is the best choice because it means a goal to be reached or attained.

30. **(A)** FACULTY (n.) means an ABILITY, talent, or skill that can be used for the purpose of attaining or fulfilling a goal.

Analogies

31. **(B)** Hide is the pelt or skin of an animal. Leather is made by drying out the hide of an animal. A raisin is a dried out grape.

32. **(C)** A terrarium is like an aquarium, except it holds land animals, such as reptiles, rodents, and insects. An iguana is a specific species of reptile. An aviary is a cage in which birds are kept. A parakeet is a specific bird species. (A) is incorrect because bird is generic.

33. **(C)** The absence of light is the state of darkness. The absence of money is the state of destitution. (D) is the only other choice that might work, but it's too much of a stretch to work. The absence of wisdom is stupidity, not immorality. This question is tricky because the student is tempted to think of light and dark as antonyms without considering that light could be used as a noun, while dark is used as an adjective.

34. **(E)** The duty of a student is to learn. The duty of a counselor is to advise.

35. **(A)** The thorax is the part of the body that comes between the head and abdomen. It comes right before and is attached to the abdomen. In a tree, the trunk comes right before and is connected to the roots.

36. **(B)** The purpose of aiming is to increase accuracy. The purpose of stretching is to increase flexibility.

37. **(E)** An actor is an active player or participant in a production. A soldier is an active player or participant in a battle.

38. **(D)** A mouse is a type of rodent. A gorilla is a type of primate.

39. **(C)** A shade of a color is a subtle variation of that color. A nuance of a word is a subtle meaning or variation in meaning of the word.

40. **(C)** Something that is invaluable has an immense or immeasurably high price. Invaluable means so precious that a price cannot be assigned to it. Something immense has an extremely large size.

41. **(B)** A trinket is a cheap artifact or souvenir. A treasure is something worth a lot. A rock is fairly worthless, but a gem is worth a lot. Thus, the analogy is one of a matter of degree.

42. **(E)** A diplomat is a type of emissary. A proxy is a type of agent.

43. **(A)** The purpose of a palisade, which is a fence or barrier of stakes or spikes, is to provide defense. The purpose of an academy is to provide scholarship. (D) is incorrect because the purpose of museums is to display and inform, not to provide tourism. (C) doesn't work because a palace itself does not provide nobility; it is where nobility resides. (E) doesn't work because the word bulk is too generic. A warehouse provides storage, not bulk.

44. **(D)** Zeal means enthusiasm and passion. Phlegmatic means difficult to excite or sluggish; it is essentially the adjective of the antonym of zeal. Opacity is the state of being opaque or

impenetrable to light. Transparent, which means see through, is the antonym of opaque.

45. **(E)** Treatment of illness leads to remission, if the treatment is successful. Therapy leads to rehabilitation, if the therapy is successful.

46. **(B)** Talkative means inclined to talk a lot. One who is talkative is not likely to be withdrawn, so the two words are almost opposite in spirit, though they're not exact antonyms. Flagrant means very obvious, usually in an offensive way. Inconspicuous means hard to detect or not obvious, so they are almost antonyms. (A), (C), and (D) are incorrect because the analogies are synonyms. (E) is the next best choice, but idiosyncratic and flattering aren't antonymous enough to be the correct answer.

47. **(B)** Dilapidated means run down as a result of neglect. Or, in other words, neglect leads to something becoming dilapidated. When one is deprived of something, he or she becomes rapacious, which means hungry or greedy, for it.

48. **(A)** Admonish means to warn or scold lightly. Lambaste means to berate severely. Thus, the words reflect a difference in magnitude of severity. Irk means to irritate. Infuriate means to anger severely, so irk and infuriate are different in magnitude of severity or intensity.

49. **(D)** A scapegoat is someone who receives the blame of a problem, while the hero is the person who resolves a problem. They are thus opposites. A hedonist is a pleasure seeker, and a puritan is one who abides by strict principles and often denies himself pleasures. Thus, a hedonist and a puritan are antonyms.

50. **(A)** Interception is a form of interference, and intercept is the verb form of interception. Divulgence is a form of revelation because to divulge information is to reveal information.

51. **(B)** Shingles comprise the outer layer of a roof. The epidermis comprises the outer layer of skin.

52. **(E)** The purpose of a ballast is to control or provide buoyancy. The purpose of a catalyst is to provide or facilitate change.

53. **(D)** A zookeeper's job is to look after the animals in a zoo. A jailor's job is to look after the prisoners of a jail or penitentiary. (A) is not as good of an answer because, while librarians do look after books, books are not living things, and there is no element of captivity. (C) is not correct because a ward and a charge are synonyms. (E) is incorrect because a hunter does not look after a victim.

54. **(A)** Nostalgia is a longing for the past or what once was. In other words, nostalgia is characterized by longing. Desperation is characterized by begging.

55. **(C)** Unorthodox is not traditional or routine. Mundane means ordinary, while illustrious means glorified, so they are antonyms. (D) is the next best choice, as cautionary means "serving as a warning," and excessive means "more than needed," so the correlation might be drawn that something cautionary is warning not to be excessive. But that is a stretch because cautionary could also warn against being too frugal or modest. Thus, (C) is the best choice.

56. **(C)** A speech is extemporaneous if it is given impromptu or without prior planning. A decision is whimsical if it is made without prior planning or thought.

57. **(A)** A pariah is someone who was exiled. A paragon is someone who is admired. Thus, the verbs used match the definition of the nouns they are paired up with.

58. **(D)** A genre is a specific type of category, as used in books, television, and music. A robbery is a specific type of theft crime.

59. **(D)** Filial means of or pertaining to a son or daughter. Thus, the word filial directly applies to the word daughter. Parental means of or pertaining to parents. A father is a parent, so parental applies directly to father.

60. **(B)** A quarry is where stones are harvested or obtained. An orchard is where fruits are harvested.

Section 4: Quantitative Reasoning

1. **(D)** Round 74,706 to 75,000 and 298 to 300. $75,000 \div 300 = 750 \div 3 = 250$. And, in fact, $74,706 \div 298 = 250.69$.

2. **(B)** $1.05 \times 24 = 1 \times 24 + 0.05 \times 24 = 24 + 1.2 = 25.2$

3. **(C)** First, find the common denominator for the mixed fractions and convert:

   $55\frac{5}{13} - 24\frac{10}{13} + 40\frac{15}{39} = 55\frac{15}{39} - 24\frac{30}{39} + 40\frac{15}{39}$
   $55\frac{15}{39} - 24\frac{30}{39} = 54\frac{54}{39} - 24\frac{30}{39} = 30\frac{24}{39}$
   $30\frac{24}{39} + 40\frac{15}{39} = 70\frac{39}{39} = 71$

4. **(A)** $2(2+5)^2 + (-18) \times 4 - 3 \div 3 = 2(7)^2 + -72 - 1 = 98 - 72 - 1 = 26 - 1 = 25$

5. **(D)** Set up the following equation:

   $225 = 1.25x$
   $x = \frac{225}{1.25} = \frac{225 \times 100}{125} = \frac{\cancel{25} \times 9 \times \cancel{100}\,20}{\cancel{25} \times \cancel{5}} = 180$

6. **(D)** Set up the following equation:

   $15 - 2T = 4 \rightarrow 2T = 15 - 4 = 11$
   $T = 5.5 \rightarrow 3T = 16.5 \rightarrow 3T + 6 = 22.5$

7. **(E)** Substitute 3 for a and 2 for b to get: $3(3)^3 + 4(2)^4 = 3 \times 27 + 4 \times 16 = 81 + 64 = 145$

8. **(B)** The plot of land has a perimeter of 50 m. If one side length is 10, then the other side length must be 15. The area is 10 m × 15 m = 150 m². If both sides are increased by 5 m, the new area is 15 m × 20 m = 300 m², an increase in area of 150 m², or 100% of the area of the original plot.

9. **(B)** If x is divisible by 9, we can write x as: $x = 9n$, where n is some integer. And since y is divisible by 5, we can write y as: $y = 5m$, where m is some integer. This means $xy = 45mn$. 45 is divisible by 15, so $45mn$ is as well. (A) is incorrect because the least common multiple of xy depends on the values of m and n. 45 is only the least common multiple of x and y if m and n

   are each equal to 1. (C) is incorrect because m and n would have to both be 1 for $x + y$ to equal 14. (D) is incorrect because the greatest common factor of x and y depends on the value of m and n. (E) is incorrect because $x - y$ isn't necessarily a multiple of 4. For instance, if x is 18 and y is 5, then $x - y = 13$, which 4 can't divide.

10. **(A)** Substitute 7 for x to get: $(7 - 5)(7 + 6) = (2)(13) = 26$. Using techniques of FOIL, we can also rewrite the expression as $7^2 + 6(7) - 5(7) - 30 = 7^2 + 7(6 - 5) - 30 = 7^2 + 7 - 30$.

11. **(D)** The value of 4 is 40,000. The value of 6 is 600. The value of 9 is 0.9. Thus, the sum of these values is $40,000 + 600 + 0.9 = 40,600.9$.

12. **(C)** If the perimeter of the field is 32 feet, then the greatest area that can result is if the dimensions of the field are 8 ft × 8 ft = 64 ft². It is not possible to get an area greater than 64 ft².

    Note: The more like a square a rectangle is, the greater the area is, assuming the same perimeter.

13. **(C)** $5\frac{3}{7} + 3\frac{1}{14} + 2 = 5\frac{6}{14} + 3\frac{1}{14} + 2 = 8\frac{7}{14} + 2 = 10\frac{7}{14} = 10\frac{1}{2} = 10.5$

14. **(C)** To find the train's rate of travel, divide 500 miles by 6 hours to get: 83.33 miles per hour.

15. **(A)** "The difference of five times a number and six times another number" can be written as $5x - 6y$, so we can write the following inequality: $5x - 6y \leq 10y$. Add $6y$ to both sides to get $5x \leq 16y$.

16. **(A)** Subtract 15 from 134 to get 119. 119 is evenly divisible by 7: $119 \div 7 = 17$, so each equal piece of string is 17 cm. To conclusively eliminate the other choices, subtract the remainder from 134 and divide the result by 7 to see that 7 does not evenly divide the quotient.

17. **(C)** 0.4 (40%) × 155 (total children) = 62 children bought cotton candy. 25% of the adults bought popcorn, so 0.25 × 104 = 26 adults bought popcorn. 62 + 26 = 88 carnival attendees bought a snack. There were 155 + 104 = 259

attendees. $259 - 88 = 171$ people didn't buy snacks. This means that $171 - 88 = 83$ more people didn't buy snacks than did buy snacks.

18. **(C)** Use elimination to solve this problem.

(A) is incorrect: If $0 < x < 1$, then $0 > -x > -1$, because the signs flip when multiplying by a negative. Adding 1 to all of the terms yields $1 > -x + 1 > 0$, which can be rewritten as $0 < 1 - x < 1$. Thus, the range of values for $1 - x$ is still between 0 and 1. **(B) is incorrect:** $1/x > 1$, since 1 divided by any number less than 1, but greater than 0, will always yield a quotient greater than 1. Thus, (B) > (A). **(D) is incorrect:** $x^4 = (x^2)^2$ will be even smaller than x^2, since x is between 0 and 1. And since we're not dividing 1 by x^4, (D) can't be the answer. $1/(x^4)$ would be the greatest possible value, but that's not an option.

Why (C) is correct: $1/(x^2) > 1$, since the square of any number between 0 and 1 is a smaller number. 1 divided by an even smaller number will give an even bigger quotient, so (C) > (B).

19. **(C)** Find the rate of cleaning for each girl. Cynthia's rate of cleaning is ½ pool per hour. Cassie's rate of cleaning is 1/3 pool per hour.

Combined, they clean at a rate of $½ + 1/3 = 5/6$ pool per hour, meaning it takes 6/5 hours to clean 1 pool. To clean a pool double the size is to clean 2 pools, so it will take $6/5 × 2 = 12/5 = 2.4$ hours. 0.4 hours $= 0.4 × 60 = 24$ minutes, so it will take them 2 hours and 24 minutes.

20. **(D)** Marla spent $\$11.20 ÷ 8$ liters $= \$1.40$ per liter. Sandy spent $\$15.60 ÷ (6 × 2) = \$1.30$ per liter. Thus, Sandy got the better overall deal, by $\$1.40 - \$1.30 = \$0.10$ per liter.

21. **(D)** Make a chart with the possible coins.

Quarters	Dimes	Pennies
3	0	2
2	2	7
1	5	2
0	7	7

It is not possible to have fewer dimes in each row because each dime would need to be replaced by 10 pennies, and that would bring the total number of pennies over 10. Thus, the above chart shows all of the possibilities by which 77 cents can be made, given the conditions.

22. **(B)** Out of the 200 students, 47 were undecided, so $200 - 47 = 153$ were interested in math, English, or both. 99 were interested in math and 87 in English. $99 + 87 = 186$, which is more than 153, indicating that some students expressed interest in both. If x is the number of students interested in both math and English, the number of students interested in only math is $99 - x$, and the number of students interested in only English is $87 - x$. We can write the following equation: $(99 - x) + (87 - x) + x = 153$, since 153 represents the sum of the number of students interested in only math, only English, and both math and English.

$186 - 2x + x = 186 - x = 153$
$x = 186 - 153 = 33$

23. **(B)** Let h represent the value of the height of the triangle:

$h = 2b - 4$, so $A = ½ × b × (2b - 4)$

$A = ½ × b × 2(b - 2) = b × (b - 2)$, since ½ and 2 are multiplicative inverses and thus cancel out. $b × (b - 2) = b^2 - 2b$

24. **(C)** The fifth person spends an average of $\$600.00$ on food per month, since his average food expenditure is double that of everyone else. The total food expenditures of the 5 people per month is $4 × 300.00 + \$600.00 = \$1,800.00$. To find the average food expenditure per person is therefore $\$1,800 ÷ 5 = \$360.00$.

25. **(D)** The larger sector formed by radii OA and OB has an angle measure of $360° - 144° = 216°$.
$\dfrac{216°}{360°} = 0.6 = 60\%$. Thus, the percent of the area that the sector comprises is also 60%.

SSAT
UPPER LEVEL
TEST KEY 3

Sections 1 & 4: Quantitative Reasoning

Directions: For each question, record your answer in the column where it says "Your Answer", next to the number of the question. If your answer does not match the correct answer, mark an 'X' in the column labeled "X|O". If you omitted the question, leave the space blank and mark 'O' in the "X|O" column.

Section 1

#	Correct Answer	Your Answer	X|O	Concepts Tested
1	E			AG
2	A			ARO
3	E			ARO
4	E			NT
5	E			ARO
6	B			AG
7	C			AG
8	B			ARO
9	E			SP
10	A			AG
11	D			AG
12	D			DSP
13	C			GM
14	A			DSP
15	B			AG
16	D			DSP
17	C			FG
18	D			FG
19	C			DSP
20	C			AG
21	D			GM
22	A			NT
23	E			ARO
24	B			GM
25	D			GM

Section 4

#	Correct Answer	Your Answer	X|O	Concepts Tested
1	E			NT
2	E			AG
3	D			ARO
4	A			GM
5	C			AG
6	D			AG
7	B			AG
8	B			AG
9	B			ARO
10	E			AG
11	B			DSP
12	D			GM
13	A			GM
14	D			GM
15	C			DSP
16	B			ARO
17	C			DSP
18	D			DSP
19	D			AG
20	D			AG
21	B			GM
22	A			AG
23	E			NT
24	B			AG
25	A			SP

CONCEPTS TESTED LEGEND

ARO – Arithmetic Operations
AG – Algebra

FG – Functions & Graphs
SP – Spatial Perception
NT – Number Theory

GM – Geometry & Measurement
DSP – Data Analysis, Statistics, & Probability

SCORING

Total Omitted (TO): _____

Total Incorrect (TI): _____

Total Missed (TM): _____
(TO + TI)

Raw Score: $50 - \mathbf{TM} - 0.25 \times \mathbf{TI}$

$50 - \underline{} - 0.25 \times \underline{} =$

$\boxed{}$

Rounded Raw Score: _____
(Round to the nearest integer value.)

Section 2: Reading Comprehension

Directions: For each question, record your answer in the column where it says "Your Answer", next to the number of the question. If your answer does not match the correct answer, mark an 'X' in the column labeled "X|O". If you omitted the question, leave the space blank and mark 'O' in the "X|O" column.

#	Correct Answer	Your Answer	X|O	Concepts Tested
1	D			INF
2	E			DEF
3	A			INF
4	D			INF
5	D			ID
6	E			MIP
7	C			ID
8	B			ID
9	D			ID
10	E			ID
11	C			MIP
12	D			ID
13	D			INF
14	D			INF
15	D			MIP
16	A			INF
17	B			ID
18	E			INF
19	A			ID
20	C			AT

#	Correct Answer	Your Answer	X|O	Concepts Tested
21	E			INF
22	B			INF
23	C			ID
24	A			ID
25	B			INF
26	C			ID
27	C			INF
28	D			INF
29	C			ID
30	B			INF
31	A			INF
32	C			AT
33	B			INF
34	B			ID
35	D			DEF
36	B			AT
37	D			ID
38	D			ID
39	A			INF
40	C			INF

CONCEPTS TESTED LEGEND

ID – Identifying Details
MIP – Main Idea or Purpose

INF – Inference & Assumption
AT – Author's Tone

DEF – Definition in Context

SCORING

Total Omitted (TO): _____

Total Incorrect (TI): _____

Total Missed (TM): _____
(TO + TI)

Raw Score: $40 - \text{TM} - 0.25 \times \text{TI}$

$40 - \text{_____} - 0.25 \times \text{_____} = $

_____

Rounded Raw Score: _____
(Round to the nearest integer value.)

174

Section 3: Verbal Reasoning

Directions: For each question, record your answer in the column where it says "Your Answer", next to the number of the question. If your answer does not match the correct answer, mark an 'X' in the column labeled "X|O". If you omitted the question, leave the space blank and mark 'O' in the "X|O" column.

#	Correct Answer	Your Answer	X|O	Concepts Tested	#	Correct Answer	Your Answer	X|O	Concepts Tested
1	C			SYN	31	E			AN
2	D			SYN	32	C			AN
3	A			SYN	33	B			AN
4	E			SYN	34	A			AN
5	E			SYN	35	A			AN
6	A			SYN	36	A			AN
7	B			SYN	37	B			AN
8	B			SYN	38	D			AN
9	C			SYN	39	E			AN
10	C			SYN	40	A			AN
11	A			SYN	41	D			AN
12	C			SYN	42	C			AN
13	D			SYN	43	C			AN
14	B			SYN	44	A			AN
15	A			SYN	45	B			AN
16	C			SYN	46	D			AN
17	B			SYN	47	E			AN
18	E			SYN	48	B			AN
19	B			SYN	49	A			AN
20	D			SYN	50	A			AN
21	D			SYN	51	D			AN
22	E			SYN	52	C			AN
23	B			SYN	53	A			AN
24	A			SYN	54	A			AN
25	C			SYN	55	C			AN
26	E			SYN	56	C			AN
27	D			SYN	57	E			AN
28	E			SYN	58	D			AN
29	C			SYN	59	A			AN
30	E			SYN	60	C			AN

SCORING

Total Omitted (TO): _____

Total Incorrect (TI): _____

Total Missed (TM): _____
(TO + TI)

Raw Score: $60 - \text{TM} - 0.25 \times \text{TI}$

$60 - \rule{2cm}{0.4pt} - 0.25 \times \rule{2cm}{0.4pt} =$

$\boxed{}$

Rounded Raw Score: _____
(Round to the nearest integer value.)

Section 1: Quantitative Reasoning

1. **(E)** If $2P - 8 = 10 \div P$, then we can rewrite the equation as:

$$2P - 8 = \frac{10}{P} \rightarrow 2(P - 4) = \frac{10}{P}$$

Divide both sides by 2 to get: $P - 4 = \frac{5}{P}$

Multiply both sides by P:

$$P^2 - 4P = 5 \rightarrow P^2 - 4P - 5 = 0$$

Factor to get: $(P - 5)(P + 1) = 0$

Thus, the possible solutions of P are 5 and -1, but since -1 is not a choice, (E) is correct.

2. **(A)** Use elimination. (B) is incorrect because 51 = 3 × 17. (C) is incorrect because 85 = 5 × 17. (D) is incorrect because 170 = 10 × 17. (E) is incorrect because 340 = 20 × 17.

3. **(E)** Carla drives a total of 15 miles and spends an hour (10 + 20 + 30 minutes = 60 minutes = 1 hour) doing so. Thus, her overall speed is 15 miles per hour.

4. **(E)** Use elimination to solve this problem.

   (A) is wrong: if either x or y is negative, then the product of x and y will be less than 0. **(B) is wrong:** $x + y$ just has to be less than 1, so if x is less than 0.5, y can also be less than 0.5. **(C) is wrong:** y can be greater than 0.5, if x is less than 0.5. For instance, if $x = 0.3$, then y could be 0.6, which is greater than 0.5. **(D) is wrong:** if x is greater than 0.5, y cannot be greater than 0.5.

   (E) is correct because if x is greater than 0.5, then y must be less than 0.5.

5. **(E)** Dividing 6 by 11 results in the decimal 0.545454..., so 54.54% is closest in percent.

6. **(B)** Let a represent the price of a cake, b that of a cupcake, and c that of a box of candles.

   Sunnie spent $a + 2b + c = \$42.35$, while Sunnie's sister spent $a + 3b = \$42.66$. Subtracting the equations, we can find the difference in price between a cupcake and a box of candles:

   $$a + 3b - (a + 2b + c) = \$42.66 - \$42.35 = \$0.31$$
   $$b - c = \$0.31 \rightarrow b = \$0.31 + c$$

   This indicates that b is \$0.31 more expensive than c. Thus, a cupcake is \$0.31 more expensive than a box of candles at the bakery.

7. **(C)** I is not necessarily true. x can be even. For instance, if $x = 2$, then $z^2 - y^2 = 2(2)^2 = 8$. If $z = 3$ and $y = 1$, the equation is satisfied, as $9 - 1 = 8$.

   II is not valid. Because x, y, and z are positive integers, if $z = y$, then $x = 0$, but 0 is not a positive integer. Also, if z is less than y, then $z^2 - y^2$ would be negative, which is not possible.

   III is valid because if z is even, then z^2 is even, and that means y must be even, since $2x^2$ is even.

8. **(B)** $\dfrac{5^4(5^3 + 5^2)}{125} = \dfrac{5^{\cancel{4}}(5^3 + 5^2)}{\cancel{5^3}} = 5(5^3 + 5^2) =$
   $5(125 + 25) = 5(150) = 750$

   The only number 740 is divisible by is 15. 750 = 15 × 50.

9. **(E)** To solve this, you must realize that, to remove a corner from a cube by removing an isosceles right triangle from corners of the numbered squares, exactly 3 corners, one from 3 different squares, must be removed. This is because each corner of a cube is formed by the meeting of three faces of the cube. Luckily, the problem makes this apparent, as each answer choice only deals with three squares.
   But because the squares fold up to create the cube, it is important that the cut off corners of the squares touch when folded.

   Use elimination to solve this problem.

   (A) is wrong: the bottom corners of square 1 won't meet with any of square 4's corners.

(B) is wrong: while the bottom right corner of square 1 and the bottom left corner of square 2 do meet, the top right corner of square 6 will not meet the aforementioned corners of squares 1 and 2. (If the choice had stated the top left corner, then that would work.)

(C) is wrong: the top left corner of square 1 will not touch any edge or corner of square 4. Only the top left and bottom left corners of square 1 make contact with the top and bottom right corners of square 4, when folded.

(D) is wrong: while the bottom right corner of square 2 and the bottom left corner of square 3 meet, neither of those corners connect with any of the edges or corners of square 4.

(E) is correct: the bottom right corner of square 3, the bottom left corner of square 4, and the bottom right corner of square 6 meet.

10. **(A)** $a - b = c \div d \rightarrow a - b = \dfrac{c}{d}$

$b = a - \dfrac{c}{d} = \dfrac{ad}{d} - \dfrac{c}{d} = \dfrac{ad - c}{d}$

11. **(D)** $4 ⚫ 3 = (3 + 4)^2 - 2(3)(4) =$
$7^2 - 24 = 49 - 24 = 25 = 5^2$

12. **(D)** The mean score is the average score, so the total score is $87 \times 4 = 348$. The median score is 85, but when there is an even number of data points, the median score is the average of the two middle numbers. Thus, 85 represents the mean of the middle two numbers, indicating that the sum of the middle two numbers is $85 \times 2 = 170$. This means that the sum of the highest and lowest test scores is $348 - 170 = 178$.

13. **(C)** If the length of a diagonal is 14 cm, then we can set up an isosceles right triangle with side lengths of x. And applying the Pythagorean Theorem, we get:

$x^2 + x^2 = 14^2$
$2x^2 = 196, x^2 = 98$

Since the area of the square is x^2, there's no need to find x first.

14. **(A)** Ronaldo has $10 + 8 + 5 + 4 + 3 = 30$ marbles in all. After withdrawing a yellow one and not replacing it, Ronaldo has left in the box a total of 29 marbles, of which 2 are yellow. Thus, the probability of drawing a yellow marble is 2/29.

15. **(B)** $(x - 5)^2 - 3x + 11 = (x^2 - 10x + 25) - 3x + 11$
$= x^2 - 13x + 36 = (x - 9)(x - 4)$

16. **(D)** Julianna can make the following pairs of letters, without regard to the order of the letters:

AB, AC, AD, AE, AF (5)
BC, BD, BE, BF (4)
CD, CE, CF (3)
DE, DF (2)
EF (1)

That's a total of $5 + 4 + 3 + 2 + 1 = 15$ pairs.

Since the order matters, for each pair, there are two possible passcodes that can be made. For instance, from AB, both AB and BA are each different passcodes. Thus, the total number of passcodes that can be generated is $15 \times 2 = 30$.

17. **(C)** The mean of the values can be found by adding all of the listed values of y and dividing by the number of data points there are: $-5.25 + -3 + -1.89 + -1.25 + 0.19 = -11.2$. Since there are 5 data points, the mean is $-11.2 \div 5 = -2.24$. The median is the middle term, or -1.89. The difference between -2.24 and -1.89 is:
$-1.89 - (-2.24) = 0.35$.

18. **(D)** To solve this problem, use elimination. Substitute each value of x into the equation listed by the answer choice and see if the resulting value matches the y value in the table. (D) is the only one that works for all of the listed x values.

19. **(C)** The two most tempting choices here are (C) and (E), but (E) is incorrect because we're not calculating the probability that both dice will be 4, which would be 1/36.

We're calculating the probability that the second die roll will result in 4. The probability of getting any of the numbers is 1/6. Thus, the probability that he will get 4 on his second throw is 1/6.

20. **(C)** Isolate the movements of the vehicles.

Car and Van:

At noon, the car leaves Town M at a rate of 70 miles per hour (mph). When the van leaves Town N at 2 pm, the car has already traveled 70 × 2 = 140 miles. Thus, the distance between the car and the van at 2 pm is 680 – 140 = 540 miles.

Because the car travels at 70 mph and the van travels at 65 mph, they travel at a combined rate of 70 + 65 = 135 mph. For the car and the van to meet, it will take them 540 miles ÷ 135 mph = 4 hours. Thus, they will meet at 4 + 2 = 6 pm.

Bus:

The bus leaves Town M at 1:30 pm at 90 mph. By the time the car and the van meet at 6 pm, the bus has traveled 6 – 1.5 = 4.5 hours. Thus, it has traveled a distance of 90 mph × 4.5 hours = 405 miles from Town M when the car and van meet. This is 680 – 405 = 275 miles from Town N.

21. **(D)** According to the coordinates given, the easiest way to think about the triangle when calculating its area is to say that the triangle's base is the segment connecting points A and C and that the height is the distance from point B to the origin of the coordinate plane.

    Using segment AC as the base, we get a base length of 7 units, since 3 – (-4) = 7. Drawing a perpendicular line segment from point B to the base results in a segment drawn from B to the origin. This segment (the altitude) has a height of 3 units. The area of triangle ABC is therefore ½ × 7 × 3 = ½ × 21 = 10.5 units^2.

22. **(A)** There are two ways to solve this.

    Method 1: Multiply

    $28 \times 28 \times 28 = 21,952$
    $37 \times 37 \times 37 \times 37 = 1,874,161$

    Thus, the sum of the unit digits is 2 + 1 = 3.

    Method 2: Look for a Pattern

Since we're only looking for the unit digits, we can concentrate our focus on the unit digits only. Find the unit's digit of 28^3 by calculating 8^3. $8 \times 8 \times 8 = 512$, so 2 is the unit digit of 28^3.

Find the unit's digit of 37^4 by calculating 7^4. $7 \times 7 \times 7 \times 7 = 2,401$, so 1 is the unit digit of 37^4.

The sum of the unit's digits is thus 2 + 1 = 3.

23. **(E)** $5^2 – 4 \times 3 + 7 \div 7 = 5^2 – (4 \times 3) + (7 \div 7) = 25 – 12 + 1 = 14$.

    To find the difference of Raymond's answer and the correct answer is 14 – 10 = 4

24. **(B)** Use elimination to solve this problem:

    (A) is wrong: 8 ft × 40 ft gives a perimeter of 2(8 + 40) = 2(48) = 96 ft; **(C) is wrong:** 32 ft × 10 ft gives a perimeter of 2(32 + 10) = 2(42) = 84 ft; **(D) is wrong:** 64 ft × 5 ft gives a perimeter of 2(64 + 5) = 2(69) = 138 ft; **(E) is wrong**: 80 ft × 4 ft gives a perimeter of 2(80 + 4) = 2(84) = 168 ft.

    (B) is correct: 16 ft × 20 ft gives a perimeter of 2(16 + 20) = 2(36) = 72 ft;

25. **(D)** To find the area of triangle BCD, we must know the height. To find the height of triangle BCD, which is an obtuse triangle, draw a perpendicular line from point B to segment AD. (Incidentally, the height of triangle BCD is the same as that of triangle ABC.)

    Because triangle ABC is equilateral, the height is the altitude from the midpoint of segment AC to point B, resulting in two right triangles. The hypotenuse of each of these right triangles is 6 in., and the base of each is half of the length of the segment AC, or 3 in. Use the Pythagorean Theorem to find the height of triangle ABC:

    $$3^2 + h^2 = 6^2 \rightarrow h^2 = 36 – 9 = 27$$
    $$h = \sqrt{27} = 3\sqrt{3}$$

    Thus, the area of triangle BCD can be calculated by ½ × 6 × $3\sqrt{3}$ = 3 × $3\sqrt{3}$ = $9\sqrt{3}$ in^2.

Section 2: Reading Comprehension

Cryptids

1. **(D)** The passage's use of such words as "many people" (line 5) and "the debate rages on" (line 8) indicates that the Yeti, Loch Ness monster, and Bigfoot have been discussed extensively. (A) is incorrect because confirmed or corroborated evidence of the cryptids does not exist. (B) is incorrect, according to lines 4-7. (C) is incorrect because it is possible that someday their existence will be completely debunked or that their existence will be proven. (E) is incorrect because the existence of cryptids has not been debunked.

2. **(E)** Lines 8-10 indicate that until the existence of these mythological creatures has either been verified or debunked, they will be referred to as cryptids, thus suggesting that the term cryptids is used to refer to creatures that may or may not be real. (A) is incorrect. If a creature's existence has been debunked, it would no longer be referred to as a cryptid. (B) is incorrect for the opposite reason of (A). (C) is incorrect because ancient mythology is not referred to. (D) is incorrect because appreciation levels are not discussed.

3. **(A)** This passage would most likely be found in a school report on cryptozoology because of the informal yet factual approach and tone it takes. It is too long for a dictionary entry for the word *cryptid*, so (B) is not correct. It is too factual and informal (the opening line) for a science fiction novel, so (C) is not correct. (D) is incorrect because this passage is not about hominids, which are humans and their ancestors. It's not (E) because it is not about a specific cryptid sighting.

4. **(D)** If an ancient diary containing the author's admission to devising the creatures of lore in order to scare children were found, that would be the best chance of disproving the existence of the creatures of lore. It would provide evidence for why people believe cryptids to exist and why they actually don't. (A) would not disprove the existence of creatures of lore because if the DNA obtained turned out to be from known species, that still doesn't deny the possibility of the existence of these cryptids. (B) is incorrect for the same reason as (A) in the sense that the absence of evidence does not disprove the existence of the creatures of lore. (C) is also incorrect for the same logical reasons as (A) and (B). (E) is stronger support for disproving the existence of (A), (B), and (C), but stating that there's a less than 50% chance of the existence of cryptids doesn't fully rule out cryptids' existence.

Ethics of Cloning

5. **(D)** Lines 18-19 indicate that Neanderthals were genetically close enough to humans to perform *many* of the same tasks, but (D) states that Neanderthals knew how to perform *all* of the same tasks. (A) is incorrect because line 16 indicates that Neanderthals probably went extinct nearly 30,000 years ago. (B) is incorrect because lines 18-20 indicate that Neanderthals were probably capable of using tools and building fires. (C) is incorrect because line 19 indicates that the Neanderthals were genetically close enough to humans to do many of the same things early humans did. (E) is incorrect because lines 16-17 indicate that the extinction of Neanderthals had something to do with competition with modern humans.

6. **(E)** This passage discusses the ethics of cloning animals and asks where we should draw the lines of ethics. (A) is incorrect because the author does not necessarily reveal new information about Neanderthals. (B) is incorrect because there is no language used in the passage to indicate a demand for animal experimentation to stop. (C) is incorrect because it makes it seem the author finds the idea of cloning Neanderthals to be acceptable. (D) is incorrect because there is no mention in the passage of whether the author would find cloning lower order species acceptable.

7. **(C)** Lines 1-7 discuss the birth of Dolly's clone and the ramifications it had on society. Lines 3-7 in particular discuss just how contentious Dolly's clone proved to be, with regard to the ethics questions cloning raises. (A) is incorrect because

there is nothing in the passage to suggest that clones are mindless bodies. (B) is incorrect because there is no reference to the possibility of widespread war. (D) is incorrect because overpopulation is not discussed. (E) is incorrect because the expenses involved with cloning sheep are not discussed.

8. **(B)** Lines 25-31 raise questions about the fairness to the Neanderthal clone. If it were kept in a laboratory setting, would that be fair to the Neanderthal? Moreover, if it were allowed to try to integrate into society, would that be fair to the Neanderthal? Either way, cloning a Neanderthal would raise many ethical questions. (A) is incorrect because the genetic compatibility of a Neanderthal fetus and human surrogate mother is not an issue raised by the passage. The passage assumes that they would be compatible. (C) is incorrect because a potential media frenzy is not discussed. (D) is incorrect because the practical knowledge of caring for a Neanderthal child is not an issue in the passage. (E) is incorrect because the cost of cloning a Neanderthal is not discussed.

9. **(D)** Lines 23-25 indicate that it is not difficult to imagine that Neanderthals would have had many of the same feelings and emotions that we do now. (A) is incorrect because the ability of Neanderthals to defend themselves is not discussed. (B) is incorrect because language barriers are not discussed. (C) is incorrect because it is not possible to assume that the Neanderthal would lament or regret being brought into the modern world. (E) is incorrect because the Neanderthal's ability to operate modern technology is not discussed.

Battery Degradation

10. **(E)** Lines 4-8 indicate that over time lithium ions cause structural damage to the battery and that this degradation in the battery's structural integrity is what causes batteries to lose charge over time. (A) is incorrect because the charges themselves don't wear out over time. (B) is incorrect because it is not known how lithium interacts with the walls of the batteries. (C) is incorrect. While batteries do not perfectly contain electric charges, this does not mean that engineers are unable to develop such technology.

(D) is incorrect because the construction of the hull of the batteries is not necessarily poorly done.

11. **(C)** The main idea of the passage is the discovery of why batteries lose their charge and how this information could be useful in building batteries in the future. (A) is incorrect because it is not known when, if ever, longer lasting batteries are coming. (B) is incorrect because the passage is not about making homemade batteries. (D) is incorrect because the latest electronic standards and their compatibility with batteries is not discussed. (E) is incorrect because the passage doesn't present a dilemma regarding batteries.

12. **(D)** Lines 20-26 discuss pothole formation. In short, potholes are formed when ice crystals cause the asphalt to break apart where the asphalt is structurally the weakest.

13. **(D)** The degradation of batteries happens when lithium ions attack the weakest areas of the battery. Thus, (D) is the best choice. (A) is incorrect because it states the opposite of what happens in lithium ion batteries. (A) could be right if it stated that the fabric was wearing thin faster at the joints. (B) is incorrect because the strength of the buildings is ignored, since the earthquake is destroying resistant and nonresistant ones alike. (C) is incorrect because strength or durability is not at issue. (E) is incorrect for the same reason as (C); a predator stalks its prey before closing in, but the only reference point of strength is between the predator and prey, not prey and other prey.

14. **(D)** Lines 14-16 indicate that the scientists from the Department of Energy used advanced electron microscopy techniques to learn more about what was happening in batteries. Thus, it would make the most sense for an electron microscope to be used. None of the other devices are mentioned in the passage.

15. **(D)** The second paragraph details how batteries become structurally degraded. (A) is incorrect because the purpose of the passage is not to compare and contrast lithium ion batteries with asphalt. (B) is incorrect because the passage does not suggest an alternative to the use of lithium ion batteries. (C) is incorrect because the purpose

of the second paragraph is to discuss lithium ion batteries; the comparison to asphalt is there to help the reader conceptualize what is going on in lithium ion batteries. (E) is incorrect because the second paragraph does not show how lithium ion batteries are used in real-world settings.

Tractor Beams

16. **(A)** Lines 4-8 indicate that the tractor beam has been confined to the realm of imagination and fantasy. Recent developments, though, may blur the lines between reality and fiction and eventually eradicate these lines altogether. This shows that the author believes that phenomena in the realm of fiction may one day become reality. (B) is incorrect because tractors and trailers are not mentioned in the passage. (C) is incorrect because the passage does not discuss UFOs or other alien spacecraft. (D) is incorrect because instant teleportation is not discussed. (E) is incorrect because it is not known if tractor beams will eventually replace machinery used for lifting heavy objects.

17. **(B)** Lines 12-14 indicate that the latest "tractor" beam represented a breakthrough in that it was able to pull objects with over a billion times more force than previous models could. (A) is incorrect because tractor beam energy is not discussed as a real type of energy. (C) is incorrect because the size and portability of the latest "tractor beam" are not discussed. (D) is incorrect because previous models could move particles at the molecular level. (E) is incorrect because it is not known how much energy was needed to pull objects a billion times more massive.

18. **(E)** Lines 9-10 indicate that the physicists at Dundee University were able to use ultrasound technology to pull a hollow triangle to the energy source. Lines 15-17 indicate that the Dundee University scientists' beam is currently only capable of moving objects approximately 1 cm in size. Putting those facts together, it's possible to see that the hollow triangle must have been about 1 centimeter in size. (A) is incorrect because neither the mass nor the density of the triangle is discussed. (B) is incorrect because it is stated that the new prototype could pull objects about 1 cm, whereas the previous models could only pull

particles of molecular size. (C) is incorrect because it assumes that the triangle was either transparent or too thin or too small to see, but none of those are supported by the passage. Hollow does not mean invisible. (D) is incorrect because the ease with which the triangle could be picked up is not discussed.

19. **(A)** Lines 1-2 indicate that the term "tractor beam" was coined in 1931 by Edward Elmer Smith in his novel *Spacehounds of IPC*, not in 1913, as (D) states. (B) is incorrect because *Star Trek* borrowed the term. (C) is incorrect, unless *Spacehounds of IPC* was the first science fiction novel, but there is no support for that assumption. (E) is incorrect because tractor manufacturers are not discussed in the passage.

20. **(C)** The primary tone of this passage is informative, although the author is also slightly optimistic for the future. Since optimistic is not an answer, informative is the best choice. (A) is incorrect because incredulous means disbelieving. (B) is incorrect because bemused means puzzled, confused, or bewildered. (D) is incorrect because jaded means tired, bored, or worn out because of something. (E) is incorrect because ambivalent means having mixed feelings about something.

Farmer and His Land

21. **(E)** This passage is about a farmer who continues to fail time and time again, until the very end. (A) is incorrect because it is not necessarily a typical farmer's life story; there is no allusion to real life in the passage. (B) is incorrect because there's no information in the passage to indicate that the farmer was arrogant. (C) is incorrect because the story is not about just the successes and achievements of an individual; it is about his growth process. (D) is incorrect because there's nothing to indicate that this is a story of rebellion against a higher power or authority figure.

22. **(B)** Lines 14-15 indicate that the moon rose and sank many evenings and the sun rose and sank many days, with the farmer promising to restore his farm. But lines 16-17 also indicate that words are only words and empty promises are no

promises at all, indicating that the farmer failed to make good on his promise for a long time.

23. **(C)** The only question unanswered by the passage is what sorts of miracles gave the farmer brief spurts of renewed energy and dedication. (A) is incorrect because line 1 indicates that it had been 18 harvests since the time the farmer acquired the plot of land. (B) is incorrect because lines 20-22 indicate that the farmer acquired the land because of the land's awesomeness. (D) is incorrect because lines 24-27 indicate the physical hardships the farmer endured as he restored his farm. (E) is incorrect because lines 5-7 indicate that the farmer fell into depression because he could not yield the abundance of crops the farm had once enjoyed.

24. **(A)** Lines 18-23 are about how the farmer began the process of restoring his farm, and it started with him waking up early one day and stopping to pick up a tomato. (B) is incorrect because first he cleaned up his farm. (C) is incorrect because there is nothing to indicate that the farmer had planned to restore his farm when he stopped to pick up the first tomato. (D) is incorrect because while the passage did indicate that the farmer told himself he'd turn over a new leaf, he didn't actually begin the process of rebuilding his farm for good on purpose. It just happened naturally and almost automatically. Lines 19-20 indicate that the farmer just started picking up one tomato after another and that before he knew it he had cleaned up a large portion of his farm. The phrase "before he knew it" implies that it was by chance. (E) is incorrect because it implies intent to clean up, but as discussed for (D), he did not intend to clean up his farm.

25. **(B)** Lines 20-22 indicate that the farmer acquired the farm because of how awesome and sublime it had been, suggesting that the farm had once yielded an abundance of crops. Furthermore, lines 5-6 indicate directly that the farm had once yielded an abundance of crops. Thus, before the farmer acquired the farm, it had yielded an abundance of crops. (A) is incorrect because it cannot be assumed that the farmer's parents were the previous owners of the farm. (C) is incorrect because the success of the farm before and after the farmer's acquisition of it cannot be compared. (D) is incorrect because there is

nothing to indicate that the farm had ever been in a state of decay before the farmer acquired it. (E) is incorrect because it cannot be assumed that the farmer had very little experience with farming.

Beaufort Sea

26. **(C)** In lines 20-22, the passage states that the size of waves is often determined by how much wind blows across the water's surface. The greater distances winds can blow over open water, the bigger the resultant waves will be. None of the other choices are mentioned or suggested by the passage, even if they are logical or reasonable.

27. **(C)** Lines 7-11 indicate that the ice thaws out somewhat during the warmer months. For the Beaufort Sea, the coldest is during April and the warmest is during September. Thus, between April and September, the temperature gets warmer, so the sea thaws somewhat. The other choices are flatly incorrect.

28. **(D)** The last paragraph (lines 28-32) discusses the consequences of having more open water available. The last thing that the paragraph mentions is shoreline erosion, so it would make the most logical sense for the passage to continue with a discussion of shoreline erosion. (A) is incorrect because the passage does not focus at all on factories. (B) is incorrect because global warming's impact on nations and industries is not been discussed. (C) is incorrect because the passage does not discuss plants. (E) is incorrect because the passage makes no reference to the quantity of greenhouse gases that have been released into the atmosphere in the past three decades by the greater availability of open waters.

29. **(C)** Line 1 indicates that the Beaufort Sea spans 184,000 square miles, so (A) is incorrect. (B) and (D) is incorrect because lines 1-2 indicate that the Beaufort sea is north of both Alaska and Canada's Northwest Territories. (E) is incorrect because lines 2-4 indicate that the Beaufort Sea has never displayed any significant wave activity until September 2012. (C) is correct because it cannot be determined by the passage if the Beaufort Sea is the northernmost arctic sea in North America.

30. **(B)** Lines 20-27 indicate that once the cycle of sea ice loss begins, wave activity will allow ice to be broken up even more quickly, which allows sunlight to help melt ice more quickly, which then yields a greater surface area of open water. This consequently results in greater wave activity. Thus, this cycle would logically lead to an accelerated loss of sea ice, until the cycle is stopped. (A) is incorrect because it is not known if sea ice loss is most heavily impacted by sunlight. Although sunlight is a factor, wave activity is also one, and it is not mentioned which results in greater sea ice loss. (C) is incorrect because the passage does not mention or state that the cycle of sea ice loss is irreversible. (D) is incorrect because it is not a logically valid conclusion that can be drawn from the passage; for instance, it could be possible that the higher summer temperatures lead to sea ice loss. (E) is incorrect because other bodies of water are not discussed.

Stupid Burglar

31. **(A)** Lines 1-5 suggest that generally people perceive burglars as being very careful and meticulous. (B) is incorrect because, if anything, the passage suggests that burglars rarely get caught, if they were careful in their planning. (C) is incorrect because there is no mention of Hollywood. Further, even if Hollywood did glamorize criminal antiheros, glamorization and getting caught aren't necessarily related. (D) and (E) are incorrect because the passage suggests that most criminals do not leave blatant traces of their presence behind at crime scenes; logging into social media websites and forgetting to log out afterwards would be a blatant trace.

32. **(C)** Lines 7-8 indicate that the author believes Warner is stupid, so the author's tone can best be said to be contemptuous. That is, the author does not think highly of Warner. The other choices, especially (A) and (B), are the opposite of how the author feels. (D) is incorrect because it is not possible to tell whether the author also feels sympathetic for Warner's idiocy. (E) is incorrect because the passage does not indicate anything to be horrified of.

33. **(B)** The moral of the passage is two-fold and can be found in lines 13-15: 1) steer clear of crime

and 2) when you sabotage yourself as you commit a crime, you will pay the price for it. Thus, the answer that best reflects the moral of the story is to think before you act. (A) is incorrect because the passage is not suggesting readers to commit crimes. (C) is incorrect because the passage is not advocating the commission of crimes. Moreover, even if the passage were advocating the commission of crimes, it would not advocate logging into Facebook at the scene of the crime. (D) is incorrect because the passage is not saying that people should get into the habit of cleaning up after themselves. While it may be related to the moral of the passage, it is not exactly on point because it is too generic. (E) is incorrect because it is not on point. The passage has nothing to do with imitating or following what others are doing.

34. **(B)** Lines 8-10 list some of the items that were stolen. Cash, credit cards, a watch, and a checkbook are the items that are specifically listed. Jewelry may have been stolen, but it is impossible to infer from the passage that it was. Thus, the other choices are incorrect.

35. **(D)** The word *wrench* is being used figuratively to talk about something that caused plans to go wrong. Thus, hindrance is the best answer. (A), (B), and (C) are incorrect because the passage is not using the word wrench to mean something physical, tangible, or palpable. (E) is incorrect because *wrench* is not being used in the context of an interpretation of something else—perhaps a metaphor, which might be interpreted, but not an interpretation in and of itself.

Healthy Food Messages

36. **(B)** The author's tone in the first passage is satirical. He is not being serious or literal and is writing in jest and poking fun at the kids who refuse to eat healthy foods. (A) is incorrect because the tone is not metaphorical. The passage does not use comparisons between things, likening them to each other. (C) is incorrect because, if anything, the author sounds underappreciative. (D) is incorrect because the author does not seem he doesn't care. (E) is incorrect because the author is not expressing dramatic, frenzied emotion.

37. **(D)** Lines 12-19 indicate that when a positive message was associated with a food item, younger children said that the food was less tasty and opted to eat those foods less. (A) is thus incorrect. (B) is incorrect because the passage does not suggest that kids became more cognizant of the health implications or consequences of unhealthy foods as a result of the positive messaging. (C) is incorrect because it is stated that the kids were less likely to go for those foods, not avoid them altogether. (E) is incorrect because the positive messaging did in fact alter the kids' preferences for certain foods.

38. **(D)** Lines 20-22 indicate that it has been hypothesized that young children cannot process the possibility that foods can serve multiple purposes. (A) is incorrect because the passage indicates that healthy foods can still be scrumptious (line 6). (B) is incorrect. If young children sought out healthier foods because their bodies crave healthier foods more, then they wouldn't be inclined to turn down foods that have positive messages associated with them. (C) is incorrect because there is no mention of babies needing proper amounts of fats in reserve. (E) is incorrect because it may be the case that children only want to eat tasty foods, not healthy foods.

39. **(A)** Lines 15-19 indicate that compared to the kids in the control group, the kids who were told that foods also served healthy purposes were less likely to describe the foods as appetizing and to prefer eating those foods. Thus, it can be inferred that the kids in the control group did not receive the same positive message for the foods. (B) is incorrect. If the children in the control group were told the foods were extra healthy, then they would likely have shunned the foods more, too. (C) is incorrect because what the children in the control group believed is not discussed; also, it is not known whether the children in the control group even knew other children were being tested, too. (D) is incorrect because the prices of the foods are not discussed. (E) is incorrect because there is no evidence in the passage to suggest that the children in the control group received such instructions. Furthermore, because this is a scientific experiment, they likely would not have tried to compromise their findings by instructing the control group to behave a certain way.

40. **(C)** Lines 24-27 indicate that the research is certainly intriguing and may be worth considering before we present food to children and telling them that the food is healthy or good for them. (A) is incorrect because there is no discussion in the passage of trying to make unhealthy foods less appetizing. (B) is incorrect because the passage is not about trying to convince kids that healthy foods actually taste better than junk foods. (D) is incorrect because there is no discussion of biologists trying to make healthy foods taste better. (E) is incorrect because there is no indication that nutritionists would come up with new charts to deemphasize the health benefits of healthy foods. If anything, nutritionists would devise charts that more strongly emphasize the health benefits.

Section 3: Verbal Reasoning

Synonyms

1. **(C)** RAMBUNCTIOUS (adj.) means hard to control or wild. BOISTEROUS means wild and noisy, uncontrolled, or unrestrained.

2. **(D)** UNKEMPT (adj.) means not cared for or messy. DISHEVELED means untidy or disarranged or uncared for.

3. **(A)** ADAMANT (adj.) means absolutely unyielding or STUBBORN.

4. **(E)** CONDONE (v.) means to forgive, overlook, or PERMIT.

5. **(E)** PROVOKE (v.) means to anger or irritate. It can also mean to stir up or stimulate. EXCITE means to arouse or stir up emotionally.

6. **(A)** IMPARTIAL (adj.) means fair or objective. UNBIASED means not taking one side or another; in other words, it means fair or objective.

7. **(B)** SOPORIFIC (adj.) means causing or leading to sleep.

8. **(B)** JUBILATION (n.) means joy. EXULTATION also means joy or celebration.

9. **(C)** UTOPIA (n.) means an ideal or perfect place or state. PARADISE is closest in meaning because it means heaven or a perfect place.

10. **(C)** INNUENDO (n.) means an indirect message or statement regarding someone or something. Thus, SUGGESTION is the best answer because it means an idea that is introduced, implanted, or brought up indirectly.

11. **(A)** ABERRATION (n.) means a deviation from the norm. ODDITY means a peculiarity or strangeness; in other words something that's not normal.

12. **(C)** ANTITHESIS (n.) means complete opposite. ANTIPODE also means direct or exact opposite.

13. **(D)** COUNTENANCE (n.) means APPEARANCE, especially the look or expression one is wearing on his or her face.

14. **(B)** BEREFT (adj.) means lacking or DEPRIVED of.

15. **(A)** GOSSAMER (adj.) means flimsy, light, or THIN—lacking substance.

16. **(C)** FALLOW (adj.) means unplowed or uncultivated. It also means INACTIVE or not ready for use.

17. **(B)** ICONOCLAST (n.) means someone who destroys tradition, in many instances religious ones. HERETIC means someone who goes against commonly established, accepted, and cherished beliefs.

18. **(E)** PLATITUDE (n.) means a common or overly used expression or saying. TRITE means common or stale from overuse. Thus, a trite remark is a saying or expression that is overly used.

19. **(B)** MYOPIC (adj.) means narrow-minded or SHORTSIGHTED, being unable to see far ahead.

20. **(D)** RENDEZVOUS (n.) means an agreement between people to meet or the actual MEETING itself.

21. **(D)** WIZENED (adj.) means withered or SHRIVELED.

22. **(E)** RECANT (v.) means to take back or WITHDRAW, as with a statement or opinion.

23. **(B)** PRECOCIOUS (adj.) means mature or developed beyond one's years. Thus, ADVANCED is the best choice.

24. **(A)** CONCUR (v.) means to AGREE or side with.

25. **(C)** GERMANE (adj.) means closely related or relevant. PERTINENT also means relevant.

26. **(E)** DUPLICITY (n.) means trickery or double dealing. In other words, it is DECEIT.

27. **(D)** ECLECTIC (adj.) means drawing from a range of different sources. In other words, it means DIVERSE.

28. **(E)** SUBLIME (adj.) means inspiring awe and respect. Thus, IMPRESSIVE is the closest in meaning.

29. **(C)** CATHARSIS (n.) means emotional relief. PURGATION is the process of purging. If something is purged, it can be said to be freed of a burden or hindrance; in other words, it means the process of relieving.

30. **(E)** BEQUEATH (v.) means to PASS DOWN or leave to another, such as a descendant or heir, as an inheritance in a will and last testament.

Analogies

31. **(E)** A waiter brings food to the patron at a restaurant. A messenger carries a missive, which is a written note or message, to the recipient. (D) is incorrect, although it is a very tempting answer choice. While a ferry does carry or transport a passenger, the

32. **(C)** A chicken lays an egg, which is then made into an omelet. A fish lays eggs, too, which are then used to make caviar. The fish eggs themselves are also called caviar, but caviar is also a dish.

33. **(B)** A trot is a faster gait than a walk. A gallop is a faster gait than canter. Also, all four of these gaits apply to horses. They are, in order of speed: walk, trot, canter, and gallop.

34. **(A)** A batter is a mixture of flour, sugar, butter, and eggs. The batter then becomes one of the ingredients of a cake. Cement is a mixture of lime stone and other minerals and rocks. It is also a key ingredient of concrete. Thus, both batter and cement are mixtures of other things and both batter and cement are key ingredients used in another item.

35. **(A)** A ring is a symbol of marriage. A trophy is a symbol of success or victory.

36. **(A)** Gambling involves trying to win money by taking large risks. Investing is a more methodical and precise method of trying to make money. In other words, gambling typically involves more uncertainty than investing does. Guessing is coming up with an answer through random chance. Deriving involves with arriving at an answer from actual facts, so guessing involves more uncertainty than deriving does. (B) is incorrect because imitate and copy are too synonymous. The same is true of (C).

37. **(B)** A doctrine is a belief, and a tenet is a foundational principle, so the two are often synonymous. Archaic means outdated or obsolete.

38. **(D)** Transactions are recorded in ledgers. Events are recorded in annals.

39. **(E)** Seawater is briny, which means salty. Tundras are flat, treeless plains in an arctic region.

40. **(A)** A tire surrounds the rim of a wheel. A scarf wraps around the neck.

41. **(D)** A filament is a component of a bulb. A bristle is a component of a brush.

42. **(C)** Debonair means sophisticated. Boorish means unsophisticated or crass. Rustic means simple, unsophisticated, or crass and rude. Thus, boorish and rustic can be synonyms.

43. **(C)** A proton is a part of the nucleus of an atom. A chromosome is a component of the nucleus of a cell.

44. **(A)** Squalor is filth due to a lack of sanitation. Indifference is not caring or, in other words, a lack of concern.

45. **(B)** An establishment can mean a place of business; the founder is the one who begins, starts, or comes up with the business. Similarly, an inventor is the one who creates or comes up with a gadget.

46. **(D)** Merchandise is usually subject to taxes. Imports are usually subject to tariffs, which are government taxes on imports and exports.

47. **(E)** Machinery is operated, so operating is the present participle form of the word *operate*. Films are directed, so directing is the present participle form of *direct*.

48. **(B)** Red and violet are on the opposite ends of the visible light spectrum. Communism and fascism are on the opposite ends of the political spectrum. Both pairs of words indicate opposite ends of some spectrum.

49. **(A)** A gourmand is one who tremendously enjoys eating good foods. Chefs provide foods. The relationship is between consumer and provider. A masochist is someone who gets pleasure from pain and punishment, and a sadist is someone who enjoys delivering pain and punishment. (C) is incorrect because a hobbyist and enthusiast are synonyms.

50. **(A)** The perimeter of a polygon is the distance around it. The circumference of a circle is the distance around it.

51. **(D)** An inkling is the start of an idea, such as a hint or clue, while a theory is well thought out idea. Thus, inkling and theories reflect difference in degrees. A suspect is someone who has possibly committed a crime and will be investigated further, while a convict is someone who has been charged with and found guilty of a crime.

52. **(C)** Ostentatious means flashy and showy; in other words, it means lacking modesty. Amorphous means without shape, so it lacks shape.

53. **(A)** Pulchritude means beauty. Compunction means remorse.

54. **(A)** Dissonance means inharmonious sound or harsh noise. In other words, it means a lack of melodiousness; dissonance is not melodious. Boorishness means lack of refinement and elegance. If someone is elegant, then he or she is not boorish.

55. **(C)** The relationship between handcuffs and gavel is that they are both items representing steps in the criminal justice process. Handcuffs are used by the police to apprehend a criminal or suspect. Afterwards, the gavel is what the judge uses during the trial process. A sickle is a tool used to cut down grains to take the grain for processing. A millstone is used to crush the grains. So both a sickle and millstone are objects used in the processing of grain, and a sickle is used before a millstone is. (A) is incorrect because an ambulance usually comes after, or at the same time as, a firefighter arrives on the scene, if there's a fire. Also, a firefighter is not an object symbolizing steps in a process.

56. **(C)** A tycoon is a well-respected leader of business and enterprise. A laureate is a person who is acknowledged as being the best in his or her field.

57. **(E)** An affidavit is a written declaration of a person's observation of facts. A contract is a written agreement. (A) is incorrect because a receipt is not a form of a product. It's a written agreement for the sale of a product, but it is not a written version of the product itself.

58. **(D)** A guerilla is a fighter or soldier who uses stealth and ambush tactics. A highwayman also often uses stealth and ambush tactics, but a highwayman is a thief. So the relationship between a guerilla and a highwayman is most analogical to soldier and bandit, which is also a thief.

59. **(A)** Destitution is the state of lacking the means of subsistence; it is utter poverty. Penury means extreme poverty. Thus, destitution and penury are synonymous. Both a soliloquy and a monologue are speeches uttered by one to him or herself.

60. **(C)** Bewilderment means confusion or puzzlement. Obfuscation is the act of confusing or bewildering someone. Bewilderment results from obfuscation. Anxiety results from stress.

Section 4: Quantitative Reasoning

1. **(E)** Use elimination to solve this problem:

    For (A): If V and W are negative, or if V = 0 and W < 0, then V^2 isn't necessarily greater than W^2.

    For (B): If V and W are negative, or if V = 0 and W < 0, then V^3 will never be greater than W^2.

    For (C): If the absolute value of V is less than 1 but greater than 0, then V^4, which must be positive, can be less than W^2, which is also positive, even if V is greater than W.

    For (D): If both V and W are negative, then V + W < 0, not > 0.

    For (E): If V > W, then no matter whether what values V and W are, V – W will always be greater than 0. Thus, (E) is correct.

2. **(E)** Let B represent the number of candies Beverly started with and C the number Chuck started with. We can write the equation:

    B – 0.5B = 7 + 2C

    Substitute 2 for C, since he originally had 2:

    0.5B = 7 + 2(2) = 11

    Multiply both sides by 2 to get B = 22.

3. **(D)** $\dfrac{13\cancel{91}}{10\cancel{0}} \times \dfrac{\cancel{10}}{\cancel{7}} = \dfrac{13}{10} = 1.3$

4. **(A)** Let r be the radius of the circle. If the radius is reduced by 40%, the resulting radius will be $r – 0.4r = 0.6r$.

    The area of a circle with radius $0.6r$ can be calculated as follows: $\pi(0.6r)^2 = 0.36r^2\pi$, which represents a 64% reduction in area, since $0.36r^2\pi = \pi r^2 – 0.64r^2\pi$.

5. **(C)** Solve the inequality:

    $2|x+3| \le 10 \xrightarrow{\div 2} |x+3| \le 5$

    With inequalities, 2 possible solutions are possible:

    $|x+3| \le 5 \rightarrow x+3 \le 5$
    $\qquad\qquad\qquad x \le 2$
    $|x+3| \le 5 \rightarrow x+3 \ge -5$
    $\qquad\qquad\qquad x \ge -8$

    Thus, the number line in (C) properly reflects that x is less than 2 but greater than -8.

6. **(D)** Let x be the original price of the shirt. If the sale price is 75% of the original price, the sale price is $0.75x$. Jo receives an additional 20% off the sale price, so $0.75x – 0.2(0.75x) = 0.6x$, which is the final price Jo paid.

    $0.6x = \$36.00$
    $x = \dfrac{\$36.00}{0.6} \xrightarrow[\times 10]{\times 10} \dfrac{\$360.00}{6} = \$60.00$

    Note: The problem does *not* state that the sale price is 75% *off* the original price. It's 75% *of* the original price.

7. **(B)** $5P + 4S = 3S – 3P$
    $8P = -S$
    $S = -8P$

    Since S is a positive square integer, P must be negative. By substituting values of values of P, we can arrive at the correct answer.

    For (A): S = -8(-4) = 32, which isn't square.

    For (B): S = -8(-2) = 16, which is square.

    For (C): S = -8(-1) = 8, which isn't square.

    Thus, (B) is the only one that works.

8. **(B)** First compare the difference between the numbers of problems Karen and Trevor solve.

    Karen solves 13 problems per day while Trevor solves 8. That means Karen solves 5 more problems per day than Trevor does. After 27 days, she will have solved 5 × 27 = 135 more problems than Trevor will have.

9. **(B)** The order amount is $25.00 + $5.00 = $30.00. The tax is 0.05 × $30.00 = $1.50. Thus, the subtotal amount is $30.00 + $1.50 = $31.50.

The diner applied the tip to the subtotal amount, so he paid 0.2 × $31.50 = $6.30 in tip. His total was $31.50 + $6.30 = $37.80.

If the diner had applied the tip to the order amount, he would have paid 0.2 × $30.00 = $6.00 in tip. His total would have been $31.50 + $6.00 = $37.50.

Thus, he paid $37.80 - $37.50 = $0.30 more than he intended to.

10. **(E)** $4(x + 2)^2 = 4(x^2 + 4x + 4) = 4x^2 + 16x + 16$

$ax^2 + bx + c = 4x^2 + 16x + 16$

Thus, $a = 4$, $b = 16$, and $c = 16$. $a + b + c = 4 + 16 + 16 = 36$.

11. **(B)** First, find the median and mode of the current data set. The median is the middle number. List out the numbers: 51, 57, 64, 64, 64, 65, 66, 68, 72, 72, 73, 73, 77, 77, 77, 79, 83, 84, 84, 86, 86, 87, 88, 88, 91, 92, 93, 95, 95, 100

The middle number is the average of the middle two numbers in this case, since there are an even number of data points. The two middle numbers are 77 and 79. Thus, the median must be 78.

If the median remains the same at 78 after the new student's score is added, that means the new student's score must have been 78, since now that we have an odd number of data sets, the new median must be the middle number.

Further Check: The mode is the most frequently occurring number. Thus, the data set was actually bi-modal: 64 and 77 both appear three times each. Adding 78 into the data set does not affect the mode. Thus, 78 is correct.

12. **(D)** Using the Pythagorean Theorem, we can solve the side lengths of triangle ABC, letting x represent the side lengths:

$$x^2 + x^2 = \left(10\sqrt{2}\right)^2$$

$$2x^2 = 10^2 \times \left(\sqrt{2}\right)^2 = 100 \times 2 = 200$$

$$x^2 = 100 \quad \rightarrow \quad x = 10$$

To find $\overline{BD}$, draw a right triangle with the dimensions 5 ($\overline{CD}$), 10 ($\overline{BC}$), and y ($\overline{BD}$). Then apply the Pythagorean Theorem again to solve for y:

$$y^2 = 5^2 + 10^2 = 25 + 100 = 125$$
$$y = \sqrt{125} = 5\sqrt{5}$$

13. **(A)** To solve this problem, subtract the area of triangle ABC from the area of the circle.

The area of triangle ABC is ½ × x × x, where x is the length of the sides of the triangle we solved for in question 12. Substituting 10 for x, we get A = ½ × 10 × 10 = 50.

The area of the circle is πr^2, where $r = 5\sqrt{2}$ because the radius is half the length of the hypotenuse of triangle ABC. Thus, the area of the circle is 50π.

The area contained in the circle but not in triangle ABC is therefore $50\pi - 50$, which is $50(\pi - 1)$ square units.

14. **(D)** This problem is asking for the difference of the perimeter of triangle ABC and circumference of the circle.

The perimeter of triangle ABC is $10 + 10 + 10\sqrt{2} = 20 + 10\sqrt{2}$.

The circumference of the circle is $2\pi r$ or πd, where $d = 10\sqrt{2}$ in the figure. Thus, the circumference is $10\pi\sqrt{2}$.

Subtracting the perimeter from the circumference, we get: $10\pi\sqrt{2} - (20 + 10\sqrt{2})$. This is equivalent to $10\pi\sqrt{2} - (10\sqrt{2} + 20)$.

15. **(C)** To solve this problem, approximate the percentages of his expenditures. About 18-19% of his allowance is dedicated to games. We'll

round this to 20% for simplicity. In one year, Connor receives approximately $15 × 52 = $780 in allowance. 20% of that goes to games. If he saved this money instead, he'd save an additional 0.2 × $780 = $156. The closest answer is therefore (C). Furthermore, since 20% is an over approximation, $150 makes even more sense.

16. **(B)** Begin by finding the least common multiple of 2 of the numbers, such as 8 and 15.

The least common multiple of 8 and 15 is 8 × 15 = 120 because 8 and 15 do not share any common prime factors. Then find the least common multiple of 120 and 36.

The prime factorization of 120: 2 × 2 × 2 × 3 × 5
The prime factorization of 36 is: 2 × 2 × 3 × 3

Because they have 2 × 2 × 3 in common, the least common multiple of 120 and 36 is (2 × 2 × 3) × 2 × 5 × 3 = 12 × 2 × 5 × 3 = 12 × 30 = 360.

17. **(C)** There are two methods of solving this problem.

Method 1:

Make a probability chart, as such:

X	P(X)	P(Y>X)
2	¼	1
4	¼	½
5	¼	½
6	¼	0

The probability of selecting each number in Set X is ¼ because there are 4 numbers. P(Y>X) means the probability that Y is greater than X. For instance, if 2 is selected from Set X, then no matter what number is picked from Set Y, Y will be greater than X, so the probability that Y is greater than X is 100% or 1. If 4 is selected from Set X, then only 6 from Set Y can be greater, and the probability of picking a number greater than 4 is ½, since there are 2 numbers in Set Y. The same is true if 5 is picked from Set X. If 6 is picked from Set X, then the probability that a number picked from Y is 0% or 0, even if 6 is picked from Y, since 6 is not greater than 6.

To find the overall probability that a number picked at random from Y is greater than a number picked at random from Set X is:

X = 2: ¼ × 1 = ¼
X = 4: ¼ × ½ = 1/8
X = 5: ¼ × ½ = 1/8
X = 6: ¼ × 0 = 0

When the probabilities are all added up: ¼ + 1/8 + 1/8 + 0 = ½.

Method 2:

Another approach to the problem, since there aren't many numbers, is to find all the possible pairings of numbers from Set X and those from Set Y. For simplicity, we'll express these pairs in the format (X, Y):

(2, 3), (2, 6)
(4, 3), (4, 6)
(5, 3), (5, 6)
(6, 3), (6, 6)

There are 8 possible pairs. (The pairs where Y > X have been highlighted.) Thus, the probability of picking a random number from Set X and one from Set Y such that Y > X is ½.

18. **(D)** Herbert caught a total of 59 + 66 = 125 fish. If this is a representative sample size of the fish population, and there are 5,000 fish, to see how many male and female fish there are in the overall population, divide 5.000 by 125 to see what multiple 5,000 is of 125: 5,000 ÷ 125 = 40

There are 59 × 40 = 2,360 male fish in the pond. The number of female fish is 66 × 40 = 2,640.

Thus, there are 2,640 − 2,360 = 280 more female fish than male fish in the pond.

19. **(D)** If the first number Jennie picked was x, the second she picked was $2x + 6$. The third number must be ½ × (2x + 6) − 3 = (3 + x) − 3 = x. Thus, the sum of the three numbers can be found by evaluating the expression $x + (2x + 6) + x$.

20. **(D)** Mildred's recipe originally calls for 3 cups of flour in a 10-cup (3 + 1 + 5 + 1) mixture. Thus, the ratio of flour to the total is 3 : 10.

If Mildred only has 0.25 cups of flour, but enough of the other ingredients, the flour will be the limiting ingredient. The total number of cups she will need to bake a mini cake can be found by using the equation $0.25 = 0.3x$, since the volume of flour is 0.3 of that of the total.

Solving for x, we get 0.25/0.3, which is 25/30 or 5/6, which in turn as a decimal number is 0.83, when rounded to the nearest hundredth.

21. **(B)** Blair drove a total of $15 + 35 + 3 = 53$ miles. Calculate how much Blair would have driven, if he had instead driven in a straight line to his destination. Draw a diagram to help. We can see that a triangle results, as such:

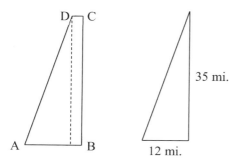

Let A be Blair's starting point. He drives 15 miles to B. Then he drives up 35 miles to C. He then backpedals 3 miles to D. What we're looking for is the hypotenuse of a right triangle with side lengths of $15 - 3 = 12$ and 35.

Using the Pythagorean Theorem, we get $12^2 + 35^2 = x^2$. Thus, $x^2 = 144 + 1225 = 1369$. Because the answer choices are all integer values, we can surmise that there is a good chance x is also an integer value. Assuming this to be the case, find what x is through some logical deduction.

Knowing that x^2 is 1369 means that we can narrow down the range of values that x can be. For instance, we know that x must be less than 40, as $40^2 = 1600$. We also know that x must be greater than 30, as $30^2 = 900$. Next, look at the unit's digit of 1369. We see it ends with 9. There are only two integers that, when squared, produce a unit's digit of 9: 3 and 7. $33^2 = 1,089$, which is not enough. Indeed, $37^2 = 1,369$, and we have x = 37.

To find how much distance Blair could have saved by driving straight from A to D: $53 - 37 = 16$, which is the correct answer.

22. **(A)** The key to deciphering this problem is understanding that $ax - bx = x(b - a)$ by way of factoring. This will give us:

$$\frac{bx - ax}{ab}\left[\left(\frac{b}{x}\right)\left(\frac{a^2}{b-a}\right)\right] = \frac{x(b-a)}{ab}\left[\left(\frac{b}{x}\right)\left(\frac{a^2}{b-a}\right)\right]$$

At this point, we can simplify to get

$$\frac{\cancel{x}\,\cancel{(b-a)}}{ab}\left[\left(\frac{b}{\cancel{x}}\right)\left(\frac{a^2}{\cancel{(b-a)}}\right)\right] = \frac{ba^2}{ab} = a$$

23. **(E)** Look for a pattern. Notice that every 5th square is white, meaning a shaded square follows every 5th square. Thus, the only answers that could work are multiples of 5 plus 1. In other words, we can determine that a shaded square will be found at $5n + 1$, where n represents the number term of the squares. None of the other choices can be represented by $5n + 1$.

24. **(B)** Multiply both sides of the equation by w: $w^2 = 25^2 - 24^2 = 625 - 576 = 49$. Thus, $w = 7$.

25. **(A)** For it to be symmetrical about the line segment $\overline{AC}$, square ABCD should look like this:

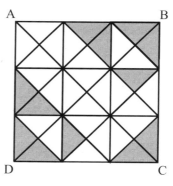

When compared to the original, we see that there are 4 more triangles shaded in.

Edited Questions
From 1st Edition

SSAT
UPPER LEVEL
TEST 1

Quantitative Reasoning – Section I

Below are the questions that were removed and replaced from the 1ˢᵗ edition of *SSAT Practice Tests: Upper Level*. The answers and explanations can be found at the very end of the book.

---

10. $\sqrt[5]{m^{13}} =$

   (A) $65m$
   (B) m^2
   (C) m^3
   (D) $8m^8$
   (E) $(m^2)\sqrt[5]{m^3}$

---

17. Marcus works full-time (40 hours per week) for a base pay of $600.00 per week. If he works overtime, he gets paid "time-and-a-half" (150% of his base wages) for each hour of overtime he works. If one week he is paid $870.00, how much overtime did he work that week?

   (A) 6 hours
   (B) 8 hours
   (C) 9 hours
   (D) 10 hours
   (E) 12 hours

---

19. Rod sold 35% of his games so he could buy some new games. The number of new games he bought was 20% of the number of games he had left, after selling some. What percent of the number of games he had originally is the number he has now?

   (A) 13%
   (B) 52%
   (C) 65%
   (D) 78%
   (E) 91%

---

23. If a line passes through the points (-1, m) and (2m, 3) and runs perpendicular to the line $2y = 3x + 8$, what is the value of m?

   (A) -13
   (B) -11
   (C) -4
   (D) 9
   (E) 13

Verbal Reasoning – Section 3

Below are the questions that were removed and replaced from the 1st edition of *SSAT Practice Tests: Upper Level*. The answers and explanations can be found at the very end of the book.

---

32. Baker is to bread as
    - (A) waiter is to food
    - (B) banker is to money
    - (C) woman is to baby
    - (D) dentist is to teeth
    - (E) sculptor is to statue

37. Microscope is to cell as
    - (A) eyeglass is to vision
    - (B) contact lens is to sports
    - (C) monocle is to fashion
    - (D) spectroscope is to radiation
    - (E) magnifying glass is to amplify

38. Cerebral is to heart as
    - (A) meticulous is to hand
    - (B) olfactory is to touch
    - (C) objective is to subjective
    - (D) osteopathic is to bone
    - (E) emotional is to brain

39. Plod is to trudge as sprint is to
    - (A) crawl
    - (B) jog
    - (C) dash
    - (D) skip
    - (E) stroll

44. Doctor is to apothecary as
    - (A) pastor is to church
    - (B) driver is to racecar
    - (C) architect is to engineer
    - (D) police is to sheriff
    - (E) captain is to first mate

45. Rural is to barn as
    - (A) urban is to freeway
    - (B) cosmopolitan is to fashion
    - (C) suburban is to mansion
    - (D) metropolitan is to skyscraper
    - (E) celestial is to sky

50. Census is to population as
    - (A) survey is to questions
    - (B) poll is to voters
    - (C) assessment is to information
    - (D) inventory is to stock
    - (E) demographic is to ethnicity

53. Key is to lock as
    - (A) password is to username
    - (B) clue is to mystery
    - (C) cipher is to codex
    - (D) index card is to notes
    - (E) alphabet is to word

58. Acre is to field as
    - (A) second is to year
    - (B) watt is to power
    - (C) millimeter is to elephant
    - (D) hour is to flight
    - (E) degree is to magnitude

Quantitative Reasoning – Section 4

Below are the questions that were removed and replaced from the 1ˢᵗ edition of *SSAT Practice Tests: Upper Level*. The answers and explanations can be found at the very end of the book.

---

1. If q is a positive real number greater than 1 but less than 100, which of the following is the greatest?

    (A) $2q$
    (B) $(1.5q^2 + 4) \times q^{-1}$
    (C) $7q^3 \times q^{-2}$
    (D) $8(q + 8)^2 \div q$
    (E) It cannot be determined from the information given.

---

17. In 1803, the United States acquired the Louisiana Purchase from France for a total sum of \$15,000,000; the size of the territory was approximately 2,140,000 square kilometers. What was the cost per hectare of the Louisiana Purchase back then, to the nearest cent? (1 hectare = 10,000 square meters)

    (A) \$0.03
    (B) \$0.05
    (C) \$0.07
    (D) \$0.70
    (E) \$7.00

---

20. A sphere's volume is given by the formula $V = (4 \times \pi r^3) \div 3$, where r represents the radius of the sphere. If a sphere has a volume of $n\pi$ centimeters cubed, and both n and r are integers, what could be the diameter of the sphere?

    (A) 4 cm
    (B) 9 cm
    (C) 16 cm
    (D) 25 cm
    (E) 54 cm

21. Which of the following gives the dollar value of $10p$ pennies, $9n$ nickels, and $3q$ quarters?

    (A) $\dfrac{p}{10} + \dfrac{9n}{20} + \dfrac{3q}{4}$

    (B) $\dfrac{p}{10} + \dfrac{9n}{100} + \dfrac{3q}{100}$

    (C) $10p + 45n + 75q$

    (D) $\dfrac{p + 5n + 25q}{100}$

    (E) $1000p + 900n + 300q$

Questions 24-25 refer to the graph.

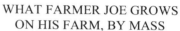

WHAT FARMER JOE GROWS
ON HIS FARM, BY MASS

24. If Farmer Joe harvests a total of 195,000 kilograms of produce from his farm year after year, how many kilograms of wheat does he harvest every year?

    (A) 24,375
    (B) 25,000
    (C) 40,000
    (D) 73,125
    (E) 78,000

25. What is the ratio of the amount, by mass, of the wheat and beets Farmer Joe grew to the amount of beans and other produce, not including corn, he grew?

    (A) $13 : 5$
    (B) $13 : 45$
    (C) $26 : 9$
    (D) $32 : 17$
    (E) $45 : 13$

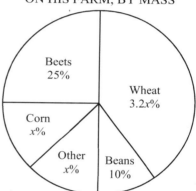

SSAT
UPPER LEVEL
TEST 2

Quantitative Reasoning – Section I

Below are the questions that were removed and replaced from the 1st edition of *SSAT Practice Tests: Upper Level*. The answers and explanations can be found at the very end of the book.

---

20. Marquis the baby manatee needs more and more food each day as his rate of growth accelerates. On the first day of the zookeepers started measuring his food intake, Marquis ate 10 pounds of food. If he needs 10 more pounds of food each day than he did the day before, how long will it take him to eat a total of 950 pounds of food, across all the days his food intake was being measured?

    (A) 10 days
    (B) 14 days
    (C) 15 days
    (D) 16 days
    (E) 95 days

---

25. A certain plot of land with an area of 163 km^2 is divided up into five regions. The smallest region has an area of 15 km^2, the largest has an area of 59 km^2, and no two of regions have the same area. If the area of each region is an integer number of square kilometers. What is the greatest possible area for the second largest region?

    (A) 56 square kilometers
    (B) 57 square kilometers
    (C) 58 square kilometers
    (D) 59 square kilometers
    (E) 86 square kilometers

Verbal Reasoning – Section 3

Below are the questions that were removed and replaced from the 1st edition of *SSAT Practice Tests: Upper Level*. The answers and explanations can be found at the very end of the book.

33. Cloud is to water as

 (A) sound is to volume
 (B) helium is to gas
 (C) air is to nitrogen
 (D) light is to ray
 (E) graphite is to lead

41. Trinket is to treasure as

 (A) tremor is to earthquake
 (B) rock is to gem
 (C) jewel is to crown
 (D) speck is to dust
 (E) gale is to breeze

43. Palisade is to defense as

 (A) academy is to scholarship
 (B) corporation is to consumerism
 (C) palace is to nobility
 (D) museum is to tourism
 (E) warehouse is to bulk

46. Gregarious is to inimical as

 (A) stingy is to magnanimous
 (B) fallacious is to nonsensical
 (C) somnolent is to lighthearted
 (D) flagrant is to fiery
 (E) jovial is to trustworthy

49. Scapegoat is to hero as hedonist is to

 (A) slave
 (B) egoist
 (C) barbarian
 (D) puritan
 (E) master

51. Shingle is to roof as

 (A) ceiling is to room
 (B) epidermis is to skin
 (C) retina is to eyeball
 (D) crankshaft is to motor
 (E) hull is to sail

53. Zookeeper is to animal as

 (A) babysitter is to child
 (B) nurse is to patient
 (C) ward is to charge
 (D) jailor is to prisoner
 (E) hunter is to victim

54. Longing is to nostalgia as

 (A) begging is to desperation
 (B) mourning is to grievance
 (C) bickering is to familiarity
 (D) chattering is to tranquility
 (E) flourishing is to mediocrity

55. Unorthodox is to traditional as

 (A) conscientious is to deliberate
 (B) apposite is to opposite
 (C) illustrious is to mundane
 (D) cautionary is to excessive
 (E) bilious is to rotund

SSAT
UPPER LEVEL
TEST 3

Quantitative Reasoning – Section I

Below are the questions that were removed and replaced from the 1st edition of *SSAT Practice Tests: Upper Level*. The answers and explanations can be found at the very end of the book.

---

6. Sunnie buys a cake and x candles for her sister's birthday for $33.91. As she's leaving the bakery, she runs into her friend, who reminds her that her sister is actually a year older than she thought. Sunnie dutifully goes back in to buy another candle. Being a cake lover, however, Sunnie ends up buying another equally priced cake for herself, along with a candle. The new cake and candle cost $32.47. If the price of a candle is c cents, what is the value of x, in terms of c?

   (A) $\dfrac{1.44 + c}{c}$

   (B) $\dfrac{1.44 - 1}{c}$

   (C) $\dfrac{144 - 1}{c}$

   (D) $\dfrac{144 + c}{c}$

   (E) $\dfrac{144 + 1}{c}$

---

11. If $m \, \bullet \, n = (n - m)^2 + m(2n - m)$, what is the value of $m \, \bullet \, (m \, \bullet \, n)$?

   (A) 0
   (B) m^3
   (C) $2mn(n - m)^2$
   (D) $n^2 + 2mn + m^2$
   (E) n^4

19. Gregory has two trick dice. For each dice, whose sides are numbered from 1 to 6, the probability of rolling an even number is twice that of rolling an odd. He rolls both dice at the same time. What is the probability that the sum of the numbers he rolls is even?

    (A) $\dfrac{1}{9}$

    (B) $\dfrac{1}{2}$

    (C) $\dfrac{3}{9}$

    (D) $\dfrac{5}{9}$

    (E) $\dfrac{3}{4}$

---

21. On the dot matrix grid, point O has coordinates of (0, 0). Points A and B have coordinates (0, 3) and (3, 0), respectively. If horizontally and vertically adjacent grid points are 2 cm apart, what would be the area of triangle ABC, if the coordinates of point C are placed at (5, 6)?

    (A) 3 cm²
    (B) 6 cm²
    (C) 12 cm²
    (D) 24 cm²
    (E) 48 cm²

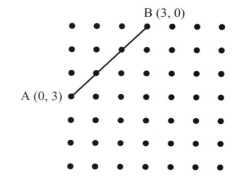

---

22. What is the sum of the units digits of 2828^{10} and 3737^{10}?

    (A) 9
    (B) 11
    (C) 13
    (D) 15
    (E) 17

Verbal Reasoning – Section 3

Below are the questions that were removed and replaced from the 1st edition of *SSAT Practice Tests: Upper Level*. The answers and explanations can be found at the very end of the book.

36. Gamble is to invest as
    (A) guess is to fabricate
    (B) derive is to copy
    (C) strike is to hit
    (D) imbibe is to food
    (E) throw is to pitch

46. Merchandise is to tax as
    (A) export is to embargo
    (B) barter is to trade
    (C) airport is to tariff
    (D) import is to duty
    (E) highway is to toll

48. Red is to violet as
    (A) green is to envy
    (B) communism is to fascism
    (C) theocracy is to oligarchy
    (D) dependence is to necessity
    (E) legitimacy is to validity

51. Inkling is to theory as
    (A) idea is to notion
    (B) likelihood is to improbability
    (C) mule is to donkey
    (D) suspect is to convict
    (E) logic is to rationale

54. Dissonance is to melodious as
    (A) machismo is to cordial
    (B) vivacity is to reluctant
    (C) dedication is to diligent
    (D) consternation is to repulsive
    (E) heterogeneity is to diverse

55. Candela is to luminance as
    (A) meter is to measurement
    (B) cup is to heaviness
    (C) calorie is to heat
    (D) gram is to density
    (E) wave is to infrared

57. Affidavit is to testimony as
    (A) receipt is to product
    (B) hieroglyph is to cuneiform
    (C) scroll is to papyrus
    (D) facsimile is to coincidence
    (E) contract is to agreement

58. Guerrilla is to highwayman as
    (A) arena is to gladiator
    (B) entourage is to group
    (C) vendor is to customer
    (D) patrol is to bodyguard
    (E) yeoman is to supervisor

Quantitative Reasoning – Section 4

Below are the questions that were removed and replaced from the 1st edition of *SSAT Practice Tests: Upper Level*. The answers and explanations can be found at the very end of the book.

---

8. Tyler is planning to train for the marathon. On the first day, he will run two miles nonstop. Each subsequent day, he will run nonstop 0.75 miles more than he did the previous day. At this rate, what is the least number of days it will take him to be able to run nonstop the full distance of the marathon (26.2 miles)?

   (A) 31
   (B) 32
   (C) 33
   (D) 34
   (E) 35

---

14. If the figure (not including the names of the points, diameter unit length, and right angle symbol) is drawn without retracing any lines or curves, what is the distance that the tip of the writing implement must travel?

   (A) $5\sqrt{2}(\pi + 1) + 20$ units
   (B) $10(\sqrt{2}(\pi + 1) + 2)$ units
   (C) $10(\pi\sqrt{2} + 2)$ units
   (D) $20(\sqrt{2}(\pi + 0.5) + 1)$ units
   (E) $20\sqrt{2}(\pi + 3)$ units

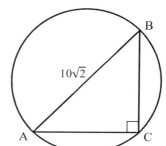

---

19. Three consecutive odd integers have a sum of 237. About what percent of the largest integer is the smallest integer?

   (A) 89.35
   (B) 91.56
   (C) 93.18
   (D) 94.67
   (E) 95.06

20. Five friends start working together to build a log cabin, which they can finish in 240 hours. Halfway through, three of the friends drop out. Assuming that everyone was building at the same rate and will continue to build at the same rate, how long will it take the remaining two friends to complete the cabin, from the time the three friends drop out?

    (A) 300 hours
    (B) 240 hours
    (C) 200 hours
    (D) 180 hours
    (E) 120 hours

---

22. Simplify the expression $\dfrac{ax - bx - ay + by}{ab}\left[\left(\dfrac{b}{y-x}\right)\left(\dfrac{a^2b}{b-a}\right)\right]$,

    where $a \neq 0$, $b \neq 0$, $a \neq b$, and $y \neq x$.

    (A) -1
    (B) 1
    (C) ab
    (D) $-(x-y)(a+b)$
    (E) $ab(x-y)(a-b)$

Edited Questions
Answers & Explanations

SSAT
UPPER LEVEL
Test 1

Quantitative Reasoning – Section I

Below are the answers and explanations to the questions that were removed and replaced from the 1st edition of *SSAT Practice Tests: Upper Level.*

10. **(E)** To rewrite this expression by extracting as many powers of m from the fifth-root radical, divide 13 by 5 to get 2 with a remainder of 3. This means that 2 powers of m can be extracted from the fifth-root radical. 3 powers of m must still be kept under the radical symbol.

    Why This Question Was Removed: For #10 of the first practice test, I believed that an easier, more concrete problem was appropriate.

17. **(E)** Marcus's base wage is $600 ÷ 40$ hours $=$ $15 per hour. 150%, or 1.5, of $15 is $1.5 × 15 =$ $22.50 per hour for overtime hours.

    If Marcus makes $870.00 in a week, that means he made $270.00 ($870.00 - $600.00) in overtime. To find out how many overtime hours he worked, we can divide $270.00 by $22.50 per hour to get: 12 hours.

    Why This Question Was Removed: I wanted to warm students up with an easier version of this problem type in the practice test, leaving this problem in the edited section if they want a more challenging version to practice with.

19. **(D)** Let G be the number of games Rod had originally. If he sells 35% of his games, he has 65% of them left.

    The number of new games he buys is 20% of 65% of G or $0.2 × 0.65 × G = 0.13G$.

    Rod now has $.65G + 0.13G = 0.78G$, or 78% of the number of games he had originally.

    Why This Question Was Removed: I removed this question from the practice test because I felt it might be too abstract for some students. I replaced it with an easier and less abstract version of the problem.

23. **(B)** The slope of the line $2y = 3x + 8$ can be found by dividing both sides by 2 to isolate y. This results in:

$$y = \frac{3}{2}x + 4$$

The line perpendicular to this line will have a slope of the negative reciprocal, which is $-\frac{2}{3}$.

Thus, $\dfrac{3-m}{2m-(-1)} = \dfrac{3-m}{2m+1} = -\dfrac{2}{3}$.

Solve for m by cross multiplying:

$3(3 - m) = -2(2m + 1)$
$9 - 3m = -4m - 2$

Solve for m by adding $4m$ to and subtracting 9 from both sides to find that $m = -11$.

Why This Question Was Removed: I removed this question from the practice test because it incorporated a combination of abstract points on the coordinate plane as well as an understanding of finding equations for perpendicular lines, which may be outside the scope of the SSAT.

Verbal Reasoning – Section 3

Below are the answers and explanations to the questions that were removed and replaced from the 1st edition of *SSAT Practice Tests: Upper Level*.

---

32. **(E)** A baker makes bread, and a sculptor makes statues. A banker makes money by investing, but the banker himself does not actually create or print money. Money is printed at a mint.

Why This Question Was Edited or Removed: I edited the answer choices for this question. Specifically, I edited choice (B) from "banker" to "bank teller" in order to avoid any possible confusion and ambiguity. A banker is someone who regularly invests money, so it could be argued that a banker makes money, although (E) is still the better choice because the sculptor actually creates statues.

37. **(D)** A microscope is a tool that can help humans study and detect small objects, such as cells. A spectroscope is a tool that can help humans study and detect radiation.

Why This Question Was Edited or Removed: I removed this question because it was too technical for some students, since many may not know what a spectroscope is, although (D) was the best choice through process of elimination, if the student knew the definitions of all of the words. There was also some potential confusion with (C), if the student thought that monocles were used for fashion and did not know what a spectroscope was.

38. **(E)** Cerebral means related to the brain or it refers to an intellectual or logical process, rather than an emotional one. Thus, cerebral is the adjective for the organ of the body "opposite" to the heart. Emotional processes are relegated to the realm of the heart and not the brain. Thus, emotional is the adjective opposite of the adjective that would be used to describe the brain.

Why This Question Was Edited or Removed: I removed this question because the flipping of the adjective and body part was confusing to students, although (E) was the best choice by elimination. Because it was the only one that had an adjective paired with the what we may consider the opposite organ. (A) is not as good as (E) because meticulous is not the opposite adjective for hand. (D) is incorrect because osteopathic does indeed relate to bone.

39. **(C)** Plod means to move slowly and heavily, as does trudge. Sprint means to run at full speed. Dash means move hurriedly or rush.

Why This Question Was Edited or Removed: I edited this question to remove potential ambiguity. The point of this question was to emphasize the synonym relationships, but some students interpreted this question as one of a matter of degree.

44. **(C)** A doctor provides prescriptions, which the apothecary, which is a pharmacist, fulfills. In other words, the apothecary is the person who comes after the doctor in the treatment process. An architect designs a building, and an engineer advises the architect what materials to use in the construction of the building. In other words, the engineer is the person who comes after the architect in the building construction process.

Why This Question Was Edited or Removed: I edited this question to remove the ambiguity with answer choice (E). When I wrote the question, I had been attempting to focus on the process. But it later became apparent that students were thinking of a synergistic or symbiotic relationship between the doctor and apothecary. Using that rationale, it could be argued that the captain and first mate of a ship also have a synergistic or symbiotic relationship. A captain issues orders, and the first mate is the one to carry them about. Here, there is a sequence in the process of issuing orders. Thus, this answer choice could also reasonably work as the correct answer.

50. **(D)** A census is a survey to measure the size of a population. An inventory is a survey to see how much stock there is. (D) is a better choice than (C) because both censuses and inventories can determine tangible objects. Furthermore, assessments do not always have to tests to see how much information one knows.

    Why This Question Was Edited or Removed:
    I edited this question because students were frequently choosing (C) as the correct answer. The rationale was that assessments are surveys of how much information one knows. Other students were choosing (B) and (E) as the correct answer using the same line of reasoning for picking (C).

53. **(B)** Keys unlock locks. Clues unlock mysteries.

    Why This Question Was Edited or Removed:
    I edited this question because many students did not know the definitions of the words *cipher* and *codex*.

58. **(D)** An acre is as unit of measurement that would be appropriate for measuring the area of a field. An hour is a unit of measurement that would be appropriate for measuring the length of time needed for a flight.

    Why This Question Was Edited or Removed:
    I edited this question to make it more straightforward. Students were too often choosing (B). A watt is the unit of measurement of power, but students confuse it to measure power. A correct analogy would be "inch is to length as watt is to power" or "acre is to area as watt is to power" because an inch is a unit of measurement of length and an acre is a unit of measurement of area. but this question was difficult because of the extreme technicality of the answer choice.

Quantitative Reasoning – Section 4

Below are the answers and explanations to the questions that were removed and replaced from the 1st edition of *SSAT Practice Tests: Upper Level*.

---

1. **(D)** Compare the different values.

   The value of (A) is $2q$.

   The value of (B) is

   $$(1.5q^2 + 4) \times q^{-1} = \frac{1.5q^2 + 4}{q} = 1.5q + \frac{4}{q}$$

   The value of (C) is $7q^3 \times q^{-2} = 7q$

   The value of (D) is

   $$8(q+8)^2 \div q = \frac{8(q^2 + 16q + 64)}{q} =$$

   $$8q + 128 + \frac{512}{q}$$

   Why This Question Was Removed: I removed this question because I felt it, along with the answer choices, might be too abstract, especially for the first problem in the section.

17. **(C)** To find the cost per hectare (ha), first convert 2,140,000 square kilometers to hectares. 1 hectare = 10,000 square meters, and 1 square kilometer = 1,000,000 square meters. To find how many hectares are in 1,000,000 square meters, divide 1,000,000 by 10,000 to get 100 hectares in 1,000,000 square meters. This means that 100 hectares = 1 square kilometer.

    $$\frac{2,140,000 \text{ km}^2}{1} \times \frac{100 \text{ ha}}{1 \text{ km}^2} = 214,000,000 \text{ ha}$$

    The cost per hectare is $15,000,000 ÷ 214,000,000 ha = \$15 ÷ 214 ha = \$0.07009/ha

    <u>Proof that 1 kilometer = 1,000 meters.</u>

    First, square both sides to get square kilometers:

    1 km = 1,000 m
    (1 km)² = (1,000 m)² = 1,000,000 m²

Why This Question Was Removed: I removed this question because there were too many conversions that the student needed to perform, making this problem cumbersome and time-consuming. Plus, not many students are comfortable dealing with hectares.

20. **(E)** Since $n\pi$ is the volume, $n\pi = \frac{4}{3}\pi r^3$

    Because n is an integer, r^3 must be a multiple of 3. This means that r must also be a multiple of 3, since r must be an integer. The diameter, which is $2r$, must be a multiple of 6. The only choice that works is 54 cm.

    Why This Question Was Removed: I removed this question because it was too abstract, since it involved not just an understanding of geometry but also rudimentary number theory.

21. **(A)** The dollar value of $10p$ pennies is $10p \times$ \$0.01, or $10p ÷ \$100$ ($p ÷ \$10$), since multiplying by 0.01 is the same as dividing by 100; the dollar value of $9n$ nickels is $9n \times$ \$0.05, or $9n ÷ \$20$, since multiplying by 0.05 is the same as dividing by 20; and the dollar value of $3q$ quarters is $3q \times$ \$0.25, or $3q ÷ \$4$, since multiplying by 0.25 is the same as dividing by 4.

    Why This Question Was Removed: I removed this question from the practice test because I felt it might be too abstract for some students. I replaced it with an easier and less abstract version of the problem.

24. **(E)** First find x. To do so, set up the following equation: $25 + 10 + x + x + 3.2x = 100$, since the sum of the percentages must be 100. We therefore get $35 + 5.2x = 100$. Rewrite the equation to isolate and solve for x:

    $5.2x = 100 - 35 = 65$
    $x = 65 ÷ 5.2 = 12.5$
    $3.2x = 3.2(12.5) = 40$, meaning that 40% of Farmer Joe's harvest is comprised of wheat. If

his total harvest is 195,000 kilograms, then 40% of that is 195,000 × 0.4 = 78,000.

25. **(C)** The ratio of the mass of the wheat and beets to the mass of the other produce (excluding corn) is the same as the ratio of the percentages. This will save time in that the masses do not need to be calculated.

The percentage of the produce by mass of the wheat and beets is 40% + 25% = 65%.

The percentage of the produce by mass of the beans and other is 10% + 12.5% = 22.5%.

Thus the ratio is 65 : 22.5 or, by multiplying both sides by 2 to get rid of the decimal, 130 : 45. Both 130 and 45 are divisible by 5, so the ratio can be rewritten as 26 : 9.

Why Questions 24 and 25 Were Removed: I removed these questions from the practice test because they required too many steps and too much computation; as a result, they were overly cumbersome and time consuming. Furthermore, some students would not expect to compute $3.2x\%$, so they would compute $32x\%$ instead.

SSAT
UPPER LEVEL
TEST 2

Quantitative Reasoning – Section I

Below are the answers and explanations to the questions that were removed and replaced from the 1ˢᵗ edition of *SSAT Practice Tests: Upper Level*.

20. **(B)** On the first day, Marquis ate 10 pounds of food; on the second day, he ate 20; on the third, 30; and so on and so forth. The total we're looking for is 950 pounds across all days. Thus, we have the following arithmetic series: $10 + 20 + 30 + ... + 10n = 950$, where n is the nth day of feeding. To find n, we can use the equation

$$950 = \frac{n(a_1 + a_n)}{2},$$ where a_1 represents the first term (in our case, 10) and an represents the last term. In this case, $a_n = 10n$. Thus, we can rewrite the equation as:

$$950 = \frac{n(10 + 10n)}{2} = \frac{10n(1 + n)}{2} = 5n(1 + n)$$

Divide both sides by 5 to get the equation:
$190 = n(1 + n)$

Find two integers that have a difference of 1 and a product of 190. Because 190 is close to 200, we can look for numbers that are relatively close together that multiply to 200. Naturally, 10 and 20 come to mind, but they are too far apart, so we need to choose numbers closer together. Because the product of the numbers is a multiple of 10, a number ending with 5 would be the perfect candidate. Try 15 and 16 and 15 and 14, since each of those pairs has a difference of 1.

$15 \times 14 = 190$, so that is correct. ($15 \times 16 = 240$, so that is too large.)

Why This Question Was Removed: For students not familiar with sequences and series, this problem may be overly complicated. I therefore replaced this problem with an easier sequences and series question that can be solved without much knowledge of sequences and series.

25. **(A)** Let a, b, and c represent the areas of the three regions of unknown areas, with a being the largest of these three, b the second largest, and c the smallest. (Note, however, that b and c must still be larger than 15 km², since 15 km² is the area of the smallest region.) The sum of the areas can be expressed as $a + b + c + 15 + 59 = 163$. Thus, $a + b + c = 163 - 74 = 89$. To find the greatest possible value of a, make b and c as small as possible. If c is 16, and b is 17, then that would maximize the value of a. This means that $a + 16 + 17 = 89$, and $a = 89 - 33 = 56$ km².

Why This Question Was Removed: Because I had decreased the difficulty of other questions, I felt it was appropriate to make the final question of the math section slightly more difficult. In other words, I replaced this question with a minimally harder version, so that students would still find the practice test a worthwhile challenge.

Verbal Reasoning – Section 3

Below are the answers and explanations to the questions that were removed and replaced from the 1st edition of *SSAT Practice Tests: Upper Level*.

---

33. **(C)** A cloud is comprised primarily of water molecules. Air is predominantly comprised of nitrogen molecules.

Why This Question Was Removed or Edited:
I edited this question because this question was too scientifically technical; not many students were aware that air is predominantly comprised of nitrogen molecules.

41. **(B)** A trinket is a cheap artifact or souvenir. A treasure is something worth a lot. A rock is fairly worthless, but a gem is worth a lot. Thus, the analogy is one of a matter of degree.

Why This Question Was Removed or Edited:
I edited this question because the relationship between a tremor and an earthquake can be construed as one of a matter of degree. A rock is to gem is a better analogy because they are both tangible objects, as are a trinket and treasure, so (B) is still technically closer as an analogy, but I thought this was nitpicking too much.

43. **(A)** The purpose of a palisade, which is a fence or barrier of stakes or spikes, is to provide defense. The purpose of an academy is to provide scholarship.

Why This Question Was Removed or Edited:
I edited answer choice (B) because the word "consumerism" was too unfamiliar with many students, so many students believed that the purpose of corporations was consumerism, when in fact consumerism means the protection of consumer rights or society's preoccupation with the acquisition of goods.

46. **(A)** Gregarious means friendly and sociable. Inimical means unfriendly or hostile, so the two words are antonyms. Stingy means unwilling to spend money or resources in a selfish way. Magnanimous means generous in character, noble, and high-minded. Thus, stingy and magnanimous are the most antonymous.

Why This Question Was Removed or Edited:
I removed this question because students were confusing the word "somnolent" with "solemn". Instead of just editing the answer choice, I wanted to provide students with additional practice opportunities, so I replaced it entirely.

49. **(D)** A scapegoat is someone who receives the blame of a problem, while the hero is the person who resolves a problem. They are thus opposites. A hedonist is a pleasure seeker, and a puritan is one who abides by strict principles and often denies himself pleasures. Thus, a hedonist and a puritan are antonyms.

Why This Question Was Removed or Edited:
I edited answer choice (A) because some students were making the argument that a hedonist and slave were antonyms in that a hedonist is a person who pursues pleasure freely while a slave is forced to suffer and is not able to pursue pleasure. Thus, to eliminate the potential confusion, I edited choice (A).

51. **(B)** Shingles comprise the outer layer of a roof. The epidermis comprises the outer layer of skin.

Why This Question Was Removed or Edited:
I edited several answer choices to eliminate possible confusion. Some were also too technical. For instance, most students know that the retina is a part of the eye, but many are unsure which part of the eye the retina composes. Most students also know what a motor is but not what a crankshaft is.

53. **(D)** A zookeeper's job is to look after the animals in a zoo. A jailor's job is to look after the prisoners of a jail or penitentiary. (A) and (B) are not correct because a child and patient are not captives.

Why This Question Was Removed or Edited:
I edited the answer choices to make it more

obvious that there was only one answer that could fit.

54. **(A)** Nostalgia is a longing for the past or what once was. In other words, nostalgia is characterized by longing. Desperation is characterized by begging.

Why This Question Was Removed or Edited: I edited answer choice (B) because too many students were confusing the word "grievance" with "grief". A grievance is a wrong that is grounds for complaint. A grievance could lead to grief, but it is not technically synonymous with grief because a grievance could simply lead to frustration or annoyance, rather than grief.

55. **(C)** Unorthodox is not traditional or routine. Mundane means ordinary, while illustrious means glorified, so they are antonyms.

Why This Question Was Removed or Edited: I edited answer choice (E) because the vast majority of students were not familiar with the word bilious.

SSAT
UPPER LEVEL
TEST 3

Quantitative Reasoning – Section I

Below are the answers and explanations to the questions that were removed and replaced from the 1st edition of *SSAT Practice Tests: Upper Level*.

6. **(D)** Let a represent the price of a cake. Since c is in terms of cents, we can set up the following system of equations:

$$a + xc = \$33.91 = 3391 \text{ cents}$$
$$a + c = \$32.47 = 3247 \text{ cents}$$

Subtract the bottom equation from the top equation to get:

$$xc - c = 144 \text{ cents}$$
$$c(x - 1) = 144$$
$$x - 1 = \frac{144}{c}$$
$$x = \frac{144}{c} + 1 = \frac{144}{c} + \frac{c}{c} = \frac{144 + c}{c}$$

Why This Question Was Removed: This problem was too abstract for many students, so I replaced it with an easier version of the problem. Also, complicating the problem was the conversion between dollars and cents. The answer choices were also extremely closely related, making selecting the correct answer difficult.

11. **(E)** $m \, \varkappa \, n = (n - m)^2 + m(2n - m) =$
$$n^2 - 2nm + m^2 + 2nm - m^2 = n^2$$

$$m \, \varkappa \, (m \, \varkappa \, n) = m \, \varkappa \, n^2$$
$$(n^2 - m)^2 + m(2n^2 - m) = n^4 - 2n^2m + m^2$$
$$+ 2n^2m - m^2 = n^4$$

Why This Question Was Removed: This problem was a bit complex for many students, requiring multiple steps. Also, the use of foreign operators (untraditional operators, i.e., those that are not $+, -, \times, \div$) frequently confused students.

19. **(D)** Let x represent the probability of rolling an odd number and $2x$ the probability of rolling an even number, since the probability of rolling an even is twice that of rolling an odd. This means that:

$x + 2x = 1$, since the probabilities must add to 1.

$3x = 1$, $x = \frac{1}{3}$ and $2x = \frac{2}{3}$

If Gregory rolls two dice, then he can get an even sum in two ways: by getting two odds or two evens. The probability of these outcomes can be stated as follows:

Possible Outcomes & Probabilities

1st Die		2nd Die		
Odd $\left(\dfrac{1}{3}\right)$	$\times$	Odd $\left(\dfrac{1}{3}\right)$	$=$	$\dfrac{1}{9}$
Even $\left(\dfrac{2}{3}\right)$	$\times$	Even $\left(\dfrac{2}{3}\right)$	$=$	$\dfrac{4}{9}$

The probability of rolling an even sum is therefore: $\frac{1}{9} + \frac{4}{9} = \frac{5}{9}$.

Why This Question Was Removed: This problem was too difficult for many students, as it required understanding more advanced concepts of probability theory.

21. **(E)** After placing point C, the following diagram results:

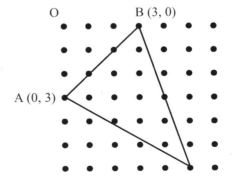

To find the area of triangle ABC, subtract the area around triangle ABC from the area of the grid matrix. A triangle exists in the upper left corner of the grid, using O, A, and B as the vertices. We'll call this Triangle M. Another triangle (Triangle N) results using the lower left grid point and A and C as the vertices.

Next, draw a vertical line extending from C to the top of the grid matrix. Let's call that point D. B, D, and C serve as the vertices for another triangle (Triangle O). Finally, using C, D, and the uppermost and lowermost right grid points, a rectangle (Rectangle P).

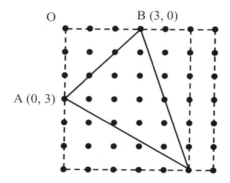

The area of the grid matrix is: $12 \times 12 = 144$

The area of Triangle M is: $\frac{1}{2} \times 6 \times 6 = 18$
The area of Triangle N is: $\frac{1}{2} \times 6 \times 10 = 30$
The area of Triangle O is: $\frac{1}{2} \times 12 \times 4 = 24$
The area of Rectangle P is: $2 \times 12 = 24$

Thus, the area of triangle ABC is:
$144 - (18 + 30 + 24 + 24) = 144 - 96 = 48$.

Why This Question Was Removed: This problem was too complex, involving taking into consideration many different factors and requiring many steps to arrive at the correct answer. As a result, this problem was too time consuming and much above the appropriate difficulty level found on the SSAT.

22. **(C)** The unit's digits of 2828^{10} and 3737^{10} can be found by looking for patterns of the unit's digit by power.

2828^{10}:
Units Digit of 2828^1: 8
Units Digit of 2828^2: $8 \times 8 = 6\underline{4}$
Units Digit of 2828^3: $4 \times 8 = 3\underline{2}$
Units Digit of 2828^4: $2 \times 8 = 1\underline{6}$
Units Digit of 2828^5: $6 \times 8 = 4\underline{8}$

Notice that the unit's digit comes back to 8 with the 5th power of 2828. This means that the unit's digit cycles after every 4th power of 2828. Thus, every 4th power of 2828 will have a unit's digit of 6. Thus, the 8th power of 2828 will have a unit's digit of 6. The 9th will have a unit's digit of 8, and the 10th will have a unit's digit of 4.

3737^{10}:
Units Digit of 3737^1: 7
Units Digit of 3737^2: $7 \times 7 = 4\underline{9}$
Units Digit of 3737^3: $9 \times 7 = 6\underline{3}$
Units Digit of 3737^4: $3 \times 7 = 2\underline{1}$
Units Digit of 3737^5: $1 \times 7 = \underline{7}$

Notice that the unit's digit comes back to 7 with the 5th power of 3737. This means that the unit's digit cycles after every 4th power of 3737. Thus, every 4th power of 3737 will have a unit's digit of 1. Thus, the 8th power of 3737 will have a unit's digit of 1. The 9th will have a unit's digit of 7, and the 10th will have a unit's digit of 9.

Because the units' digits of 2828^{10} and 3737^{10} are 4 and 9, respectively, the sum of the units' digits of 2828^{10} and 3737^{10} is $4 + 9 = 13$.

Why This Question Was Removed: Not many students are familiar with finding number patterns using the units digits of large exponents. I replaced this question with an easier one that could potentially still involve a great deal of multiplication, if the student is not actively looking for the shortcut.

Verbal Reasoning – Section 3

Below are the answers and explanations to the questions that were removed and replaced from the 1st edition of *SSAT Practice Tests: Upper Level*.

36. **(E)** Investing is a carefully calculated form of gambling, and pitching is a directed, focused form of throwing.

    Why This Question Was Removed or Edited: I edited the answer choices because although the correct answer is (E), many students could not draw the link; they felt it was too abstract. Also, a throw can be directed, so it is not necessarily more random than a pitch is. I made the answer choices less ambiguous in this sense.

46. **(D)** Merchandise is usually subject to taxes. Imports are usually subject to duties, which are government taxes on imports and exports.

    Why This Question Was Removed or Edited: I edited the answer choices to make it more apparent that (D) is unequivocally the correct answer. (A) and (E), which are the next best answers, were barely not as good as (D), since the analogy presented in (D) is more directly analogous, but I didn't want the decision to be so difficult for students.

48. **(B)** Red and violet are on the opposite ends of the visible light spectrum. Communism and fascism are on the opposite ends of the political spectrum. Both pairs of words indicate opposite ends of some spectrum.

    Why This Question Was Removed or Edited: I edited answer choice (C) because students were often unsure how theocracies and oligarchies were related. Because oligarchies are not familiar to many students taking the SSAT, I removed it.

51. **(D)** An inkling is the start of an idea, such as a hint or clue, while a theory is well thought out idea. Thus, inkling and theories reflect difference in degrees. A suspect is someone who has possibly committed a crime and will be investigated further, while a convict is someone who has been charged with and found guilty of a crime.

Why This Question Was Removed or Edited: I edited the answer choices to make the correct answer less ambiguous and easier to discern, as (A) and (E) both pertained to ideas and reasons; this caused students to spend too much time trying to figure out if there were shades of difference between idea and notion and between logic and rationale.

54. **(B)** Dissonance means inharmonious sound or harsh noise. In other words, it means a lack of melodiousness; dissonance is not melodious. Vivacity means eagerness. If someone is eager, then he is not reluctant.

    Why This Question Was Removed or Edited: I edited answer choices (A) and (B) to remove potential ambiguity. While machismo is not exactly the opposite noun of cordial, it is nearly opposite enough to warrant an edit.

55. **(C)** A candela is a unit of measurement for luminance. A calorie is a unit of measurement for heat. (B) and (C) are incorrect because while the specified units can be used to derive heaviness, in the case of (B), and density, in the case of (D), the units do not directly measure those things.

    Why This Question Was Removed or Edited: I removed this question because it was too scientifically technical.

57. **(E)** An affidavit is a written testimony. A contract is a written agreement.

    Why This Question Was Removed or Edited: I edited the question to make the definition of affidavit more accurately represented. An affidavit is a written declaration of facts.

58. **(D)** A guerilla is a fighter who uses stealth and ambush tactics, as does a highwayman. In other words, they both carry out similar actions. A

patrol and bodyguard both protect, so they carry out similar functions.

Why This Question Was Removed or Edited:
I edited answer choice (D) to make it more apparent that it was the right answer. Through elimination, the other choices could have been ruled out. The best choices would be (B) and (D). Between (B) and (D), however, (D) would work better, as a patrol and bodyguard are two different classes, whereas an entourage is a specific type of group, and a group is a generic word. Neither guerilla and highwayman are generic classes, making (D) the better choice. To make the answer more obvious, though, I edited answer choice (D) to soldier and bandit.

Quantitative Reasoning – Section 4

Below are the answers and explanations to the questions that were removed and replaced from the 1st edition of *SSAT Practice Tests: Upper Level*.

8. **(D)** The simplest way to solve this problem is to use an arithmetic sequence. If n represents the number of the day Tyler started training, i.e., $n =$ 1 for Tyler's first day of training, $n = 2$ for his 2nd day, etc., then we can represent the arithmetic series as:

Distance run $= 2 + 0.75(n - 1)$

If we want to see how many days it took Tyler to run the 26.2 miles, we can solve the following equation: $26.2 = 2 + 0.75(n - 1)$

$24.2 = 0.75(n - 1)$
$n - 1 = 32.267$ (to the nearest thousandth)
$n = 33.267$

As we can see, If Tyler runs 33 days, then he will run less than 26.2 miles. (Check: $2 + 0.75(33 - 1) = 2 + 0.75(32) = 26$ miles.) Thus, Tyler needs to run 34 days, to be able to run at least the full distance of the marathon. (Check: $2 + 0.75(34 - 1) = 2 + 0.75(33) = 26.75$ miles.)

Note: It's $0.75(n - 1)$ and not $0.75n$ because on the first day the 0.75 doesn't apply.

Why This Question Was Removed: This problem was too complex for a sequences and series problem for a significant number of students.

14. **(B)** This problem is asking for the sum of the perimeter of triangle ABC and circumference of the circle.

The perimeter of triangle ABC is $10 + 10 + 10\sqrt{2} = 20 + 10\sqrt{2}$.

The circumference of the circle is $2\pi r$ or πd, where $d = 10\sqrt{2}$ in the figure. Thus, the circumference is $10\pi\sqrt{2}$.

Adding the perimeter and circumference, we get: $20 + 10\sqrt{2} + 10\pi\sqrt{2}$. Since none of the answers are in this format, we must find a way to rearrange the solution. Notice each term possesses 10 or a multiple thereof, so we can factor 10 out from each term:

$$10\left(2 + \sqrt{2} + \pi\sqrt{2}\right)$$

From this, we can factor out $\sqrt{2}$ from each of the second and third terms:

$$10\left(2 + \sqrt{2}\left(1 + \pi\right)\right) = 10\left(\sqrt{2}\left(1 + \pi\right) + 2\right)$$

Why This Question Was Removed: The answer choices involved too much conversion between PEMDAS formats.

19. **(E)** To find the integers, set up the following equation:

$x + (x + 2) + (x + 4) = 237$
$3x + 6 = 237$
$3x = 231$
$x = 77$ (smallest integer), $x + 4 = 81$ (largest integer)

$77 \div 79 = 0.9506 = 95.06\%$

Why This Question Was Removed: This problem was removed because it was too time consuming, although conceptually not particularly challenging for advanced students.

20. **(A)** To find how long it will take the friends to finish the cabin, first determine the rate at which each friend can work.

If 5 friends can build a cabin in 240 hours, then it will take 1 friend $240 \times 5 = 1,200$ hours to build the cabin by himself.

If 2 friends are working on the cabin, it will take them $1,200 \div 2 = 600$ hours to build the cabin from start to finish. Since they are only working on half of the cabin, however, because that's how much needs to be completed after the halfway point, they need to work for $600 \div 2 = 300$ hours.

Why This Question Was Removed: This problem required too many steps and could thus confuse students, especially considering that many students are not strong with inverse variation rate problems.

22. **(C)** The key to deciphering this problem is understanding that $ax - bx - ay + by = x(a - b) - y(a - b)$ by way of factoring. From here, we can further factor out $(a - b)$ to get: $(a - b)(x - y)$. This will give us:

$$\frac{ax - bx - ay + by}{ab}\left[\left(\frac{b}{y - x}\right)\left(\frac{a^2b}{b - a}\right)\right] =$$
$$\frac{(x - y)(a - b)}{ab}\left[\left(\frac{b}{y - x}\right)\left(\frac{a^2b}{b - a}\right)\right]$$

The next key to solving this problem is recognizing that $(b - a) = -(a - b)$. Similarly, $(y - x) = -(x - y)$. If we make those substitutions in, we get:

$$\frac{(x - y)(a - b)}{ab}\left[\left(\frac{b}{-(x - y)}\right)\left(\frac{a^2b}{-(a - b)}\right)\right] =$$
$$\frac{\cancel{(x - y)}\,\cancel{(a - b)}}{ab}\left[\left(\frac{b}{-1\cancel{(x - y)}}\right)\left(\frac{a^2b}{-1\cancel{(a - b)}}\right)\right] =$$
$$\frac{a\,\cancel{a^2}\,\cancel{b^2}b}{\cancel{a}\,\cancel{b} \times (-1)^2} = ab$$

Why This Question Was Removed: This problem required too advanced of an understanding of factoring for most 7th and 8th grade students.

NOTES

NOTES

Made in the USA
Middletown, DE
31 August 2018